DATE DUE

DEC 0 4 1996	

"Sumter Is Avenged"

The Siege and Reduction of Fort Pulaski

Painting of an aerial view of today's Fort Pulaski from the west shows the plan of the fort;

"Sumter Is Avenged"

The Siege and Reduction of Fort Pulaski

Herbert M. Schiller

White Mane Publishing Company, Inc.

This White Mane Publishing Company, Inc. publication
was printed by
Beidel Printing House, Inc.
63 West Burd Street
Shippensburg, PA 17257 USA

In respect for the scholarship contained herein, the acid-free paper used in this book meets the guidelines for permanence and durability of the Committee on Production Guidelines for Book Longevity of the Council on Library Resources.

For a complete list of available publications
please write
White Mane Publishing Company, Inc.
P.O. Box 152
Shippensburg, PA 17257-0152

Library of Congress Cataloging-in-Publication Data

Schiller, Herbert M., 1943–
        Sumter is avenged : the siege and reduction of Fort Pulaski /
Herbert M. Schiller.
            p.   cm.
        Includes bibliographical references (p.) and index.
        ISBN 0-942597-86-9 (alk. paper)
        1. Fort Pulaski (Ga.)--Siege, 1862.   I. Title.
E472.79.S25 1995
973.7´31--dc20   95-39922
                                                                         CIP

For my son,
Stephen Miles Schiller

*T*able Of *C*ontents

List Of Illustrations

*L*ist Of *M*aps

$\mathcal{A}$cknowledgments

This is probably the most enjoyable part of any book to write. I had help from many people over the years which I spent gathering material for this book. The earliest was Richard McMurray, who generously shared with me his microfilms of Savannah newspapers from late 1861 and early 1862. Talley Kirkland, historian at the Fort Pulaski National Monument, was helpful in making copies of the manuscript material in the park's collection and in answering questions about the structure of masonry forts and the location of Federal batteries. Ed Olmstead read my appendix and section dealing with the James and Parrott guns and offered both corrections and helpful suggestions. Dick Sommers and Mike Winey were invaluable during a visit to the Unites States Army Military History Institute; Dick with the great collection of manuscript material and Mike with the wonderful collection on images, many of which have been included in this book. Michael Musick explained the accessioning system of the adjutant general's office in the 1860's and guided me through the microfilm records while providing me with copies of individual reports and letters. I owe a great debt to the librarians and curators at the various institutions listed in the bibliography for their help in suggesting manuscripts and pointing me directions I would not have found myself. Finally, Martin Gordon and the entire staff at White Mane Publishing Company have been a joy to work with.

My son Stephen was a great help in the preparation of this book. Having finished college and again living at home while awaiting graduate school to begin, he edited the manuscript and made many valuable suggestions. He learned a little about nineteenth-century siege warfare, and I learned a lot about writing. It was great fun to work on this together.

Winston-Salem, N.C.   Herbert M. Schiller, M.D.

August, 1995

*I*ntroduction

I first visited Fort Pulaski twenty-five years ago. During a warm, lazy December afternoon my brother-in-law and I drove to see it. I still remember the visit. During winter there were hardly any visitors. The fort, completely intact, was a beautiful example of an early nineteenth century masonry fort. One of the officers' rooms had been made into a museum and displayed hundreds of exquisite iridescent bottles, recovered from the moat during restoration efforts in the 1930's. The story of the bombardment was amazing. Batteries on Tybee Island, about a mile away, had opened on the fort and in less than two days had breached the wall and hit the magazine, threatening to explode the fort, along with its garrison. Walking around the wall, I could see the site of the breach, repaired in 1862. The part not replaced still had craters where shells had exploded, and embedded in the wall were the projectiles which had not detonated! Exhibits in the visitor center showed a brief history of the fort's construction and examples of the guns and shells used by the Federal besiegers, along with the Confederate commander's sword and letters to his wife.

Over the years, I was always intrigued by the novelty of the first use of rifled artillery by the Federal army against the masonry fort. The Union siege commander, Brigadier General Quincy A. Gillmore, later said that he cleverly planned to breach the wall at just the correct angle for his shells to cross the parade and hit the fort's magazine and threaten the fort with explosion. I have since learned this was not true.

Little had been written about the siege and reduction of Fort Pulaski. Gillmore wrote several accounts, both during and after the war. Official "after action" reports are few and little official correspondence was published. I first decided to see what manuscript material I could find about Pulaski in 1988 and began in earnest the following year. I found diaries and letters written by participants scattered in repositories across the United States. As I worked with the material, an elaborate story unfolded. At the beginning of the war, Savannah was one of several major ports of the new Confederacy. As the Federals organized their efforts, they decided to blockade the Southern coast to close the rebellious nation to international commerce. A successful blockade demanded fueling stations for the fleet; Port Royal Sound and Hilton Head Island along the southern South Carolina coast were selected and captured in November, 1861. Fernandina, Florida, was selected as the other Federal station but, as will be seen, not taken until the following year. Commander of the Federal expedition Brigadier General Thomas W. Sherman conceived of a plan to take the port city of Savannah with the cooperation of the United States Navy in January, 1862. Although Savannah was largely defenseless, naval vacillation resulted in postponement, then cancellation, of the expedition. Rather than capture the city, Federal authorities decided to close it to blockade runners. Taking Fort Pulaski, which controlled the entrance of the Savannah River, would free many vessels from blockading duties. Thus the siege was undertaken.

Until this time, masonry forts were considered impregnable to smoothbore artillery fire from great distances. The islands which would be suitable sites for Federal batteries were too far from the fort for guns to be effective. Rifled guns had been developed in Europe and were being developed and tested in the United States a few years prior to the outbreak of the Civil War. They had shown their effectiveness against masonry works in European tests but had never been used in combat. Gillmore decided to equip two of his eleven batteries with rifled guns as an experiment. He relied on mortars and large smoothbore guns for the other nine batteries. The results of the rifled gun fire exceeded all expectations; revolutionized siege warfare; and made masonry forts, previously thought to be impregnable, obsolete. The technological significance of the successful use of rifled artillery was a turning point in warfare as important as the use of iron plating on wooden vessels—the *Monitor* and *Virginia.*

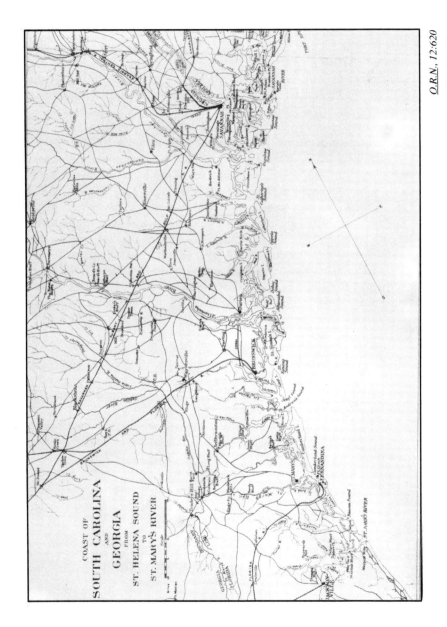

Map of the coast of Georgia extending from Hilton Head Island, South Carolina, southward to Jacksonville, Florida.

Chapter 1

Seizing Fort Pulaski

Originating on the slopes of the Appalachian Mountains, the Savannah River forms the boundary between South Carolina and Georgia as it flows three hundred miles east. East of Savannah, Georgia, the main channel courses twelve miles farther to the Atlantic while numerous lateral channels twist their way into the sea between dozens of marshy islands. Formed of soft mud, these islands are scarcely exposed at high tide and frequently lie submerged at high spring tide. Covered with tall grass and reeds, they convey the appearance of a savannah. Several islands lie in tandem within the river, and closest to the ocean is Cockspur Island. Cockspur Island is a deposit of mud lying between the two main channels of the Savannah River. Although a mile long and less than half a mile wide, only a few acres remain above water during high tide. In 1862, a Connecticut soldier described the "solid" part of this island as clay that became "minute pudding" after a storm.[1]

Cockspur Island is ten miles east of the city of Savannah, the most strategic point on the one hundred mile long Georgia coast. Three railroads, the Charleston and Savannah, the Georgia Central, and the Savannah, Albany, and Gulf linked the city with the north, west, and south. Ship building, marine industries, and railroad shops were the primary industries of military importance.[2]

* * * * * * *

The only choices for coastal defense in the eighteenth and early nineteenth centuries were either a large fleet, in need of constant repair, at each harbor or well constructed, properly sited forts; the latter were far more economical. Sea coast forts, armed with heavy artillery, were an integral part of America's defense. Harbor and waterway protection was a vital part of United States' defensive requirements. With her enemies an ocean away, American forts provided defensive points, en-

1

abling militia to assemble for defense. Seacoast forts also insured the possession of commercial and naval harbors, and denied their use to the enemy. Historically, nations reserved their navies for offensive actions and defended their ports with fortifications. The development of steamships made the idea of coastal fortification even more important.[3]

Of such forts and their armament, chief engineer Colonel Joseph G. Totten wrote:

> Various forms of heavy artillery . . . [are] the only effectual instrument of defence. This artillery being in adequate numbers, properly placed, sufficiently manned, out of the reach of seizure by the enemy, and too powerful to be silenced by him—all, conditions indispensable, . . . is prepared with all useful accessories and ready for its great functions, independent of any aid from without.[4]

Coastal fortifications had two separate and distinct qualities—to prevent the passage of ships and to resist land attack. Stopping ships required the proper number and type of heavy guns. To be secure from ground forces' shot and shell meant a fort had to be inaccessible. The fort to be built on Cockspur Island—Fort Pulaski—would well fulfill both requirements. Its armament would assure the former; its location would provide the latter. Totten later said specifically of the fort: "You might as well bombard the Rocky Mountains as Fort Pulaski. . . . The fort could not be reduced in a month's firing with any number of guns of manageable caliber."[5]

Cockspur Island had been the site of forts since pre-Revolutionary War days. First was Fort George in 1761, a palisaded log blockhouse dismantled and abandoned by patriot forces in 1776 because it was undefensible against the British fleet. Fort Greene, named for the Revolutionary War patriot Nathaniel Greene buried on nearby Mulberry Grove Plantation, was built in 1794-1795. In 1804, a hurricane swept Cockspur Island, destroying the fort and drowning part of the garrison. The island remained unused until 1821.[6]

During the War of 1812, British forces had ascended American rivers and come ashore with impunity. To remedy this problem, President James Madison urged Congress to appropriate money to extend and complete the system of coastal fortification. French Brigadier General Simon Bernard, distinguished chief military engineer to Napoleon, had come to the United States in 1815. Armed with high recommendations from Lafayette and former Secretary of the Treasury Albert Gallatin, he was selected for the project. Madison commissioned Bernard brevet brigadier general in the Corps of Engineers. At the end of 1816, Bernard, Colonel William McRee, and Colonel Joseph G. Totten were constituted as the Board of Engineers and began to devise a system for seacoast defense. It would be under Totten, a major general at his death in 1864, that Fort Pulaski and most of the other works would be completed.[7]

The Board's first complete report was submitted in February, 1821. It noted the primacy of the navy in the total defensive system and envisioned forts as protectors of naval facilities and commercial ports. Forts were usually hexagonal, because casemate guns carriages could only traverse 60 degrees of lateral movement. Built near sea level, forts could use ricochet fire against enemy ships.[8]

Early coastal surveys had recognized that a system of interior water communication existed from the Savannah River down the Georgia coast to the Saint John's River in northeastern Florida. (Parts of this system are included in the intracoastal waterway.) The city of Savannah could be approached not only from the primary river channels but also from a host of secondary inter-island channels, lying mainly to the south. Although the defense of these individual inlets, like Wassaw and Ossabaw Sounds, remained unresolved, the fort on Cockspur Island easily covered the Savannah River approaches to the city. (Fort Jackson, a 14-gun masonry fort begun in 1842, was a second barrier on the river and located between the city and the entrance of the channels entering the river from the south.)[9]

Although Bernard had surveyed the river approaches to Savannah in 1821, construction of Fort Pulaski did not begin until 1829 due to a lack of congressional funding. Bernard's initial plans had called for a fort architecturally identical to Fort Sumter, i.e., a two-story pentagonal fort with three tiers of guns. However, Cockspur's muddy composition could not support the weight. Despite extensive wooden pilings and grillage foundations to support the masonry, the walls were modified to one story: a single row of casemate guns, and a row of parapet (barbette) guns above.[10]

Major Samuel Babcock, of the Corps of Engineers, supervised the initial construction in the spring of 1829. That November, Lieutenant Robert E. Lee, newly graduated from the United States Military Academy, arrived as Babcock's assistant. Ill health prevented Babcock from taking an active role, so Lee oversaw the project for a year until Lieutenant Joseph K. F. Mansfield superseded Babcock in January, 1831. Lee directed the surveys that would determine the permanent site of the fort; he then began the system of drainage canals and dikes. Assigned to Virginia in April, 1831, Lee took no further role in the fort's construction.[11] Mansfield supervised the construction of the fort from 1831 to 1845. In 1833, the partially completed fort was named for Count Casimir Pulaski, a hero of the American Revolutionary War mortally wounded in the 1779 battle of Savannah.

Twenty-five million bricks were used on the fort; they were brought in lots varying from one to seven million. Hermitage Plantation, two miles west of Savannah, manufactured the rose-colored bricks used in the walls. Harder bricks used in the embrasures, arches, and interior walls were shipped from Virginia and Maryland. New York granite and Connecticut River valley sandstone provided finishing trim. The Corps of Engineers rented slaves from neighboring plantations for hard labor; masons and carpenters came from Savannah and the North. Malaria, yellow fever, typhoid, and dysentery halted work each summer.

Congress frequently lapsed in appropriating money; once Mansfield borrowed on his own credit to pay for labor and supplies. Construction was nearly finished by 1847; a million dollars had been spent. Construction of the island dike system, barracks, quarters, storehouses, and an advanced battery outside the fort cost an additional $35,000. Fort Pulaski was designed to be armed with 150 guns: 65 32-pounders, 53 24-pounders, four 18-pounders, four flank howitzers, twelve 8-inch heavy howitzers, two 8-inch light howitzers, one 13-inch howitzer, seven 10-inch heavy mortars, and two coehorn mortars. Twenty 32-pounder guns were mounted in the casements in 1840. Twenty years later, the United States government had added not a single gun.[12]

Fort Pulaski has five sides, called faces. Two guard the south channel; two guard the north channel. The least vulnerable side of Fort Pulaski, called the gorge, faces west. The three ocean-facing angles of the fort—northeastern, eastern, and southeastern—redans, have a short face, the *pan coupé,* in the salient angle. Each *pan coupé* has a single casemate and embrasure (opening) for a gun to protect the potential blind spot. Seven and one-half foot-thick walls stand 25 feet above the water-filled moat. The gorge was covered by an "earthen outwork (demilune) in bold relief." (The demilune has been remodeled and differs today from its original design.) The brick-walled moat around the main fort is 48 feet wide; around the demilune it is 32 feet wide. One must cross over the demilune on a drawbridge and from there a second drawbridge to enter Fort Pulaski.[13]

* * * * * * *

South Carolina passed her Ordinance of Secession on December 20, 1860; six days later, Major Robert Anderson's Federal troops left Fort Moultrie and occupied Fort Sumter in Charleston harbor. Outraged Georgians protested in Savannah.[14]

The 1st Volunteer Regiment of Georgia, commanded by Colonel Alexander R. Lawton, was comprised of men from Savannah and the surrounding Chatham county area. It included the Savannah Volunteer Guards, Republican Blues, Oglethorpe Light Infantry,[15] Phoenix Riflemen, Irish Volunteers, German Volunteers, DeKalb Volunteers, Chatham Artillery, Irish Jasper Greens, and Pulaski Guards. The Montgomery Guards were added later.[16]

On January 2, Lawton, together with Captain John W. Anderson of the Blues; Captain John Screven of the Guards; Captain Joseph S. Claghorn of the Chatham Artillery; Captain Francis S. Bartow of the Oglethorpe; and Major General Henry R. Jackson, to be later appointed commander of the Georgia militia, met in Savannah with Governor Joseph E. Brown. Regimental adjutant Captain Charles H. Olmstead also attended. They drew plans and issued orders to seize Fort Pulaski the following day, two weeks before Georgia passed her Ordinance of Secession.[17]

At 8:00 a.m. the next morning, the city rang with martial music. Lawton had selected details of 34 men from the Claghorn's Chatham Artillery, and 50 men each of the Screven's Savannah Guards and Bartow's Oglethorpe Light Infantry. He led the men to the foot of West Broad Street and boarded the sidewheel steamer *Ida.* The Chatham Artillery brought along two 12-pounder howitzers and four 6-pounder field guns. The *Ida* descended the Savannah River and landed at the north wharf of Cockspur Island. "With drums beating colors flying and hearts swelling we marched over the drawbridge, under the portcullis, and into the Fort," Olmstead later wrote. "I can shut my eyes and see it all now, the proud step of the officers and men, the colors snapping in the strong breeze from the ocean; the bright sunlight of the parade as we emerged from the shadow of the archway."[18]

After taking Fort Pulaski, Lawton raised a flag—a solitary red star on a white ground—and then fired a salute. Ordnance Sergeant ,Walker surrendered the fort, twenty guns, and a small supply of ammunition. Captain William H. C. Whiting, of the U.S. Army Engineer Department, was in Fernandina at the time Fort Pulaski was taken. He rushed to his office in Savannah on January 6 to notify Totten of the fort seizure.[19]

Captain Bartow now commanded the fort. Within two days the Georgians had established their quarters, set guards, and organized the kitchens. They found the twenty captured 32-pounders mounted on useless, rusted iron carriages within the casemates. Powder stores were small; the magazine contained many solid shot but only a few shells. During the first month the guns and carriages were refurbished, the magazine stocked, and additional larger guns requested. The fort was in a sorry state; quarters were unfit to live in. The overgrown parade was unusable. A morass of silt and marsh grass filled the moat. One hundred and twenty-five slaves from neighboring plantations worked for months to restore the fort to a habitable and defensible condition.[20]

By mid-January, Olmstead observed that the entire garrison was "cleaning up the fort, casemates, parade, and every other part of it." "Here a wheelbarrow party gravely marching in column of platoons, there a squad with shouldered brooms going from casemate to casemate, and everywhere nothing but cheerful obedience to the proper authority." During these first months of 1861, Olmstead spent his time between the fort and Savannah. The First Volunteer Regiment of Georgia was divided among Fort Pulaski, Tybee Island, Thunderbolt Island, Fort Jackson, and Green Island.[21]

Alexander Lawton, original commander of the 1st Volunteer Regiment of Georgia, became brigadier general on April 13, 1861, and military commander of the state of Georgia, still a separate military department. General Lawton's departmental headquarters were in Savannah, and it was with the city's defenses that he was primarily concerned. Hugh W. Mercer became the regimental colonel; William S. Rockwell, the lieutenant colonel and Olmstead, the major.[22]

Olmstead served in Fort Pulaski as Mercer's second in command in the spring of 1861. He found his duty boring: drilling at the guns; studying drill and regulations; worrying about hygiene, food preparation, garbage disposal, the cleanliness of quarters and the men. During the summer of 1861, the "cooks were all Negroes and it goes without saying that strong measures had to be used to keep them up to the mark. If a kitchen did not meet the requirements of authority, the cook was

U.S.A.M.H.I.

Alexander R. Lawton

promptly laid across the brass drum and a good paddling administered with a shingle while his associates stood grinning around." This occurred only twice.[23]

On May 1, 1861, *Harper's Weekly* correspondent Theodore R. Davis, along with London *Times* correspondent William Russell, visited Fort Pulaski. They found tents arranged around two sides of the ramparts. Several hundred recruits were drilling. Other men were busy mounting guns newly arrived from Virginia. The 8- and 10-inch columbiads *en barbette* had the name "Beauregard," "Davis," "Tattnall," "Sumter," "Lawton," "Lane," "Twiggs," "Wigfall," among others, the names painted on the gun's cascabels. Lieutenant Theodorick W. Montfort had three casemate guns and named them for his wife—Louisa—and for his mother and a close family friend. Other casemate guns were named "Big Hannah" and "Nancy Heart," and a mortar was called "Crasher." Commodore Josiah Tattnall was present and "expressed his determination, in the event of an attack, to point the monster dispenser of iron favors with his own hand." Russell had private reservations that the Confederates "do not understand the nature of the new shell and heavy vertical fire, or the effect of projectiles from great distances falling into open works."[24]

The first Federal blockading ship arrived at the entrance to the Savannah River on May 27, 1861, closing the port to all but a few blockade runners. When additional Union vessels arrived, the Confederates constructed a two gun battery near the lighthouse on Tybee Island, across the south channel of the Savannah River from Fort Pulaski, to keep away the ships and prevent a landing.[25]

* * * * * * * *

F.P.N.M.

Colonel Charles H. Olmstead, commander of the Confederate garrison in Fort Pulaski during the siege.

Charles H. Olmstead was born in 1837 and reared in Savannah. His father was a business man and banker. He began four years at the Georgia Military Institute in Marietta, Georgia, in 1852. He later began a business career and three years afterwards married Florence Williams. The then Colonel Lawton offered him the adjutancy of the 1st Volunteer Regiment of Georgia in early 1860.[26]

Olmstead's first independent command was on Tybee Island during the summer of 1861. Various bodies of troops garrisoned the small island earthwork, but it was exposed and "incapable of a stout defense." Olmstead stationed pickets a mile apart along the coastal shore to the southern end of the island. He rode the beach at night so the men could see they were "under supervision." He recalled, "I do not know that I have ever felt more lonely than in the performance of that duty. . . . As I rode from one to the other in the black

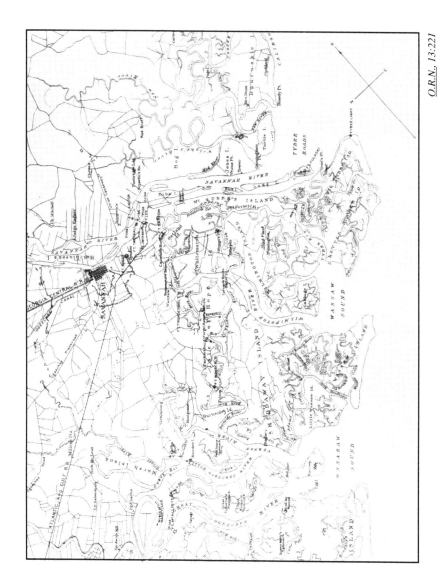

O.R.N., 13:221

Map of the coastal area east of Savannah, Georgia, showing the Confederate river defenses.

night, with the bare sand dunes on one hand and the rolling waves of the ocean upon the other I seemed to be the only person in the Universe."[27]

Shortly after Lawton's promotion, Colonel Charles J. Williams' 1st Georgia Regulars Infantry arrived on Tybee, temporarily relieving Olmstead's companies. Williams' regiment was ordered to Virginia on July 10, and Olmstead's men returned to the island and the fort. During summer, mosquitos plagued the Confederates on Tybee. Olmstead's wife sent netting for his head and arms. He could then sit in front of his tent at night "calmly serene while the other fellows had to slap right and left." A Georgia soldier described conditions and routine at Camp Mercer, the Tybee encampment, in late August, 1861: Revilee at 5:00 a.m. followed by roll call. Breakfast at 7:00 a.m. consisted of black coffee and a hard biscuit. The camp guard formed at 8:00 a.m. and drilling began for an hour at 10:00 a.m. The mid-day dinner was "fresh beef and rice or, less often, bacon and bread." Drill was repeated at 5:00 p.m. followed by dress parade an hour later and then supper. Surf bathing followed until 9:00 p.m., then roll call and taps at 9:30 p.m., "but candles are permitted in the tents until 11:00 p.m. Great banks of oysters "of good quality" filled the tidal waterways; the men broke them off and steamed them. Crabs were abundant, and in the cooler weather ducks were also plentiful.[28]

Work continued in the fort. Quadrants and sights for the guns arrived in May. The garrison on Tybee sent a hydraulic jack to help "put the barbette guns in order." In September, Captain Joseph S. Claghorn commanded Fort Pulaski. He worried over the lack of small arm and artillery ammunition. He feared the newly constructed pine gun carriages would not withstand repeated firing and wanted to replace them with oak carriages. Claghorn reported 45,000 pounds of cannon powder on hand.[29]

In early October, Colonel Mercer took command on Tybee and assigned Olmstead to command Fort Pulaski. By the end of the month, all but one of the fort's earthen rampart traverses had been completed. Olmstead drilled the artillery so that ten-twelve guns could coordinate their fire on different fronts. "The officers seem to think it is just the thing. "Your 'boy',"' he wrote his wife, "will be quite an artillerist before we leave this Fort."[30]

The Georgia Confederates developed a strong defensive line, extending on the right from Fort McAllister on the Ogeechee River, sixteen miles south of Savannah, northward through Fort Beaulieu on the Vernon River, a series of strong batteries at Thunderbolt, Bonaventure and Causten's Bluff, then to Fort Jackson with its associated earthworks on the Savannah River. The line continued into South Carolina all the way to Charleston harbor. The forward line in Georgia was Fort Pulaski and in South Carolina the New River Bridge, Bluffton, Port Royal Ferry, and north to the works below Charleston. To compel the Federals to pass under the guns of Fort Pulaski, Confederates drove piles into the channels leading into the Savannah River from the north (Wall's Cut) and south (Saint Augustine Creek).[31]

In October, 1861, Major Olmstead commanded Fort Pulaski, now garrisoned by seventeen officers and 210 men. Thirty-six guns now defended the fort. The battery on Wassaw Island contained five heavy guns served by six officers and 120 men. Three officers and 100 men garrisoned the four heavy guns of Thunderbolt

Battery. Isle of Hope Battery had six field guns manned by two officers and 50 men. Skidaway Island had 28 officers and 498 men garrisoning a main battery, with a water battery above and a "Lower Battery" below, near an "old mansion." Tybee Island was then occupied by 54 officers and 896 men, and had a battery near the Martello tower containing two heavy guns. Nearly five thousand officers and men defended the remaining Department of Georgia, most being stationed in Savannah and other at coastal points.[32]

In early November, 1861, General Lawton ordered Major Olmstead to have the two heavy guns in the battery by the Martello tower on Tybee moved to Fort Pulaski. Further, he directed Olmstead to add one or two companies to the fort's garrison. Olmstead ordered the guns to be moved without the Federals seeing. Further, he ordered the leveling of the sand banks at Kings Landing at the northwest end of the island.[33] Tybee Island was abandoned.

Chapter 2

"$\mathcal{E}$veryone seems impatient to be doing something"

On November 5, 1861, General Robert E. Lee assumed command of the newly consolidated Confederate Department of South Carolina, Georgia, and East Florida. President Jefferson Davis told Lee that he would go as a full general in the regular Confederate army and be senior officer in the department. Lee was concerned because of his earlier problems with indefinite authority and divided command in western Virginia. Secretary of War Judah P. Benjamin assured Lee that "you are authorized to use the entire resources of South Carolina and Georgia that are under control of the Confederate Government for your defense, whether troops, munitions of war, or supplies of every kind." South Carolina did not receive Lee's appointment with uniform favor, but Georgia's Governor Brown was enthusiastic.[1]

U.S.A.M.H.I.

Robert E. Lee

Lee arrived in South Carolina on November 7, the day Port Royal Sound fell to a joint Federal army-navy expedition. He hastened to Coosawhatchie, on the Charleston and Savannah Railroad and nearest inland station to the sound. Halfway between Savannah and Charleston, the station was on

10

the Coosawhatchie River that flows into the Broad River, which in turn, empties into Port Royal Sound. Lee and his staff heard the bombardment. The commander of local Confederate troops, Brigadier General Roswell S. Ripley, had already ridden down river to examine the situation; Lee followed later.[2]

Lee ordered the Confederates to evacuate Hilton Head and Phillips Islands bordering the sound and then returned to Coosawhatchie to begin organizing the defenses of his department. Although the Confederates escaped safely, they abandoned all their tents, clothing, provisions, and artillery. A thousand Georgia troops sent earlier by Lawton returned to Savannah without orders. The fall of Port Royal Sound and the adjacent islands convinced Confederate authorities that they could not hold every outlying island.[3]

Lee organized his new department into military districts; Georgia fell under Lawton's command. On November 10, Lawton wrote Lee, pledging his full cooperation and informing him of the number and disposition of troops in Georgia. Brigadier General Hugh W. Mercer, recently promoted from colonel of the 1st Volunteer Regiment of Georgia, was in Brunswick with 2,000 men. Thirty-five hundred more were north of the Altamaha River above Brunswick, all but 500 within twenty miles of Savannah. That same day, the 25th Georgia on Tybee was ordered to evacuate; one company, the Wise Guards, was moved into Fort Pulaski, raising the defenders there to 450 men. Lawton concentrated his 2,800 men around Savannah for easy maneuverability. Two hundred men held the Green Island Battery on the Vernon River, securing an important approach twelve miles below Savannah. Five hundred cavalry, "well mounted and armed," were near the city. Three thousand more infantry, organized by the state of Georgia, were encamped along the Savannah, Albany and Gulf Railroad and were available in Savannah within a few hours. Of all these men, only 2,000 of Lawton's infantry were well drilled and disciplined.[4]

* * * * * *

On July 5, 1861, Federal naval Captain Samuel F. DuPont had chaired a committee appointed by the Secretary of the Navy, Gideon Welles, to evaluate the expeditions to the southern coast. It recommended Hampton Roads, Virginia, and Fernandina, Florida, as the "most suitable point[s] for a place of deposit" for supplies of the blockading squadron. The Secretary of War, Simon Cameron, ordered Brigadier General Thomas W. Sherman to lead the army in cooperation with newly promoted Commodore

U.S.A.M.H.I.

Samuel F. DuPont

U.S.A.M.H.I.

Thomas W. Sherman

DuPont. The two officers were "to decide upon the points of assault after the expedition has sailed." As Sherman's fourteen regiments and DuPont's fleets were assembling at Fort Monroe, Virginia, DuPont, along with his flag captain, Captain Charles H. Davis, Sherman and his three brigade commanders met and decided to seize Port Royal Sound before taking Fernandina. Since only the harbors were to be taken, no preparations were made "to march into the interior at all." DuPont supplied all water transportation; he had fifty surf boats constructed for the expedition. Two shallow draft steamboats and two steam tugs, previously requisitioned, never arrived.[5]

After DuPont occupied the Sound, the Confederates abandoned its bordering islands and the adjacent South Carolina islands. General Sherman, commander of the army, was a native Rhode Islander. He was one of the first brigadiers appointed in the Federal army; directing the land forces after the seizure of Port Royal Sound was his first important service. He had graduated from the United States Military Academy in 1836, became an officer of artillery, and served in the army in Mexico and various other posts during the years before the Civil War.

Naval commander of the expedition, Commodore Francis DuPont, in mid-1861, characterized Sherman as a "very superior military man" but noted that he was also reputed to be "ugly tempered and morose." This was bad, DuPont added, "for a naval cooperation where the two branches are so apt to come in collision." However, after working with Sherman for three months, DuPont considered him to be "a *thorough officer* and understands what he is about and what is before him." By late October, DuPont would say of Sherman, "he is more able than I thought as a general; instead of being a mere sabreur, he studies maps, has informed himself well of his work." The two men shared quarters aboard DuPont's *Wabash* during the Port Royal expedition.[6]

After the fall of Port Royal Sound, General Sherman's thirteen hundred-man Expeditionary Corps landed on Hilton Head Island. Sherman's men were in two groups of transports, one of which had been designated to continue to Fernandina. However, because DuPont had expended three-fourths of his ammunition in taking Port Royal Sound, all the men disembarked at Hilton Head Island while DuPont requested additional ordnance.[7]

Sherman's force consisted of three regularly organized brigades and an additional three attached regiments. The troops were largely unexperienced; some had never been drilled; some came without arms. Brigadier General Egbert L. Viele commanded the First Brigade that consisted of the 8th Maine, 3rd New Hampshire,

46th, 47th, and 48th New York Infantry. Brigadier General Isaac I. Stevens commanded the Second Brigade, composed of the 8th Michigan, 79th New York, 50th and 100th Pennsylvania Infantry. Brigadier General Horatio G. Wright commanded the Third Brigade, composed of the 6th and 7th Connecticut, 9th Maine, and 4th New Hampshire Infantry. Attached but not brigaded were Colonel Edward W. Serrell's 1st New York Engineers, the 3rd Rhode Island Heavy Artillery, and Battery E, 3rd

U.S.A.M.H.I.

General Sherman's headquarters on Hilton Head Island, March 8, 1862.

U.S. Artillery. All of the brigade commanders were West Point graduates and engineer officers.[8]

Sherman's staff consisted of adjutant Captain Louis H. Pelouze, chief engineer Captain Quincy A. Gillmore with First Lieutenant John A. Tardy and Second Lieutenant Patrick H. O'Rorke as assistants, chief of ordnance Captain John McNutt with First Lieutenants Francis J. Shunk and Horace Porter as assistants, chief of artillery Captain John Hamilton, and chief topographical engineer First Lieutenant James H. Wilson.[9]

Eight days after the occupation of Hilton Head Island, Sherman was still having difficulties landing his stores. With the cooperation of DuPont's fleet, Sherman strengthened his position on Hilton Head and Phillips Island. The earthworks he built on Hilton Head were about a mile in circumference and mounted with heavy guns; they could be held with 2,000 men. Sherman then planned to occupy Beaufort, Port Royal Island, and the Savannah and Charleston Railroad at Pocotaligo. Further, he wanted either to move into lower coastal South Carolina counties and threaten Savannah, or move through the interior creeks and channels connecting with the Savannah River below Savannah and begin a siege against the city while isolating Fort Pulaski. To move on Savannah, Sherman would need additional boats.[10]

Two days later, November 17, Sherman reported that he had secured the harbors at Port Royal and Saint Helena. Unfortunately, manning these points and establishing a secure operational base on Hilton Head, left few men for inland expeditions. He therefore asked for 10,000 reinforcements. To ascend the coastal rivers and creeks he needed four steamers and two shallow draft ferry boats, each of which to transport 800 to 1,000 men. Sherman also asked for 100 rowboats, each able to carry 40 to 50 men, for transporting men, artillery, field carriages, and siege

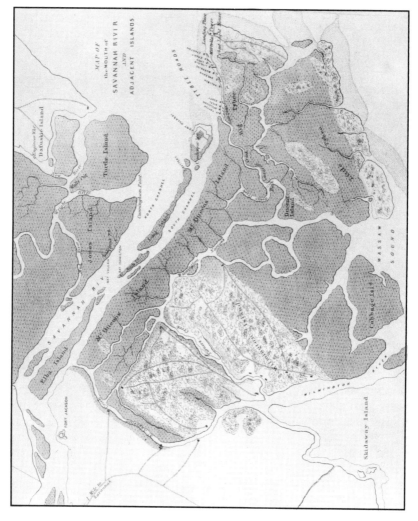

Gillmore, Siege, pl. I

Map of the Savannah River and adjacent islands.

guns. Finally, he requested additional engineer officers to repair captured fortifications and erect new ones.[11]

On November 22, twelve days after the Confederates had pulled back, the Federals learned Tybee Island was unoccupied. Commodore DuPont realized that "with Tybee Point, a large ship can command the roads and cork up Savannah as tight as a bottle and hoist the flag in Georgia." Before its complete Federal occupation, one Union observer described the island:

> The sand is thrown rather into dunes than into hills. These are covered by bushes and low trees, mostly deciduous. Inside this outer strip of sand are strips of salt marshes, alternating again with stretches of sandy dunes. The uplands covered with stunted growth of live oak, long-leaved pine, cedar and an occasional palmetto. The marshy strips are clothed in grasses, reeds, strange looking willows. Along the edges, the border land between the two is usually a most luxuriant, almost tropical growth, of those trees constituting something almost a jungle where tied together with grapevines and other climbers, notably the yellow jessamine.

Many sand hills were twenty feet high. At the northeast corner were the lighthouse, a Martello tower, and an abandoned sand fort.[12]

On November 24, Commander John Rodgers' squadron, including the *Pocahontas* and *Seneca*, both 5-gun screw steamers; *Flag*, a 7-gun screw steamer; and *Augusta*, a 9-gun sidewheel steamer, anchored off Tybee Island. Among their armaments were 11-inch shell guns and 6-inch rifles. Rodgers' orders were to learn the most suitable place to sink navigation obstructions in the Savannah River, to ascertain remaining enemy forces on the island, and to evaluate the possibility of gaining the inner bar.

The following day, Rodgers fired at the Martello tower and lighthouse and randomly "in every direction along the shore," trying to draw fire from Confederate pickets. The nine pickets on Tybee rowed to the safety of Fort Pulaski. Once the Federals saw that Tybee was quiet, they landed 200 men. They placed a battery at the Martello tower. Because Fort Pulaski remained occupied, Rodgers did not steam further up the river. A member of the *Augusta*'s crew, Francis McCarten, took the flag from his boat and raised it on the 108-foot lighthouse. This was the first United States flag raised in Confederate Georgia. McCarten was later admonished for acting "without orders" and placed in irons for ten days.[13]

Later that day, more vessels joined Rodgers. After Tybee was secured, Sherman and a few staff members came ashore. They made a reconnaissance of Tybee to learn its topography and the range of Fort Pulaski's guns. Sherman noted that the barbette guns could explode shells on the western end of the island near Lazaretto Creek. Sherman believed that Federal artillery could reduce the fort from Tybee, using a combination of mortars and breaching guns.[14]

DuPont ordered Commander John S. Missroon to occupy the Tybee roadstead "giving him a fine anchorage for the winter and *sealing* Savannah for the remainder of the war." Missroon helped reconnoiter Tybee; he felt its immediate occupation by marines and the placement of artillery in the Martello tower would enable the Federals to maintain possession.[15]

U.S.A.M.H.I.
John S. Missroon

That night, Confederate Captain James B. Read and a squad of ten men from his Irish Volunteers within Fort Pulaski crossed to Tybee and beached at Kings Landing. Although encountering Federals, they burned the interior of the lighthouse, two houses nearby, and a house at Kings Landing. Before withdrawing, they also burned the abandoned hospital and houses at the western end of the island. Within two weeks, the Federals repaired the gutted lighthouse interior, and it subsequently served as a signal station. Read later saw the Northerners searching for cotton and rice on the island and dispersed his men to neighboring islands to burn all stores which might be valuable to the Federals.[16]

On November 26, while the Union forces strengthened Tybee, Confederate Commodore Josiah Tattnall steamed down the Savannah River in his *Savannah* with a large hulk lashed to her side serving as a platform for two guns. Accompanying the *Savannah* were two two-gun paddle vessels, the *Resolute* and *Sampson*. These two sailed a short distance below the fort and fired at Union vessels in the Roads before slowly withdrawing and anchoring near the fort. Federals moved forward to return fire but carefully kept out of range of Fort Pulaski's guns. DuPont's *Flag* and the *Pocahontas* returned fire. In all, fifty shots were exchanged during the hour-long encounter, but neither side inflicted any damage. Federal vessels fired occasional shots at the fort until December 3, when Tattnall's vessels returned upriver.[17]

At sunset of November 29, five days after the Federal landing on Tybee, Captain Quincy A. Gillmore, chief engineer of Sherman's expeditionary force, arrived aboard the army steamer *Ben De Ford*. The next morning, he disembarked with three companies of the 4th New Hampshire under the command of Major Jeremiah E. Drew. Gillmore learned that most of the marshy island was subject to tidal flooding from the Tybee River that centrally divided the island, leaving only the sandy north and northeast shores above water. On the

U.S.A.M.H.I.
Josiah Tattnall

F.P.N.M.

The Martello tower on the northeast corner of Tybee Island.
The tower is no longer standing.

U.S.A.M.H.I.

Lighthouse at Tybee Island viewed from the top of the Martello tower.

Quincy A. Gillmore

west end of the island across the sandy neck of land he found an abandoned 100-yard parapet built to prevent Federal forces from approaching Fort Pulaski from the east. Beyond the earthwork Gillmore saw abandoned brush shelters. Returning to the lighthouse, Gillmore inspected the nearby abandoned concrete three-story Martello tower, which had been built during the War of 1812, and found its walls varied in thickness from ten feet at the base to four at the top. The ground floor was a magazine, the second story had one opening facing west, and the third story was a room with twelve evenly placed loop-holes around the periphery. The wall rose an additional four and a half feet above the roof. At the base of the tower were incomplete sand gun emplacements. Gillmore felt that one or two siege guns mounted on the tower could control the principal channel of the Savannah River.

After inspecting the north shore of Tybee and examining Fort Pulaski through field glasses, Gillmore concluded that he could reduce the fort with batteries of mortars and guns. He postulated that batteries might be established closer than Tybee Island, but he never explored McQueens Island, across Lazaretto Creek west of Tybee, to realize that it was an unsuitable marsh.

Gillmore initially proposed that the besieging batteries, each containing one gun, be placed twenty to twenty-five yards apart. He suggested placing the batteries immediately west of the lighthouse and recommended excavating each battery site as low as possible to protect the mortars and to allow high parapets for the other guns. The engineer proposed high mounded sides and back walls for the batteries and recommended covering each gun with a bombproof of earth-covered logs. He wanted the embrasure of each battery to be as narrow as possible. Gillmore estimated that five of every eight of the mortar shells fired would hit the fort. He wanted enough mortars to allow one shell to land in the fort every minute, and a number of guns to also strike the fort once a minute. In total he wanted ten 10-inch mortars, ten 13-inch mortars, eight heavy rifled guns, and eight columbiads. To maintain fire continuously day and night he needed 900 shells/mortar, 900 rounds of solid shot/gun for the guns and columbiads, and 300 rounds of shells/gun for the columbiads, too. Gillmore recommended that two or three flat-bottomed bateaux be built at Hilton Head to land guns and supplies. Finally, he recommended that Tybee Island be immediately occupied by at least a full regiment to prevent the reoccupation of the island by Confederate forces.[18]

Gillmore had confidence in the effectiveness of the newly developed rifled artillery.[19] He would request two types of rifled guns for the investment of Fort

Pulaski. First was the Parrott gun, developed by Robert P. Parrott, a West Point graduate who served as inspector of cannon for the army until he resigned in 1836 with the rank of captain, and until his death in 1867, as supervisor of the West Point Foundry. Parrott developed a manufacturing process for cast iron rifled cannon before the Civil War. The tube was rotated horizontally after casting and was cooled from the inside with a stream of water, which allowed the more slowly cooling exterior to compress and strengthen the interior. While the hot tube rotated, a wrought iron band was slipped over the breech and, because the tube was rotating, it cooled and clamped itself uniformly, providing even reinforcing strength. Gillmore would use five "30-pounders" during the siege. These guns were rifled with five lands and grooves and fired a 30-pound solid projectile or a 25-pound shell with a plate of soft metal at the base to take the rifling.[20]

Ripley, Artillery, p. 301

The other type of gun Gillmore would use was the rifled smoothbore using the James system of projectiles. Rhode Island militia general Charles T. James developed this system using a 6-Pounder Model 1841 smoothbore gun rifled with 15 lands and grooves; by the time of the siege of Fort Pulaski, several large caliber smoothbore guns had been rifled with fewer grooves for use with the distinctive James projectile.[21] The James system involved a unique projectile, a cast iron body with a conical anterior and a cage of slanted iron ribs that started near the middle and extended to a solid ring at the lower end. The core of the lower half was hollow, and the spaces between each of the eight ribs communicated with the central core at their lower ends. The ribbed lower half of the projectile was encased with soft lead and covered with a greased sewn canvas jacket. When the gun was fired, the expanding gases entered the open center of the cage and swelled through the openings between the "ribs" and forced the soft lead into the grooves that the greased canvas served to lubricate.[22] The eight elongated ribs and openings resembled a wheel hub, and Confederates in the fort would later refer to

42-pounder (7 inch) James shell with sheath removed, showing the slanting ribs comprising 3/5 of the projectile. The outer lay of lead and greased canvas are absent. The discharge of the gun forces gases into the open center of the base and out through the openings between the ribs, thus forcing the soft metal into the rifling; the greased canvas lubricated the rifling.

these projectiles as "cartwheels." Gillmore would employ five of these guns: one 24-pounder, two 32-pounders, and two 42-pounders. James shot generally were double the weight of the similar smoothbore caliber roundshot, e.g., a 42-pounder

(7-inch) James projectile weighed 84 pounds. The James projectiles were considerably heavier than those fired by the Parrott guns. Ammunition subsequently developed during the war was superior to the James system and the latter fell into disuse. For its time, however, it was an effective projectile.[23]

Sherman agreed with Gillmore about the guns and supplies necessary for the bombardment and ordered armament sufficient for the reduction of the fort. Sherman had reservations about rifled artillery and suggested that the guns be more fully tested before being employed. He reasoned that the closest battery would be one and a half miles from Fort Pulaski and if the rifled shells did not strike the wall point foremost, then 10-inch columbiads could be used along with the mortars. Sherman had great confidence in mortars dropping explosive shells into the fort and shattering the casemate arches from above. He also knew that columbiads could shatter the brick wall with their large iron balls.

Sherman had reason to be concerned about placement of the batteries. During his reconnaissance of the island on November 27, he had drawn fire from the fort. Although Fort Pulaski's casemate guns were ineffective, its barbette guns easily reached the western end of Tybee Island. Sherman realized that western Tybee, potential site of the batteries, was closest to the fort. Like Gillmore, he did not explore McQueens Island. Sherman believed that siege mortars would achieve Fort Pulaski's reduction, and concluded that if the fort's casemate guns proved effective, it would not be reduced.[24]

In early December, Sherman ordered Colonel Rudolph Rosa's 46th New York Infantry to occupy Tybee Island. Sherman planned to quickly land sea coast artillery for batteries at the tower and lighthouse. These guns could control the channel entering the Savannah River without the navy's assistance.[25]

Without orders from the War Department, Sherman made plans to take advantage of the good weather before the onset of the hot, semi-tropical, enervating summer. Since most of his force consisted of volunteer soldiers, he felt acutely the need for additional experienced engineer, ordnance, artillery, and quartermaster officers. Sherman alerted the War Department that he was rapidly diluting his numbers by occupying increasing numbers of coastal islands. He requested more reinforcements: ten regiments of infantry, one regiment of cavalry, and one regiment of regular artillery.[26]

Sherman also realized early that he required additional ordnance for the reduction of Fort Pulaski and submitted a detailed list of his needed supplies. But the necessary guns, chiefly mortars and columbiads, would not arrive for over two months; they had to be cast in Pittsburgh. Again Sherman asked for an experienced ordnance officer. It is not clear if he wished to replace or help his staff ordnance officer, Lieutenant Shunk, whose problems with alcohol would become apparent in the following months.[27]

After observing the volunteer troops aboard the *Wabash,* DuPont's appraisal was even more severe than Sherman's. In mid-December he recalled that if the volunteers had "had the discipline of this ship's crew, with the relationship between them and their officers which exists between the sailors and theirs, they could destroy the railroads and take both Charleston and Savannah in the next week."[28]

Before this operation, Sherman and DuPont had worked closely for months. The commodore wrote his wife on December 1 that he was still getting on well with the general, "having determined to do so, and look over, as you advise, all little things and some big ones; he means well."[29]

On December 1, DuPont ordered Commander C. Raymond P. Rodgers to lead a naval force into Wassaw Sound, south of Tybee Island, to discover the position of Confederate batteries.[30] The 4-gun screw steamers *Ottawa* and *Pembina*, and the *Seneca*, departed on December 5. Rodgers learned that the Confederates had removed eight guns and abandoned Wassaw Island's fortifications.[31]

Since Wassaw and Ossabaw Sounds allowed passage to Savannah and Fort Jackson, bypassing Fort Pulaski, DuPont reasoned that 10,000 men could take the city. Although lamenting that "there seems no plan," DuPont was only partially correct in his evaluation of the approaches to the Savannah River.[32] There were two routes from Wassaw Sound up Wilmington River or Wilmington Narrows to Saint Augustine Creek and hence the Savannah River. There was no navigable water connection between the Savannah River and the rivers that flowed into Ossabaw Sound.

U.S.A.M.H.I.

C. Raymond P. Rodgers

On December 11, DuPont ordered further investigation of the inlets and sounds below Tybee Roads. With the *Ottawa*, *Seneca*, *Pembina*, and *Henry Andrew*, the latter a 3-gun screw steamer, Rodgers entered Ossabaw Sound, and discovered another fort at the eastern end of Green Island on the Vernon River. Rodgers' vessels withdrew when this fort fired on them, and the shells fell short. The Confederate fort commanded the Vernon River, Little Ogeechee River, and Hell's Gate, the passage between the Vernon and Great Ogeechee Rivers.[33]

By mid-December, on Tybee Island members of the 3rd Rhode Island Artillery were mounting guns in the sand fort at the lighthouse on Tybee Island. From this site they closed the channel of the Savannah River but could never reach, much less reduce, Fort Pulaski.[34]

On December 14, General Sherman summarized the situation of his forces thus far. They occupied a coastal line from South Edisto to Tybee. Wassaw and Ossabaw Sounds had been abandoned by the Confederates. Facing Sherman was a strategic line with its right resting on Burnside Island, site of the village of Montgomery on the Vernon River. To the north, Confederate Fort Wimberly stood on Isle of Hope on the Back River. Farther north, Battery Daniels on the same island covered the Skidaway River.[35] Still farther north, at the village of Wassaw on Thunderbolt Island, facing Saint Augustine Creek, stood Fort Thunderbolt,[36] then

**Fort Jackson (1900) viewed from the west;
the Savannah River is on the left.**

Bonaventure Battery on Saint Augustine Creek, and yet farther north, a battery at Causten's Bluff, also on Saint Augustine Creek at the junction with Oatland Creek. A mile overland to the north was old Fort Jackson, a brick work mounting nine guns,[37] and nearby earthen Fort Lee with places for nine guns. The Confederate lines then skipped across the Savannah River into South Carolina. The Federals had further learned of Confederate troop concentrations between the Vernon and Savannah Rivers, in Savannah, and north across the river at Hardeeville and other towns along the railroad, with advanced posts in Fort Pulaski and in South Carolina at New River Bridge, Bluffton, Port Royal Bridge and points farther north.[38]

General Sherman was unsure where to concentrate his force, but by December 14 decided that if he had sufficient men Savannah should be his object. He saw that, while Fort Pulaski was being shelled, naval gunboats could bombard the garrisons in the Confederate river forts on the Vernon and Saint Augustine Rivers. Federals could then land at Montgomery and neighboring Beaulieu, both on the Vernon River, and march overland to seize in reverse the fortifications on Saint Augustine River, Fort Jackson, and Savannah. Sherman believed this southern approach of Savannah should be coordinated with penetration into South Carolina at Hardeeville, Bluffton, and New River Bridge to capture part of the Savannah and Charleston Railroad. Unsure of the number of opposing Confederates, Sherman revised his estimate of late November and doubled his request for reinforcements to twenty infantry regiments. He also requested as many bridge pontoons as possible. Sherman promised that if the troops he requested exceeded his needs, he would use the surplus to move against whatever objectives next presented themselves. Again, the general requested "experienced staff officers, particularly a quartermaster of rank and great experience, artillery officers, and, if they cannot be had, ordnance officers." Sherman noted that he had immense work to be done, and it was performed by inadequate volunteer soldiers: "It drags for want of a sufficient number of able directors." He further added that Black labor was a total failure because the former slaves would not work in their new state of apparent freedom without "those aids to which they have ever been accustomed, viz., the driver and the lash."[39]

On December 19, Sherman wrote Major General George B. McClellan, General-in-Chief of the United States Armies, explaining his anticipated movements on the south Atlantic coast. DuPont received his ammunition at the end of November, and Sherman had hoped to send part of his force south to Fernandina, but the Navy again was detained with sinking the recently arrived "stone fleet" in a channel of Charleston harbor. DuPont believed the navy would be ready in two weeks, but Sherman feared that the obligations at Tybee and in South Carolina would divide his infantry forces and leave insufficient men for an expedition to northeast Florida. Sherman and DuPont then decided to "indefinately" postpone the Fernandina expedition. Sherman added that Confederate threats against his small force on Tybee Island had forced him to reinforce the New Yorkers with seven companies of the 7th Connecticut on December 18 and 19. Three of DuPont's gunboats joined two vessels already at Tybee Roads. Infantry observers on Tybee had reported that Fort Pulaski had also been reinforced and that Commodore Tattnall was constantly reconnoitering with his fleet. Although Sherman was optimistic about severing the Charleston and Savannah Railroad south of Coosawatchie, he was primarily concerned about a possible Southern counteroffensive.[40]

On December 20, Sherman provided Brigadier General Lorenzo Thomas, Adjutant General of the United States Army, with his assessment of the defenses of Savannah. Sherman knew of an earth fort near the mouth of Saint Augustine Creek (Causten's Bluff) and another on Green Island. Although both contained heavy caliber guns, he felt gunboats could shell them. In addition, masonry Fort Jackson protected Savannah on the right bank of the Savannah River. Escaped slaves had told Sherman that strong entrenchments guarded the south side of the city. Sherman estimated that he would need forty pieces of siege artillery to take Savannah, excluding any to be used to bombard Fort Pulaski. He requested five 10-inch siege mortars, two coehorn mortars, two stone mortars, five 18-pounder siege guns, ten 8-inch siege howitzers, twenty 24-pounder siege guns, and five 18-pounder siege guns. He requested an "able ordnance officer" to superintend the siege.[41]

On December 20, Commander John S. Missroon blocked the Wilmington River to prevent egress by the *Fingal*, a British twin screw blockade runner that had reached Savannah five weeks earlier. He sent the *Seminole*, a five-gun screw steamer, and the *Henry Andrew* to the entrance of the river into Wassaw Sound near Cabbage Island. The *Andrew* was subsequently relieved by the *Pembina*.[42]

* * * * * * *

Accompanied by Lawton, Governor Brown, Commodore Tattnall, and "some ten or twelve army and naval officers or high rank," General Lee paid a hurried visit to Savannah and Fort Pulaski on November 10-11. He told Olmstead: "They will make it very warm for you with shells from that point [Kings Landing] but

Leslie's Weekly

**Somewhat fanciful depiction of Fort Pulaski during the
Confederate occupation.**

they cannot breach at that distance." The greatest distance that balls could be effective against masonry walls was eight hundred yards and Tybee was over 1,700 yards away. Lee directed Olmstead to build traverses between the barbette guns, dig ditches on the parade ground to catch shells, tear down the porch along the officer's quarters, and erect blindage around the entire interior circuit of the fort to cover the casemate doors and to cover the blindage with several feet of earth. After Lee's visit, Confederates floated rafts of timber for the blindage down the river into the south channel and up the small irrigation canal into the moat.[43]

On November 13, Secretary of War Judah P. Benjamin ordered Lawton to move to Savannah "all unarmed troops offered for the war" and to arm them with rifles from the *Fingal*. The War Department authorized Lee to use 4,500 rifles. In addition, 1,100 rifles had been brought in by the state of Georgia on the *Fingal* for her own troops; Lee was authorized to use these, too, giving him a total of 5,600 rifles. On November 19, Lee was further directed to retain 10,000 pounds of cannon powder from the supplies brought by the *Fingal*. Also on this day, Colonel Augustus R. Wright, with his 38th Georgia (Wright's Legion), was ordered to Savannah to aid coastal defense.[44]

Two days later, Lee, now in Charleston, candidly wrote his daughter Mildred that his assignment was "another forlorn hope expedition. Worse than West Virginia." Although privately discouraged, Lee began designing his regional defensive system. He devised a three-part plan for his 300-mile coastal front which extended from Georgetown, South Carolina, to the Saint John's River in Florida. First, he would prepare the defenses of Savannah, Charleston, and Fort Pulaski for a more serious bombardment than they had thus far anticipated. Second, he planned to block waterways with obstructions and batteries to deny their use to the Federals. Third, he would concentrate Confederate forces near the most probable points of Federal attack, taking advantage of the mobility offered by the Savannah and Charleston Railroad. He planned assembly points inland beyond the range of the Federal gunboats. Sixty-eight hundred men were stationed between Charleston and the Savannah River. Fifty-five hundred more were around Savannah but few could be withdrawn without exposing the city. Many of the poorly equipped Georgia troops had little field artillery. By the first of the year, Lee had assembled almost 25,000 men in his department. He finalized his defensive strategic concepts in late November, and he would adhere to them during his time of service in the department.[45]

On November 18, Lee visited Savannah on a departmental inspection tour. He continued to Brunswick, Georgia, and later to Fernandina, Florida. Upon his return to Savannah three days later, he wrote Samuel Cooper that he had removed guns from the less important points and sent them to "those considered of greater consequence." He added, "the entrance to Cumberland Sound and Brunswick and the water approaches to Savannah and Charleston are the only points that it is proposed to defend." The next day, Lee wrote his daughters about his inspection tour to the south. Of the defenses he wrote, "They are poor indeed & I have laid off work enough to employ our people a month. I hope our enemy will be polite enough to wait for us. It is difficult to get our people to realize their position." During these days, Lee, based at Coosawatchie, made frequent long trips of inspection. Riding up to 35 miles on "Greenbrier," a young gray horse Lee purchased from one of his staff, this animal soon earned the name of "Traveller" because of the distance he covered on these journeys.[46]

By the end of the month, Lee had accumulated at least 50 rounds for each artillery piece in his department; he had reached half of his goal. He further asked the Confederate War Department for experienced artillerists to come and serve as instructors.[47]

Federal occupation of Tybee Island neither alarmed Lee nor deterred him from continuing on his plan of earthwork construction along the river. From Fort Pulaski, Olmstead wrote his wife that he had seen "nothing more than what we expected ever since we gave up Tybee." Although preparations at Fort Pulaski had not gone as rapidly as Lee had hoped, Fort Jackson was fully armed. Lee believed the Federals could force their way up the river. He was unsure whether Savannah was the object of Federal activity and cautioned Ripley, now in command of the Charleston defenses, to maintain his alertness. Lee was unconcerned about the Federal occupation of most coastal islands because he believed once the Northerners had pillaged them they would not find them worth holding.[48]

On November 27, Lieutenant Colonel William G. Gill, Lee's ordnance officer, reported on the status of Fort Pulaski's defenses. The fort now had five 10-inch columbiads *en barbette*, six 8-inch columbiads *en barbette*, and two 10-inch mortars *en barbette*. There were three 8-inch columbiads, two 42-pounder guns, twenty 32-pounder and one 24-pounder guns in casemates. The magazine held 120 rounds of shot and shell for each gun. The two mortars shared 70 shells between them. Gill ordered two 12-pounder field howitzers to be placed to flank the gate.

U.S.A.M.H.I

John C. Pemberton

He found many fuses "imperfect" and ordered replacements from the arsenal in Augusta, Georgia.[49]

On November 20, Olmstead wrote Lawton to express his fears that the Federals would bypass the fort from Hilton Head Island using the channels north of the river. He requested that one of Tattnall's steamers come down at night to cruise the channels north of the fort. The next day, Olmstead had the spars removed from the ship the Confederates had earlier sunk to obstruct Wall's Cut. He brought them to the fort to be placed on the inside of the parapet to throw down on any possible scaling parties. Chain from the hulk was placed in bags and attached to sabots for use in place of canister. The next day, Brigadier General John C. Pemberton, Northern-born but secessionist in philosophy and married to a Virginian, reported for duty to Lee as his second in command.[50]

On December 1, the Fort Pulaski garrison began in earnest the work that Lee had suggested to strengthen the fort. The men built sand bag traverses on the ramparts between the guns. Enough twenty-foot lengths of fourteen inch squared pine were accumulated, and they were tipped upright at a 20 degree angle before the casemate doors to form the blindage; dirt was piled against them. This work was completed by the end of the year.[51]

On the tenth, Lee reorganized South Carolina into five military districts and appointed Brigadier General Thomas F. Drayton commander of the area north of the Savannah River. During the remainder of December, Lee asked Secretary of War Benjamin for twenty more heavy guns. Many guns that Lee found in place on the coast had been there for over 30 years and were of "too light a calibre to cope with the powerful ordnance facing them in the Federal navy." Benjamin sent nine 32-pounders, one 24-pounder, three 8-inch columbiads and eight 42-pounder carronades from the Norfolk Navy Yard.[52]

On December 24, Walter H. Taylor cautioned Lawton against firing artillery at Federal ships that were out of range. The threat of enemy vessels, Taylor added, should "stimulate the officers and the troops of your district to press forward the projected earthworks and defenses to a speedy completion." Taylor noted that further reinforcements must come from the state of Georgia.[53]

On December 26, Tattnall's squadron, consisting of his flagship, the steamer *Savannah*, the *Resolute, Sampson, Ida,* and *Bartow*, sailed down the river to try newly received guns and give the men artillery practice. Tattnall fired at the Federals' vessels in the mouth of the river, forcing them out to sea. The Confederates pursued for several miles, and, after demonstrating the "inefficient character" of their guns, returned to their anchorage.[54]

On December 28, newly appointed commander of the Georgia forces, Major General Henry R. Jackson, offered his full cooperation with Lee. He had enjoyed a long and cordial relationship with Lawton and hoped to help in the defense of Georgia with his reserve forces. On January 3, Lee assigned Jackson to serve under Lawton, who would designate where the reserve troops were to be employed.[55]

Tattnall anticipated a Federal approach along the waterways south of the Savannah River and had a battery built on the small island across from Fort Jackson, which he named Battery Cheves. Part of its armament was some 32-pounder ship's guns from the Navy Department. Tattnall prepared fire rafts in the Savannah River near Fort Jackson.[56]

On the afternoon of December 29, the newly promoted Colonel Olmstead was working with a casemated 32-pounder.[57] Three Federals walked out on Kings Point, and standing on the ruins of a burned house, made "defiant and indecent gestures toward the fort." Olmstead

> wanted to get the elevation of our 32 Pounders for that particular spot, and accordingly had one of the guns trained upon the group, but without the slightest thought that there would be anything more than a scare for the men. But the shot hit the middle man and probably tore him to pieces. Through my glasses I could see the two others crawling up to the body on hands and knees, and then getting up and running away as fast as their legs could take them. It was a very extraordinary shot; its probability of its being made again with a smooth bore gun at that distance, (a few yards short of a mile), is infinitesimally small.[58]

Olmstead did not know, but he had cut in half a private in the 46th New York. This event made a big impression on the New Yorkers, many of whom were still talking about it a month later. Rumor among the Federals on Tybee Island was that because of the incident, Olmstead had been promoted to colonel. Olmstead had received his new rank on December 26.[59]

As the new year began, the garrison of the fort consisted of the Irish Jasper Greens (Captain John Foley), the German Volunteers (Captain John H. Stegin), the Washington Volunteers (Captain John McMahon), the Irish Volunteers (Captain James B. Read), and the Oglethorpe Light Infantry, Company B (Captain Thomas W. Sims).[60]

* * * * * * *

At the end of December, Gillmore interviewed a "colored man Brutus" who was "the most intelligent slave I have met here." Brutus had reached Tybee in a canoe from Wilmington Island. Gillmore told Sherman that Brutus said Confederate pickets went daily to the eastern edge of Wilmington Island. Further, Brutus reported on the armaments of Skidaway Battery and Thunderbolt Battery further up the river. The road from Skidaway Battery to Savannah passed within a half mile of Thunderbolt Battery. Brutus affirmed that boats of ten feet draft could pass through Wassaw Sound to the Savannah River, at high tide, through Wilmington

Narrows and Saint Augustine Creek, leaving Wilmington Island on the left and by-passing the Skidaway and Thunderbolt Batteries. Brutus said no guns covered Wilmington Narrows. Saint Augustine Creek could be entered by that route three miles north of Thunderbolt Battery. He added that the steamer *St. Mary* had been plying this route for the last two summers. Brutus apparently was unaware of the battery at Causten's Bluff. Gillmore continued, "If we can get into Savannah River, by a line of communication that we can retain and control, it seems to me a far better policy to reduce Pulaski by cutting off its supplies, than by the very doubtful and very expensive operation of bombardment from Tybee Island." He recommended "a gun boat reconnaissance up Wilmington Narrows, and solicit[ed] the privilege of accompanying it." Gillmore estimated it would take a month to prepare batteries on Tybee.

If we suppose all the mortars to be 13-inch, and all the solid shot to be thrown from 8-inch Columbiads, we require storage room and transportation for 300 tons of powder, 1,900 tons of shells, and 470 tons of shot. . . . As there seems to be at least two ways of accomplishing the reduction of Pulaski, we ought to select the one offering the greatest advantages as regards rapidity and economy. . . . My chief reliance would be, as I have already intimated to you, in heavy rifled guns, to be used in breaching the walls and dismounting the guns.[61]

Also by year's end, the blockading fleet, under Commander Percival Drayton, was in place in Tybee Roads. It consisted of the *Pawnee*, a 10-gun screw steamer, *Wyandotte*, a 5-gun screw steamer, and *Ben De Ford*. Lieutenant Cornelius M. Schoonmaker, on the *Wyandotte*, told his family what blockading duty was like: just out of Fort Pulaski's range "we can see the Rebel flag floating, but with our present force we are unable to take it. We use every precaution to prevent a surprise by the enemy. I always have a whole watch on deck at night the look outs are armed with pikes, while loaded muskets and pikes are ready for the rest of the watch."[62]

By the end of December, Sherman had completed the sand fort near the light-house on Tybee Island and had mounted one 8-inch columbiad, one 32-pounder gun and one 24-pounder gun; he believed these guns could close the ship channel. Sherman had planned to install two 30-pounder Parrotts on the Martello tower, but decided instead to mount them a half mile west of the lighthouse behind sand hills. He realized Tattnall's small gunboats could come down the south channel of the Savannah River, pass the fort, and assail his positions "without much resistance on the part of our vessels laying in the main channel." Sherman subsequently mounted several more columbiads near the Parrott guns to strengthen this defensive position and to "assist the work of the mortar batteries destined for the bombardment whenever they arrive."[63]

* * * * * * *

The capture of Port Royal was only the first stage of the Navy's plan to seize two harbors for the South Atlantic Blockading Squadron. The July, 1861, plan designated Fernandina as the other harbor, and DuPont wanted to secure the port before becoming more involved in helping the army. Increasing criticism in Northern newspapers over lack of progress angered General Sherman and on December 21 he complained to Secretary of War Simon Cameron. For some time Sherman had troops ready to move against Fernandina, but the Navy had first been halted while awaiting ammunition and supplies and then further delayed when sinking the "stone fleet" in Charleston harbor. Disgusted with the lack of cooperation, Sherman told Cameron that he had developed a plan that would require little naval assistance. When the expedition to Port Royal Sound was originally planned, there was no thought of taking Savannah and, therefore, Sherman did not have cavalry or field artillery. Although Sherman was anxious to "push on and crush out this rebellion," he had not yet been provided with proper reinforcements and felt that neither the public interest nor his professional reputation would be served by making "dashes without object and without lasting results." Everything required "thought, system, and prudence."[64]

Cameron agreed with Sherman, and observed that "there has been too great a desire to avoid responsibility rather than force the enemy into early action." The Secretary wisely noted that "while we are preparing our enemy is also engaged in preparation, and that, being in his own country, he can do so much more rapidly than ourselves." Cameron offered to send to Sherman whatever reinforcements and supplies he needed but concluded that, given his distance from Washington, he must rely on his own judgment.[65]

Sherman continued to plan. He was aware of additional Confederate batteries being built on Skidaway Island below Thunderbolt. He felt, however, that once he received the requested cavalry and field artillery, he could dash into the South Carolina mainland, destroy the railroad, and cut off Savannah from above. Such a movement could be made together with one directly on Savannah or independently, since "every one seems impatient to do something." He believed movement against Savannah from the south would be easy and would eliminate the need to bombard Fort Pulaski.[66]

Chapter 3

"We are all disgusted with the Navy"

As the *Seminole* patrolled in the Wilmington River on January 2, she picked up a contraband. He was one of several escaped slaves and deserters who brought word of Savannah and Fort Pulaski over the next four months. Although he incorrectly reported fifteen thousand troops in and around Savannah, he knew that provisions and ammunition were scarce. The slave added the fort had provisions for three months and enumerated the armament of the batteries on Skidaway, Thunderbolt, and Green Islands. Finally, he said that the *Fingal*, unable to escape to sea, had unloaded its cargo of three hundred bales of cotton.[1]

That same day Commander John Rodgers wrote Captain Davis about information from Isaac Tatnall Gillis, another contraband from the *St. Mary* in Savannah. Gillis had detailed the water route from Ossabaw Sound to Montgomery, a village ten miles below Savannah, and reported that a good road joined the two. Gillis also wrote that Freeborn Cut was 24 feet deep, although Rodgers had sounded it at low tide at nine feet.[2]

Explorations continued for future operations against both Fort Pulaski and Savannah. On January 2, 1862, First Lieutenant James H. Wilson, Sherman's chief topographical engineer, destined to be a major general, reported on his reconnaissance of the land and streams north of the Savannah River.

U.S.A.M.H.I.

James H. Wilson

On December 30, General Sherman had sent Wilson with forty men from Company A, 3rd Rhode Island Artillery under First Lieutenant Thomas W. Fry and forty men of Company E, 3rd Rhode Island Artillery under Captain James E. Bailey. That night they pulled through Skull Creek and Calibouge Sound in four large boats and made for the New River, landing on Pine Island at 9:00 p.m. The Rhode Islanders killed the few Confederate pickets they encountered as the boats continued. The following day, they passed through Pull-and-Be-Damned Creek and that night landed on Daufuskie Island.[3] Wilson knew the Confederates were aware that his party was behind their lines because a series of Confederate signal rockets had streaked across the daylight sky.

Wilson selected a single boat for the final, longest part of the reconnaissance. He, Bailey, and a small boat's crew set out to get their bearings while the remaining men returned to Pine Island. Ten artillerymen kept lookout and eight Black boatmen carefully rowed down the Wright River, through Wall's Cut west through Mud River into the Savannah River. While Wilson took soundings and made observations, the Rhode Islanders watched for Confederates. At night they ascended within three miles of Savannah. Coming unexpectedly within twenty yards of the *Sampson*, they quietly drifted back down river. After exchanging a few shots with Confederate pickets the following morning, they reached Daufuskie Island about 10:00 a.m. and slept. The following day they returned to Hilton Head.[4]

West of Daufuskie Island, Wilson had sounded the New River up to fifteen feet deep. Wall's Cut, which joined the New and the Wright Rivers west of Turtle Island south of Daufuskie, was 250 yards long and 100 feet wide. The Wright River continued south into the Savannah River about two miles above Fort Pulaski and varied in depth to fifteen feet. When Wilson had gone west on Mud River, a branch of Wright River along the north shore of Jones Island, he had found the water scarcely eight feet on the flood tide; at low tide it was little more than a marsh with current. Mud River, however, continued six miles before it merged with the Savannah River six miles above Fort Pulaski.

A 90-foot sunken bark with a 24-foot beam partially obstructed the middle of Wall's Cut. In addition, three rows of square piles blocked the cut. The sunken vessel contained little ballast and its free swaying with the tide had dislodged several piles. Wilson decided the obstructions could be easily removed. Earlier, General Lee had also come to the same realization, "yet as the marsh is too soft and impassable to admit the construction of a battery, it is the only obstacle that could be opposed to its navigation."[5]

Several days later, Sherman ordered Major Oliver T. Beard, of the 48th New York, to remove all obstructions from Wall's Cut. Beard led a party composed of Company I, 1st New York Volunteer Engineers under Captain Joseph Walker, twenty picked men of the same regiment, and sixteen men from Company G, 3rd Rhode Island Heavy Artillery, under Sergeant Hudson. On the night of January 8, the men loaded tools into surf-boats, and *Mayflower* towed them to the Dunn Plantation on the south end of Daufuskie Island. They began the removal of the obstructions the next night. On the north side they sawed off the piles level with the bottom of the channel, and the hulk swung to the south side, leaving the passage 53 feet wide and thirteen and one-half feet deep at high tide. They completed their work in three days. Major George F. Gardiner and three companies of the 7th Connecticut were stationed on Daufuskie and assigned to guard the channel. Sherman hoped that navy gunboats passing through Wall's Cut, down the Wright River, and up the Savannah River, could cover either a movement against Savannah or "the erection of the investing batteries."[6]

Sherman considered building batteries on the islands between Savannah and Fort Pulaski to close the river and avoid the need to bombard the fort from Tybee Island. Wilson reported, however, that Jones Island and Long Island, upstream in the Savannah River from Cockspur Island, were entirely marsh and unsuitable for battery sites. Elba Island, upstream from Long Island, had not been explored but might be suitable.

Sherman also wanted to evaluate the water channels south of the Savannah River. On January 7, Gillmore, John Rodgers, and a small crew embarked up the Wilmington River in a howitzer-mounted launch from the *Seminole* and explored the Little Tybee River from Wassaw Sound and Freeborn's Cut to the first firm ground on Wilmington Island, Mrs. Barnard's house. Above this site, the passage was known as Wilmington Narrows until it reached Saint Augustine Creek. At Mrs. Barnard's house the party learned of a Confederate force located near Dr. James P. Screven's house, also on Wilmington Island. Having ventured nine miles and afraid of alerting enemy pickets and causing them to obstruct the Narrows, the party halted. At half tide, the depth of the water varied from eighteen to forty feet; the channel was "wide, deep, and practicable." Isaac Tattnall, the Black pilot, and other contrabands said that the unexplored portion narrowed but was suitable for vessels up to 170 feet long.[7] Rodgers and Gillmore felt gunboats could pass through Freeborn's Cut into the Savannah River without hindrance. If they encountered unanticipated obstructions, they could easily return; so both men believed that their ships could enter the Savannah River, ascend rapidly, fight past Fort Jackson, and reduce it from above. Transport vessels could then easily journey up the river. After Fort Jackson fell, Gillmore and Rodgers anticipated that the Confederates would abandon the then useless batteries on Skidaway and Thunderbolt Islands. Fort Pulaski would then be isolated and starved into surrender.

Gillmore and Rodgers had studied coastal survey charts and knew that Federal gunboats in the Savannah River and Saint Augustine Creek could protect the land approaches to Fort Jackson after it had been occupied by Federal forces. An occupying force in Fort Jackson with easy means of resupply and reinforcement could serve as an excellent base for operations against the city of Savannah.[8]

On January 14, Sherman and DuPont conferred aboard the *Wabash* with Wright, Gillmore, Captain Davis, and Commander C. Raymond P. Rodgers. A strong storm prevented Commander John Rodgers from attending. From Wilson's and Gillmore's expeditions, Sherman had learned the strength and condition of the Savannah defenses and believed "there was an excellent prospect of capturing the city if set about soon." DuPont was concerned about passing Fort Jackson with his gunboats; Sherman said he would land at the mouth of Saint Augustine Creek and

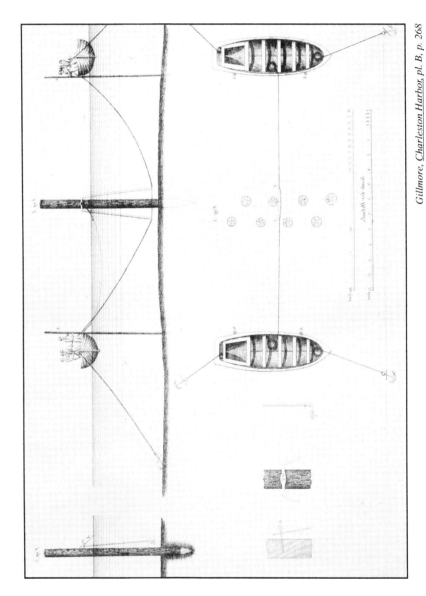

Gillmore, Charleston Harbor, pl. B, p. 268

Diagram of Federal method for sawing obstructing river pilings below the surface of the water.

take the fort from the land side. After a thorough discussion, Sherman stated everyone agreed that:

> a sufficient number of the gunboats could be got up the river as to make it not only a practicable but a profitable operation. It was decided to immediately move on Savannah with all the gunboats of practicable draught, in the absence of light draught steam transports, which I had expected, but had not arrived, the Navy was to give me all the assistance it could render me.

Sherman planned to use the many sail vessels in Port Royal harbor to transport men and material. The shallow draft gunboats would tow a few light draft steamers. DuPont "thought it was an excellent thing" and would provide all the necessary vessels. Sherman remembered that "every officer present regarded the thing as very feasible, indeed."[9]

Two days later, Sherman wrote DuPont asking about the proposed combined operations. Sherman had learned that the only land battery covering the Savannah River above Fort Pulaski was Fort Jackson. Although a battery was being constructed at the lower end of Hutchinson Island, near Fig Island, it yet mounted no guns. "It appears to me," DuPont read, "that if the Savannah River is to be entered, now is the time, before these batteries can be completed."[10]

On January 17, John Rodgers, Lieutenant John S. Barnes of the *Wabash*, James Wilson, Acting Master John W. Godfrey, and contraband pilot William Haffards made a nighttime boat reconnaissance along the Wall's Cut, Wright River, and Mud River route and found it practicable with at least five feet of water at low tide and twelve feet of water at high tide. That confirmed Wilson's January 2 observations that gunboats and light transports could pass at high tide. However, Rodgers still thought the channels too shallow and that his gunboats risked grounding. After conferring with DuPont, Rodgers decided against passage up the Savannah River, concluding "the attempt, then, is not advisable until after the channel shall be staked or buoyed." Upon further reflection, the cosenior naval officers felt that portions of the Savannah River were "too hazardous to attempt the running of gunboats and transports up the river without further examination" and, therefore, Sherman and DuPont decided to begin further investigation immediately. Meanwhile, a balloon went up from Hilton Head Island to observe enemy activity and chart their positions.[11]

During the navy's dilatory efforts, Sherman prepared a force to be ready when and if the navy bypassed Fort Pulaski. It consisted of the 48th New York, two companies of the New York Volunteer Engineers, two companies (Cos. E and G) and a select group from the 3rd Rhode Island Heavy Artillery, part of the 8th Maine— all under the command of Brigadier General Egbert L. Viele. They were to take twenty guns: two 8-inch siege howitzers, four 30-pounder Parrotts, three 20-pounder Parrotts, three 24-pounder James rifles, and eight 24-pounder field howitzers. Half the guns would be on flats towed by the transport steamer *Mayflower*. The others were to be on a schooner that also carried ammunition and intrenching tools. The troops would rendezvous at Daufuskie Island, where Major Gardiner's three companies of the 7th Connecticut had been guarding Wall's Cut since mid-January. DuPont would provide three gunboats.[12]

An optimistic member of Sherman's staff, First Lieutenant Horace Porter, wrote his father that "our forces are to move at once on Savannah," and added that he had "been appointed Chief of Ordnance for the expedition" and was busy preparing a proper siege armament "for our operation in the interior." Porter added that Shunk remained at Port Royal with the reserve. "He has not been doing very well lately and I dare not tell the particulars" Porter added, alluding to Shunk's worsening alcohol problems. Porter cautioned his family to "not mention even our destination until it appears from other sources. If we get started properly we will be entirely successful."[13]

U.S.A.M.H.I.

Egbert L. Viele

Thus, although all had agreed, "within thirty-six hours the naval commander had changed his mind." Sherman later reflected, "could Savannah have been captured, the siege of Pulaski would have been unnecessary." Although Sherman still preferred isolating the fort and avoiding the "slow and expensive process of bombarding Pulaski by cutting it from Savannah," the continuing absence of boats, wagons, and field artillery, caused him by January 20 to abandon further thought of inland operations north of the Savannah River.[14]

Late in the afternoon of January 26, Confederate Commodore Tattnall came down in the *Savannah*, accompanied by the steamer *St. Johns*, to observe Federal activity at Wall's Cut. John Rodgers' gunboats were anchored off Hauge Point at the west end of Daufuskie Island. Tattnall saw the Federals removing the obstructions; they saw him and fled. The *Savannah* moved forward and destroyed "all their implements, which were left behind, together with their shanties on the bank."[15]

That same day, Porter, Sherman's ordnance officer, left Port Royal for the New River. There he found three flats anchored loaded with four 30-pounder Parrotts, three 20-pounder Parrotts, two 8-inch siege howitzers, and one 24-pounder field howitzer. Each boat was towed by steamers and carried equipment and ten rounds for each gun. A schooner accompanied the flat boats with five 24-pounder field howitzers, three 24-pounder James rifles, one 8-inch siege mortar and one 10-inch siege mortar, and 200 rounds of ammunition for each piece. This artillery had been assembled for the now-abandoned joint operation against Savannah. The boats remained in the New River until February 10, guarded by two companies of the 3rd Rhode Island Volunteer Artillery, under the command of Captains William G. Bailey and John H. Gould.[16]

* * * * * * *

On January 8, Lee told General Samuel Cooper that the defensive works and batteries protecting Savannah and Charleston were complete, armed, manned, and sufficient to successfully resist the enemy. Lee felt that he could gather sufficient troops to protect the entire coast line.

> Wherever [the enemy's] fleet can be brought no opposition to his landing can be made except within range of our fixed batteries. We have nothing to oppose to its heavy guns, which sweep over the low banks of this country with irresistible force. The farther he can be withdrawn from his floating batteries the weaker he will become, & lines of defence, covering objects of attack, have been selected with this view.[17]

At the end of the second week in January, Lee inspected Savannah and from there the east coast of Florida. He stopped at Cumberland Island on the Georgia coast and visited for the first time the grave of his father at "Dungeness," the post-Revolutionary War home of General Nathanael Greene. Lee returned to Coosawhatchie on January 16. Three days later he wrote to his eldest son, Colonel George Washington Custis Lee: "Matters are encouraging & if the enemy does not approach in overwhelming numbers we ought to hold our ground. He is quiescent still. What he is preparing for or where he will strike I cannot discover."[18]

On January 8, Captain James B. Read led a detachment of ten-fifteen men of his Irish Volunteers again over to Kings Landing on Tybee to learn Sherman's position there. Moving toward the Martello tower, they encountered Federal pickets who fired and fled. Drums awakened the Union camp. Read escaped to the fort. The Savannah *Republican* concluded, "Whatever may be his faults, he [General Sherman] will never be court-martialed for caution."[19]

On January 12, another company of Confederates rotated through Fort Pulaski. One group was assigned to live in a casemate known as "Christians Rest," "exceedingly airy and heavenly in many of its aspects." The neighboring casemate was called "Purgatory," and "Christians' Rest" was only accessible by passing through "Purgatory." "The morning gun was fired from Purgatory, and the noise and smoke that invaded our 'Rest' were suggestive of those reflections that obtrude themselves even upon the good." Drill on the guns began the first day of arrival.[20]

Next day the 1st Volunteer Regiment of Georgia elected a new major. Captain John Foley (Irish Jasper Guards) received more votes than Captain William R. Pritchard (Coast Rifles), Captain James B. Read (Irish Volunteers), and Lieutenant Black (Phoenix Riflemen).[21]

On January 25, the Irish Volunteers returned to Savannah on the *Ida*, their term of service having expired. Union soldiers on Daufuskie Island clearly saw the comings and goings of Confederate steamers; on a clear day they could see the steeples in Savannah. Private James M. Green, of the 48th New York, wrote that "with a glass [he could] look in the streets of the city. . . . We have a clear view of the rebel steamers from the time they leave the wharf at Savannah till they reach Pulaski."[22]

In mid-January, Confederates observed fourteen blockading vessels outside the bar at Wassaw Sound: eight steamers and six schooners. Three steamers were inside the sound, along with two dismantled hulks that had been there for some time. Five days later, a few Federals from ships in Wassaw Sound landed on Skidaway Island near the Adam's Place and skirmished briefly with the Louisiana pickets, then withdrew. Because of the Federal skirmishing, two days later, the Confederate "Bartow Artillery" of Griffin, the "Coast Rifles" of Chatham county, six companies of Lieutenant Colonel William H. Stiles' regiment (4th Georgia Battalion), the "Sappers and Miners" of Atlanta, and two companies of Wright's Legion (38th Georgia) occupied Skidaway Island.[23]

On January 25 and 26, a second Federal "stone fleet," 12 hulks, was sunk in Maffit channel at Charleston harbor. Lee then learned of Federal activities to clear Wall's Cut and, fearing a move against Savannah, he visited the city on the twenty-eighth and moved his headquarters there six days later. In Savannah he enjoyed the hospitality of the Mackay family, with whom he had spent much time during his assignment at Fort Pulaski thirty years before. Lee was also a frequent guest of the Minis family and that of Moxley Sorrel. From Savannah he continuously urged the War Department to send heavier guns for the fort and the batteries being erected to defend Savannah, and to withdraw "all cannon from the river below the fort."[24]

On January 26, a reporter for the Savannah *Republican* visited Fort Pulaski. He saw the lights of Federal work parties to the north and thought they were "seeking for a channel through which they may enter the river out of reach of our guns." On January 25, Confederates watched Federal vessels enter Wall's Cut; Fort Pulaski fired at them. On the night of the twenty-sixth, an observer at Skidaway saw thirteen Federal vessels crossing the bar into Wassaw Sound while two remained outside.[25]

* * * * * * *

Having abandoned all thought of capturing Savannah, Sherman and DuPont now planned a combined reconnaissance and demonstration to focus Confederate attention on the city before sending the delayed Federal expedition to seize Fernandina. As mentioned, Fernandina was to be the second harbor for the Southeast Atlantic Blockading Squadron. Both men hoped a move toward Savannah would cause the Confederates to abandon the fortifications along the lower Georgia and upper Florida coast. Transports carrying Wright's brigade destined for Fernandina were anchored at Wassaw Sound while Captain Davis and Commander Rodgers led their respective expeditions. Davis' command consisted of the *Ottawa* (Lieutenant Thomas H. Stevens), *Seneca* (Lieutenant Daniel Ammen), *Potomska*, a 5-gun screw steamer (Lieutenant Pendleton G. Watmough), *Isaac H. Smith*, a 9-gun screw steamer (Lieutenant James W.A. Nicholson), *Ellen*, a 2-gun side-wheel steamer (Acting Master Thomas A. Budd), and *Western World* (Acting Master Samuel B. Gregory), along with two armed launches from the *Wabash* and the transports of Wright's brigade; all rested at anchor in Wassaw Sound by early afternoon on January 26.[26]

The next morning the southern portion of the reconnaissance began. Captain Charles H. Davis was aboard the gunboat *Ottawa* along with Lieutenant Stevens, General Wright, and Major John Spidel with part of Company C of the 6th Connecticut. Lieutenant Ammen was in the *Seneca*, along with Company D of the 6th Connecti-

U.S.A.M.H.I.

Horatio G. Wright

cut, and Commander Rodgers. This reconnaissance was similar to the smaller expedition of January 7. At 8:00 a.m. they entered Little Tybee River (or Freeborn's Cut) where the vessels were clearly visible to, but seemingly unnoticed by, Fort Pulaski. At 1:30 p.m. they passed the fort. Continuing west and passing the solid ground of Wilmington Island, they found a fork in the channel. The passage leading to the right that continued into Saint Augustine Creek was blocked by a double line of large timber pilings, placed months before. Reconnaissance on the north shore Wilmington Island revealed that part of the City Light Guards from Savannah had recently left Dr. Screven's plantation. The Federals burned the house and outbuildings. That night, Lieutenant Ammen and several Connecticut men crossed the marsh to the north and cut the telegraph line to Fort Pulaski; they returned with several lengths of wire. The Federals anchored between the Screven and Gibson plantations, the latter on the east corner of Whitemarsh Island, at the junction of Turners and Oatland Creeks with the Wilmington Narrows. On the morning of the twenty-eighth, the *Wabash*'s Lieutenant Barnes along with Wright rowed a small boat above the obstructions and into Saint Augustine Creek. As they had learned from contrabands, the waterway was deep and wide enough for gunboats if the obstructions were removed.[27]

On January 28, the northern part of the reconnaissance began. John Rodgers took the 6-gun screw steamer *Unadilla* and the *Henry Andrew* through Wall's Cut at the morning high tide. The *Pembina* grounded in the soft bottom mud near the entrance. The site where she had grounded was a good location for a battery; danger from the Confederates could only come at high tide and then the *Pembina* would float free. Unfortunately, the *Pembina* was clearly visible from Fort Pulaski.[28]

Rodgers was still apprehensive about participation in any river operation:

> I think that gunboats can be carried into Savannah River at high tide. I am not yet, however, prepared to report the fact as certain. When in, the force will, at most times of tide, be cut off from retreat or help, and must stand all that the South can bring against them.[29]

U.S.A.M.H.I.

Charles H. Davis

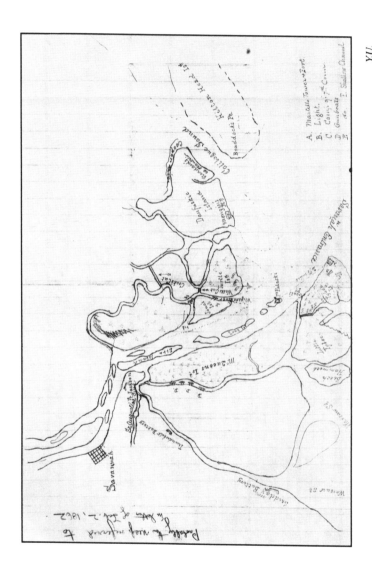

Y.U.

Alfred H. Terry's map of the Savannah River and connecting channels at the time of the January 28, 1862, reconnaissance up Wilmington Narrows. The site of his regiment's camp (7th Connecticut) on Tybee Island is south of the lighthouse ("B") and is indicated as "C." Federal gunboats in Wilmington Narrows are indicated as "D" while those stalled in Mud River are indicated as "E." Confederate batteries along the Wilmington River are marked as is Fort Jackson.

The next day, Rodgers sent Lieutenant John P. Bankhead to measure, yet again, the depth of the Mud and Wright Rivers at high tide. The latter was nine and a half feet deep; the former was five feet deep. Only the Wright River, Rodgers realized, was practicable for gunboats.[30]

During the naval reconnaissance of January 28, Gillmore had checked Jones Island for a possible battery site. He suggested that, if the Mud River proved too shallow, a sidewheel steamer running up and down the channel could stir up the mud, and the action of the tides would easily increase the depth by one and one-half feet. It was Sherman's plan that part of the force assembled by Viele, both men and guns, be landed on Jones Island from the Savannah River side, to construct a battery. The navy's gunboats would provide protection during the landing and construction. The navy feared that entering the Savannah River from the Wright River would place vessels in direct fire from Fort Pulaski. This concern about exposure meant that the much shallower Mud River must be used to enter the Savannah River.[31]

At the time of the Federal reconnaissance, Lawton had ordered Commodore Tattnall to begin reprovisioning the Fort Pulaski. At 5:00 p.m. on the twenty-seventh, five Confederate steamers descended the Savannah River and anchored below Fort Jackson at the mouth of Saint Augustine Creek. Unaware of the Federal reconnaissance, shortly before noon the next day, Tattnall continued down the river in his flagship *Savannah* with the armed steamers *Resolute* and *Sampson* escorting the steamers *Ida* and *Bartow,* the latter with a barge lashed to either side filled with enough supplies and provisions for six months. Captain John Rodgers' squadron on the northern side of the Savannah River and of Captain Charles H. Davis' on the south had their guns trained on the channel down which Tattnall must pass. The distance between the Federal fleets was three miles, and their guns could easily reach across the intervening flat marshy islands. Tattnall sent down the transports in advance, with the *Sampson* closely following. The Federals saw the Confederates, and hoping to destroy the entire Rebel squadron, allowed the first vessels pass. Tattnall followed in the *Savannah,* along with the *Resolute.* The *Sampson* accompanied the steamers to the fort's wharf and then turned to rejoin the other two armed vessels. Around 2:00 p.m. at high tide, Tattnall's three armed vessels returned up the river, and the Federals opened fire, hitting the *Sampson* several times but not damaging her engines. Tattnall's lightly armed vessels were no match for the Federals. The artillery exchange lasted half an hour. Tattnall reached Savannah at 3:00 p.m. With the onset of firing, Confederate reserves rushed to the batteries along the waterways. The Confederates gone, Davis returned down the narrows and passed Fort Pulaski in the darkness. Rodgers' vessels remained at Wall's Cut. It had been a worthwhile mission. Besides cutting telegraphic communication with the fort, the Federal reconnaissance learned Wilmington Island had been abandoned by Confederate troops.[32]

Sherman later observed that although the reconnaissance forced the Confederates to withdraw armament from the lower Georgia coast, the navy failed to keep the Confederates from resupplying Fort Pulaski. Had the navy succeeded in stopping Tattnall "the bombardment of Pulaski would have been rendered unnecessary for in less time than it took to besiege the work would have brought about a capitulation from the effect of starvation."[33] Sherman was incorrect; several ships subsequently reached the fort.

Horace Porter had observed the naval reconnaissance from Daufuskie Island and wrote his father that the navy would not venture into the river until they were reinforced and, thus, the army could do nothing. "We are all disgusted with the navy. They have detained us in everything we have yet undertaken." Two weeks later, Porter added:

> You see we are not yet at Savannah and I fear the attack is given up for the present. . . . The troops removed sunken vessels piles & c., and opened a good channel which would bring our Navy into the Savannah two miles above Pulaski. They [the Navy] got near the river, then got scared about torpedoes, infernal machines, fire-rafts, & c. and positively refused all cooperation on the Savannah attack, and have actually started back for Port Royal. You can imagine how disgusted we all are.

That was just the opposite of the feelings among naval officers before the expedition. Adrian Terry wrote, "The naval officers have no doubt of the result and confidently predict our entrance into Savannah within two days."[34]

Sherman said that "the naval officers are the best judges of their own area," yet he believed "Savannah would have been at this time in our possession had we carried out the plan for entering the river with our combined forces as early as the 18th or 20th January, and secondly that Pulaski should have been cut off at the time of the reconnaissance." The infantry and guns were ready to go; they "wanted only a few gunboats to protect the erection of the batteries." The gunboats had sat above Wall's Cut for thirteen days. When Viele brought Sherman word that he was establishing his island battery, the navy sent word that their gunboats were passing through Wall's Cut. Sherman felt the delay now made operations on the mainland impossible and he was sending Wright to Fernandina "whenever the Navy is ready."[35]

Sherman also complained to Major General Montgomery C. Meigs, Quartermaster General of the United States Army, that none of the supplies he had requested in the last several months had arrived: no boats, no wagons, no light-draught steamers. With the onset of warm weather, Sherman feared he was doomed to "do little but simply garrison the coast." "I am not my own master," Sherman lamented. "My master thus far have been the exigencies created by want of means and facilities for operating in a way desirable to both ourselves and the country at large." He felt Savannah should already have been taken, not by direct march after the fall of Port Royal but by combined operation with the navy, either from the south by way of Montgomery, or by bold ascent of the Savannah River under cover of the gunboats. He felt that the total absence of supplies for a siege had prevented him from moving south. DuPont's lack of cooperation prevented ascent up the Savannah River. Sherman felt that had the gunboats passed Wall's Cut once it had been opened in mid-January, a coordinated land force on the right bank of the Savannah River could have taken Fort Jackson in reverse. Savannah, essentially without artillery defenses, would too have fallen. Now, he lamented, it was too late. Savannah was too well defended, and chances for a successful joint operation had passed. The city seemed "out of our grasp at present." At best, Sherman now hoped to cut off Confederate communication with the fort. Perhaps when the navy was ready, he would use some of his ample land forces to take Fernandina and the incomplete Fort Clinch at the mouth of the St. Mary's River in Florida.[36] (The expedition for Fernandina did not sail until February 28.)[37]

Reports about the lack of progress Sherman received from friends and Northern newspapers heightened his uneasiness.[38] On February 12, a letter arrived from Major General McClellan reviewing Federal successes in Tennessee at Forts Henry and Donalson and in North Carolina on Roanoke Island. Noting that forty-eight surf boats were ready for shipment to Sherman's command, McClellan casually mentioned that he had "been daily expecting to hear more definite accounts of what can be done in the Savannah River and of the possibility of starving out Fort Pulaski." While the Confederacy was being pushed all along its perimeter, could not Sherman reduce his garrisons to a minimum and move on Savannah, after Fort Pulaski had been starved into submission?[39]

Meanwhile, McClellan finally received Sherman's request for siege materials for use against Savannah. On February 14, he wrote Sherman that "the siege and capture of Savannah do not promise results commensurate with the sacrifices necessary." Now ended all thought of an overland operation against the city in 1862. McClellan felt Savannah itself was still a prize worthy of capture, and he suggested two alternatives. First, he mentioned Sherman's idea for an army-navy *coup de main,* but that both men knew the time for that had passed because of DuPont's inertia. McClellan then suggested that Sherman continue his efforts to take Fort Pulaski by a combination of isolation and bombardment. Occupation of Fort Pulaski by Federal forces, McClellan correctly noted, would gain "all that is really essential" in the area. McClellan was sure that once Sherman received the 13-inch mortars and heavy guns he could reduce the fort. McClellan concluded, "I do not consider the possession of Savannah worth a siege after Pulaski is in our hands."[40]

On February 15, Sherman reluctantly had come to the same conclusion, but felt "grieved . . . almost [to] a state of mortification." He felt the season for campaigning along the southern coast would end in six to twelve weeks. The great extent of coast he was to cover soaked up many troops. Only part of the requested siege material had slowly arrived; the 13-inch siege mortars, indispensable for the reduction of Fort Pulaski, had yet to be seen. Sherman reluctantly sent detachments to Fernandina and Edisto Island, South Carolina, because a lack of shallow draft transportation prevented his forces from establishing themselves on the mainland.[41]

The Confederates realized that Union navy had gained control of the river east of Fort Jackson. The Savannah *Republican* observed: "Should they [the Federal vessels] be allowed to remain where they are, the navigation of the river may be considered as closed to unarmed vessels." Other Southerners regarded the lack of a Northern advance as "inexplicable."[42]

Confederate Lieutenant Cornelius R. Hanleiter felt Southern military officers "—having charge of this Military Department—have been criminally neglectful of the defense of this Island [Skidaway] and other approaches to Savannah." He had observed the Northerners for the previous three weeks and was "thoroughly convinced that they could have driven us from this position in three hours, at any time, during that period."[43]

Union officers judged Sherman harshly. Lieutenant Colonel Joseph R. Hawley, of the 7th Connecticut on Tybee Island, felt that Sherman had "utterly failed in trying to cut off Pulaski." Complaining about Sherman's inaction, Hawley noted the Confederates had now had months to strengthen Savannah's defenses, had "fortified every channel," and had 20,000 troops in and around the city. "The attempt to harness the Savannah River, either for the purpose of going up to the city or of cutting off Pulaski is abandoned." Five weeks later, Hawley's feelings had changed. "If our naval leaders had allowed the gunboats to imitate the pluck of Comm. Foote, as they would gladly have done, Savannah would have been ours long ago."[44]

U.S.A.M.H.I.

Joseph R. Hawley

The lack of movement bothered many men in the department. Corporal Charles Lyons, of the 48th New York, wrote his father about the inaction and wished "Fremont, Sigel, or Butler" was there; "I think we would get something done." Colonel James H. Perry, of the 48th New York, made a speech to the regiment on Washington's Birthday critical of Sherman for not having taken Savannah when he had the opportunity months before. Another private added, "I think Savannah could have been taken last fall with 2,000 men."[45]

Even Wilson, Sherman's topographical engineer, wrote his friend Lieutenant Colonel James B. McPherson serving on General Henry Halleck's staff in St. Louis:

U.S.A.M.H.I

James H. Perry

You know I was happy when I was ordered to join Sherman, the prospect was fair for an active, energetic, exciting campaign, but alas! Our General was not a genius and in addition was battered by the conditions of the venture. . . . The day for taking Savannah has been allowed to slip away from us by the culpable inactivity of the Navy. . . . Nothing now remains for us but to maintain the blockade of Pulaski. From this it is easy to see there is no chance here for an active campaign, unless indeed we are reinforced by 20,000 men.[46]

In Savannah, Lee was concerned about the two Federal expeditions and the removal of the obstructions in Wall's Cut. Confederate scouts found those in Wilmington Narrows remained yet intact. Lee realized that the way could be opened to the Savannah River, "and we have nothing afloat that can contend against them." On January 29, Lee strengthened the obstructions in the Southern approach by having the "floating dock of this city" towed to be sunk in Wilmington Narrows. Federals observed the steamers towing a "large wreck" into Saint Augustine Creek and realized that, along with the piles, major obstructions now blocked the Southern passage.[47]

That same day, Sherman wrote DuPont about another Confederate deserter's report that Lee had visited the fort the previous day and there spent the night. The deserter said the fort held enough food for six months but confirmed that drinking water was scarce.[48]

Also on January 29, Gillmore sent Lieutenant Patrick H. O'Rorke, of the Engineers, and Major Oliver T. Beard, 48th New York, to examine Long and Elba Islands in the Savannah River. The two men went by way of Wright River to the Savannah River around the west end of Elba within two miles of Fort Jackson. They reported the upper end of Long Island was as suitable for a battery as was Venus Point. On a small island opposite Fort Jackson, the men saw a Confederate battery under construction, later Fort Tattnall, with two mounted guns and three

Patrick H. O'Rorke

more ready to mount. The battery was in the river south of Barnwell's Island. An 800-foot raft—20 to 30 feet wide—extended across the channel. Pitch and irregularly spaced piles of cord wood covered the raft. It seemed a "harmless thing and poorly gotten up" and apparently designed to serve as a fire raft to prevent an ascent of the river. Beard saw 700 men in a camp south of Fort Jackson but no Confederates on the north bank of the Savannah River. Returning to Daufuskie, Beard saw 200 Confederates along the upper reaches of the New River in South Carolina.[49]

O'Rorke, separated from Beard the night of their return, became lost. In a driving rain, Porter returned in a boat to rescue O'Rorke who was perched in a tree to escape the rising tide. Each initially thought the other was the enemy; Porter was ready to shoot. After the two men recognized each other, Porter threatened, "the next time you go out I will have a bell tied to you."[50]

Four days later, Beard made another reconnaissance of the Wright River, taking soundings and modifying maps. He found that Hog Island, west of Jones Island and south of the Wright River, had only a few dry spots less than 100 feet in size.[51]

Confederates had observed O'Rorke, Beard, and Porter. General Lee felt that "it seems probable that the enemy is meditating an advance from New River to the bank of the Savannah." Lee ordered Brigadier General John C. Pemberton, stationed at Pocotaligo, South Carolina, to be ready to move to Hardeeville to take command of all troops north of the Savannah River and help in the city's defense, should the enemy move in that direction.[52]

On February 3, Brigadier General Thomas F. Drayton, commander of the Fifth Military District of South Carolina, in Hardeeville, wrote Colonel Walter H. Taylor on Lee's staff that he had evacuated Red Bluff on the New River on February 1 and moved four miles inland. Drayton found it "indefensible against gunboats armed with heavy pieces." That same day, four gunboats shelled the abandoned fort. The Federals removed the chain obstructions across the New River and ascended further. Soldiers disembarked along the shore and burned two plantation houses. One company took river soundings. Drayton had one company of cavalry and three of infantry observe the Federals and was prepared to attack, but the Federals did not move inland away from their gunboats.[53]

On February 4, Naval officers again sounded the Mud and Wright River. They found Mud River one and one-half feet deep at low tide "with a very soft, almost semi-fluid bottom." That same day to the south, six companies of the 25th Georgia were ordered to Thunderbolt Island. On February 8, Confederates cut all of the trees along the roads leading inland from the island batteries. They fell randomly across the swampy ground and would force any advancing forces to keep to the roads and to prevent flanking by cavalry or artillery.[54]

* * * * * * *

In late December, seven companies of the 7th Connecticut, under Colonel Alfred H. Terry, had landed on Tybee Island. The remaining three companies, under Major Gardiner remained on Daufuskie, guarding Wall's Cut and would not rejoin the regiment until mid-March. On Tybee the men prepared their encampment and helped in the construction of the defensive works near the lighthouse. The first days were also spent in drill. One member wrote his mother that he was "to stay here some time and to build mortar batteries for throwing heavy shell."[55]

Terry was a lawyer and before the war had served as clerk of the New Haven Superior Court. On January 18, he wrote a "private" letter to his wife, explaining that private meant that it was not to be shown to "*all* the family." He gave details of the new uniform she was to have prepared for him and recounted on page after page his merits, comparing himself advantageously to the other colonels with whom he was serving. Throughout the coming months, Terry would scheme, successfully, with Connecticut politicians for promotion to brigadier general.[56]

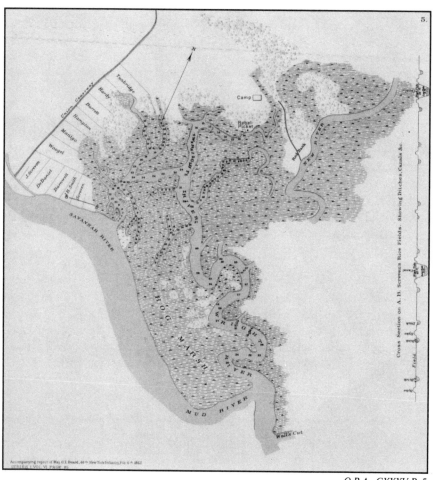

O.R.A., CXXXV-B, 5

**Map submitted by Colonel Oliver T. Beard of his reconnaissance of
the Wright River on February 6, 1862**

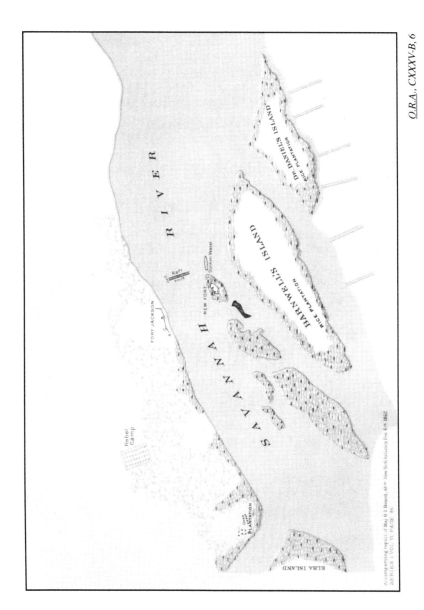

Map submitted by Colonel Oliver T. Beard with his observations of the vicinity of Fort Jackson, based on his February 6, 1862, reconnaissance. (South is uppermost).

Alfred H. Terry

Lieutenant Horace Porter was assigned to Tybee Island in mid-January after the joint army-navy move on Savannah had been cancelled. His orders were to put the island in a state of defense. Arriving, he found 1,400 men of the 46th New York and 7th Connecticut under the command of General Wright. Porter's first responsibility was to construct an earth fort to be armed with eleven guns northwest of the lighthouse. He also directed the completion of two additional batteries, farther west, to bear on Fort Pulaski. Porter anticipated that the construction would take two weeks and guessed he would then be transferred from Tybee.[57]

In late January, Private Milton M. Woodford of the 7th Connecticut wrote a friend that although they had been on Tybee for about six weeks, the regiment had done nothing but build forts and batteries and mount guns. "We expected to see something before now." The earth fort was about two and a half miles from Fort Pulaski and the batteries about a mile closer. Each time the Southerners saw men on the beach who might be in range, they "blaze away at them generally without doing any damage." Although the Confederates had fired at the sand fort near the lighthouse often, their rounds fell short. Woodford added: "A man needs a good deal of *patriotism* to live on *pork* and hard bread, week after week, shovel sand and roll a wheelbarrow, and be *snubbed* by men with stripes on their arms, or straps on their shoulders, who *at home* we should consider no better than ourselves."[58]

By mid-January, the Rebels had almost ceased shelling the island. Every so often, however, Fort Pulaski would remind the Federals of its presence. Adrian Terry, brother of the regimental colonel, reported that "Fort Pulaski appears to feel a little more spiteful than usual and throws some 10-inch shells at us that as usual fall just short doing no damage." A Confederate reconnaissance party would occasionally land on Tybee; one night in mid-January, twenty men landed but were quickly driven off. For their part, Federal forces had reconnoitered Cockspur Island, "getting up nearly to the walls of the fort."[59]

Horace Porter

Porter chose to mess with officers of the 46th New York, the "German regiment." During this time he lived "principally on sour kraut and cheese." Like so many others, Porter commented on the abundance of oysters in the tidal channels. "We have enough oysters here to fill ten ships. We used to make a big fire, get Gen. Wright to join the party and amuse ourselves roasting them."[60] Wright by this time had left Tybee to prepare for the expedition to Fernandina.

By February 2, Terry's regiment had worked on the sand fort and the two batteries. "Nearly all the works which we came down to construct are completed, but there are as yet no indications of a change of post. Our life here is monotony in the extreme." Terry, too, was astounded by the abundance of shellfish in the tidal inlets. "The one thing which we have the greatest abundance that is to say oysters. The creeks here are filled with them between high & low water mark; in many of them there is a solid *wall* of oysters and they are very good."[61]

By February 7, the fort at the base of the Martello tower had been completed and most of its guns mounted. The two western batteries were also completed. Six days later, John B. Marchand and Percival Drayton visited Tybee Island and crept to one of the two sand batteries, one armed with three 8-inch columbiads, to view Pulaksi. Peering through the brush cover, they saw "men working around the fort at ordinary occupations, the lookout on the walls watching closely everything and sometime seeming to look directly at us."[62]

Although the 7th Connecticut and 46th New York shared Tybee Island, the Connecticut officers were disdainful of their relaxed, easy living compatriots. Adrian Terry noted that he had thus far avoided the "rather undesirable proximity to the German Regiment which shares the island with us." They frequently got drunk. "As the Dutch sutler sells liquor and our camp butts right against theirs, we can not prevent some of the detestable alcohol passing into our camp." Because of this, Colonel Terry had decided to move the 7th Connecticut to a plateau a quarter of a mile away.[63]

Having escaped the unwholesome influence of the 46th New York, Terry was most pleased with his new camp. The location was "a most delightful sight." Lieutenant Colonel Hawley boasted, "Our new white tents are white as snow and pitched with beautiful regularity." The ground was all the "whitest sand." "Picturesque live oaks and pines give diversity to the ground." Many men decorated their tents, "laying turf and transplanting flowers before them and sticking up little pines and cedars and making arches." Other observers later described the camp as having perfect "policing and general management."[64]

* * * * * * *

On January 30, the transport *Leesburg* steamed down with a load of provisions and landed at the south wharf of Fort Pulaski. Federal vessels in Wall's Cut did not fire at her; three shots from Tybee fell short. The fort returned fire. Another boat came down the following day with lumber and more provisions. On February 1, yet another boat arrived at the fort. The Oglethorpe Light Infantry spent the day unloading flats of wood. The *Ida* came down on February 3. Lee felt Fort Pulaski was well provisioned to withstand a long siege.[65]

On February 7, Captain Francis Circopeley brought his *Ida* down to Fort Pulaski. He saw four vessels in Wall's Cut and two on the Red River. At Tybee, four steamers and one large sloop of war moved slowly off shore. On February 10, the *Ida* again landed at the wharf at Fort Pulaski, where men loaded supplies onto carts and drove them into the fort. The gunboats in the creeks north of the Savannah River edged a little nearer but none tried to intercept communications.[66]

The following day in Savannah, Lee summarized the situation:

> Guns are scarce, as well as ammunition, & I shall have to break up batteries on the coast to provide, I fear, for this city. Our enemies are endeavoring to work their way through the creeks that traverse the impassable & soft marshes stretching along the interior of the coast & communicating with the sounds & sea, through which the Savannah flows, & thus avoid the entrance of the river commanded by Fort Pulaski. Their boats only require 7 feet water to float them & the tide rises 7 feet, so that on high water they can work their way & rest on the mud at low. They are also provided with dredges & appliances for removing obstructions through the creeks in question which cannot be guarded by batteries.[67]

From Savannah on February 10, Lee told the Secretary of War Judah P. Benjamin that Brigadier General Hugh W. Mercer had reported that the batteries on Saint Simon's and Jekyl Islands were unable to withstand attack. Lee had advised Mercer that "should he adopt this course [evacuation], the heavy guns at those batteries will be sent here for the defence of Savannah River where they are much needed & cannot otherwise be obtained." Lee also informed Georgia governor Joseph E. Brown of his instructions to Mercer. Eight days later, Lee wrote Cooper that "the guns have been withdrawn from the batteries on Saint Simon's & Jekyl Island and the troops removed to Brunswick. The former are now in progress of transportation to this place, to be used in the defence of the city of Savannah, & the latter directed to occupy a position to command the [Charleston and Savannah] Railroad & protect the back country." Lee concluded that the Confederates should destroy Brunswick, as its "convenient harbor & salubrious climate, & comfortable buildings might tempt [the Federals] to hold it for the continuance of the war." Mercer withdrew the 4th Georgia Battalion and Colonel Cary W. Styles' 26th Georgia.[68]

Despite Lee's concentration of men, guns, and supplies, some remained critical of his efforts. On the islands east of Savannah, Lieutenant Hanleiter, by February 10, was still "mortified at the inactivity of our officers in command of this Department." He lamented the absence of batteries on Wilmington Island opposite those on Skidaway, the absence of one at Adams' Place, one at Pritchard's Landing, one at Whitemarsh opposite Thunderbolt, and more on Skidaway itself. Colonel William Phillips, Phillips Regiment, previously stationed at Beaulieu, was transferred to Pritchard's Place on Skidaway Island, lately the temporary headquarters of General Lawton.[69] This move merely shifted men already on the islands.

On February 11, the screw steamer transport *Robert Habersham* arrived at Fort Pulaski, bringing the Wise Guards to relieve the Irish Jasper Greens. This would be the last change of personnel in the fort. Lieutenant Theodorick W. Montfort in the garrison confirmed that telegraphic communication between the fort and the city of Savannah had been severed.[70]

A few days later, Lee began to arrange for obstruction of the Savannah River between Savannah and Augusta. Major George W. Rains located a site at Shell Bluff, 45 miles below Augusta, which had an elevation suitable for a battery.[71]

By February 16, all guns were removed from Saint Simon's and Jekyl Islands to Brunswick. All but four guns were shipped to Savannah; those remaining hauled to Fernandina. Further, Mercer felt that to burn the town of Brunswick would show the enemy that the Confederates would make "every sacrifice," but he wanted "precise orders to destroy all the buildings that can afford shelter and comfort to the enemy." Lee requested and received approval for Mercer, who left Brunswick in flames on February 22.[72]

Because of the fall of Forts Henry and Donelson in Tennessee (February 6 and 15) and the loss of Roanoke Island, North Carolina (February 8), Judah Benjamin directed Lee on February 24 to withdraw all units from the coastal islands to the mainland and to abandon Florida except the line of the Apalachiocola River. He further directed Lee to send 4,000 men from Florida to General Albert Sidney Johnson in Tennessee. Lee now realized he could expect no reinforcements for the 18,000 men remaining under his command.[73]

* * * * * * *

On February 7, General Sherman wrote DuPont, ten days after the January 28 reconnaissance, that the army troops for the move on Savannah were still bivouacking on Daufuskie Island, awaiting the movement of the gunboats. Gillmore, in turn, informed Sherman that Captain Rodgers was "still awaiting orders." DuPont ordered Rodgers to cover the proposed battery to be soon built at Venus Point on Jones Island but Rodgers did nothing but continue to take river soundings.[74]

Furthermore, Wright and his Fernandina-bound force had been afloat in Wassaw Sound for fifteen days, and none of the troops had been ashore. Sherman feared the imminent onset of "ship fever" among the men "huddled up on those little steamers."[75] Sherman's concern for Wright's division was warranted. The experience of the 6th Connecticut was typical. On January 20, they hurriedly boarded the *Cosmopolitan*, a steamer too small to hold the entire regiment. Initially kept in harbor at Hilton Head because of storms, they then sailed to Wassaw Sound, where most of the men remained on board for almost a month, with only short intervals ashore to allow the boat to be disinfected. One soldier recalled that for sixteen days they ate salt pork and beef, vermin-ridden hard tack, no vegetables and "water that had been put in kerosine oil barrels three months before. The water was so thick in one barrel that . . . could be lifted up on the finger. It was so nauseating and foul that when poured into the sea, the water was discolored by it." Private Martin Emmons wrote that his companions "were a week without anything cooked to eat." He added that "the water was thick and stringy like frog spittle and stank so that we had to hold our breath to drink it." Eventually, a severe sickness, described by survivors as "spotted fever" broke out and claimed four or five men a day. The condition of the 6th Connecticut became so critical that after 31 days at sea the regiment returned to Hilton Head Island to convalesce and never took part in the expedition to Fernandina.[76]

* * * * * * *

During January and February, Sherman continued having the water routes bypassing Fort Pulaski into the Savannah River evaluated and approaches against the city of Savannah explored. He also continued to plan to isolate the fort.

On December 15, 1861, Sherman had written Adjutant General Lorenzo Thomas informing him that engineer operations were progressing at such a rate that he required someone above the rank of captain to manage them as chief engineer. Sherman reminded Thomas that after Gillmore had been assigned to him, Governor William Dennison of Ohio had asked President Abraham Lincoln to have Gillmore promoted to brigadier general. Lincoln then had declined on grounds that Gillmore's position with the force did not require such a rank. Sherman felt, however, that the time had now come for the promotion. Sherman emphasized that "it is desirable, too, to remove [Colonel] Serrell's battalion of artizans from the anomalous position in which the rank of its commander places it in relation to the Chief Engineer." Sherman added that Gillmore had been "active, energetic, and able" and "in consequence of his will and capacity, the Engineer Dept has been more successful in its work than any other." Gillmore's abilities were so obvious, Sherman concluded, that Captain Gillmore must be promoted to the senior rank. Sherman felt to reward such obvious merit would serve as an example and "urge others to greater zeal."[77]

U.S.A.M.H.I.

Edward W. Serrell

Colonel Edward W. Serrell, commander of the 1st New York Engineers, was a civil engineer of excellent reputation. Thirty-three years old, Chief Engineer of the Raritan and Delaware Bay Railroad at the war's outbreak, he had volunteered his services directly to Lincoln. Trained as a topographical and mechanical engineer, he had built the largest suspension bridge then in North America. Serrell had also designed railroads, water works, tunnels, and enjoyed international acclaim for his bridge design theories.[78]

As preparations for the coming siege and possible bombardment of Fort Pulaski continued, Sherman realized he needed to better organize the engineers in his command to put them "into a working condition." By

January 22, Sherman was convinced that it was "absolutely necessary to place Capt. Gilmore [*sic*] of the Engrs, for the time being, in such relation to the Engineer Rgt. of Vols as to fully effect that object." This was the only way to achieve that end "without a loss of time that cannot be spared." On January 22, Sherman appointed Gillmore Brigadier General of Volunteers, subject to approval of the President, and was "directed to immediately assume military command of all engineer forces in the Expeditionary Corps."[79]

On February 26, Sherman wrote McClellan, explaining that McClellan's help was imperative in pushing Gillmore's appointment with Lincoln. Sherman insisted he had "found it absolutely necessary, on the strength of my own appointment of him alone to place Gen. Gilmore [*sic*] in charge of the siege of Pulaski and consequently in command of all the troops of Tybee Island. War creates necessities that cannot be overlooked. The dearth of the proper kind of officer here for such work must justify me I think, in your eyes, in taking the course I have." To further justify his action, Sherman said that Vicle was busy with his forces above the Savannah River, General Wright's division was being sent to Fernandina, and that General Stevens was occupied on the South Carolina islands.[80]

Gillmore lost no time promoting his own case. On February 7, he had written Brigadier General Joseph G. Totten, Chief Engineer of the Army, enclosing a copy of Sherman's January 22 letter to Thomas. Gillmore pointed out that only a brigadier general's rank would do. "In fact, nothing short of this would better matters at all, as Col. Serrell's rgt. of Vol. Engrs is the force (and the only Engineer force) with which we have to work." He further added:

> It became a matter of such importance, in the opinion of Genl. Sherman, to inaugurate this change without delay, that about two weeks since—(I cannot remember the exact date being absent from Head Quarters)—he issued an order appointing me "Brigadier General of Volunteers, subject to the approval of the President of the United States."

From that time on, Gillmore was in charge of all engineer duties, which he managed "directly through the Colonel of the Engineer Regiment." Sherman was pleased with the arrangement, Gillmore added, and operations were running more efficiently than before. Gillmore then reflected that if the President did not act favorably, it would "place me in a very embarrassing position, and will utterly disorganize the system now successfully established, beside placing me in a ridiculous light before whom I am dependant on for such work." Disingenuously, Gillmore added that he would have not troubled Totten with the matter "were it not for the urgent necessity of it." Gillmore concluded by requesting that, if he could not be confirmed, a brigadier general be sent to replace him.[81]

On February 15, General Totten endorsed Gillmore's letter:

> I feel assured that the promotion of Capt Gillmore, asked for within, is really and greatly required by the public interests connected with Genl. Sherman's expedition. Should the rank which Genl. Sherman has conferred upon Capt. Gillmore, provisionally, be confirmed by the President,

his high qualities will, I am confident, justify the selection, by contributing with increased force to the advancement of the operations in progress.[82]

James Wilson wrote his friend McPherson approvingly of Gillmore's appointment: "Gillmore has conducted his department with eminent ability, so much indeed, as to meet the warmest commendation of the General commanding. He is a noble fellow, a fine officer, and will reflect credit on his new grade. I hope the president will confirm it."[83]

The appointment of Captain Gillmore to the rank of acting brigadier general was not universally popular. Major Charles G. Halpine, Major General David Hunter's adjutant general, later recalled an incident surrounding the action. Halpine attributed the appointment to "a fit of his jocose but dyspeptic humor" by Sherman. Halpine added, incorrectly, "Of course, for this act, Gen'l Sherman had about as much authority as he would have had to nominate Gillmore for Chief Justice of the U.S., but the latter at once accepted the honor as if seriously given, and proceeded by the first mail from New York to array himself in a brigadier's double buttons, velvet cuffs, and a star on either shoulder."[84]

Shortly before the beginning of the siege, Sherman directed his chief of artillery, Captain John Hamilton, to report to the new General Gillmore. Both men had been captains in the regular army and Hamilton's commission predated Gillmore's. Hamilton peremptorily declined because he had been Gillmore's senior in actual rank. Hamilton added that "nobody but the President could ask or compel him to waive his rights and take orders from a junior." Sherman explained the reasons for Gillmore's promotion and asked Hamilton what he should do. Hamilton said that he understood completely Sherman's reasons and added, "I see no way out of the difficulty except for you to appoint me a major general and direct Gillmore to report to me." The impasse was unresolved before Sherman was transferred from the department. Major Halpine retold the episode in more detail: "One day as Gillmore, thus arrayed [as brigadier general] was talking to Gen'l Sherman, Capt. Jack Hamilton . . . strolled up to them and commenced abruptly: 'Brigadier General Sherman, I want you right off to appoint me Major General, for I have already my doublebreasted coat, with velvet collar and cuffs, buttons in bunches of three, and strips with double stars.' Gen'l Sherman saw the joke at once, but asked Hamilton what he meant. 'Why,' said honest Jack—than whom the old army never had a finer officer—'I see you have appointed Capt. Gillmore there, my junior on the file, to be a Brigadier; and so the only justice you can do me is to make me a Major

U.S.A.M.H.I.

John Hamilton

General—once step above yourself.'" Although Gillmore eventually rose to the rank of Major General of Volunteers, Hamilton never received a promotion in volunteer rank.[85] Thus did Quincy A. Gillmore come to be a brigadier general as he directed the engineering operations during the siege of Fort Pulaski.

Chapter 4

"We had to work all night"

Sherman had envisioned a battery upstream from Fort Pulaski to close the Savannah River to the Confederates. During the naval reconnaissance on January 28 Gillmore had explored Jones Island and selected Venus Point, midway on the river side, as the site. It was one of the few elevated points of land on the island and was covered by a dry crust of mud "3 or 4 inches in depth." Gillmore found a 1,300-yard path for the causeway across the island from Mud River to the battery site. The original plan was to tow Viele's guns, ammunition, and men on flats down the New River, through Wall's Cut, up the Wright River and Mud River into the Savannah River under the protection of Rodgers' gunboats. Sherman wanted the causeway across the island so that if the Confederates attacked, reinforcements from Daufuskie could rush to the battery site. Delays, bad weather, and the navy's fear of torpedoes caused Sherman to change the plan; in early February he ordered the army to build the battery without naval assistance.[1]

On January 26, the 48th New York left Hilton Head for Daufuskie Island, four miles east of Jones Island. During the following days, the regiment camped near the southern end at Dunn Plantation and explored its surroundings. The regiment had been divided for a few days when one of its two transport vessels broke apart after grounding on one of the many oyster beds thriving along all of the tidal waterways; the regiment reunited on February 1.[2]

During the first four days of February, Captain Alfred F. Sears and two companies of New York Engineers, along with the 48th New York and the three companies of the 7th Connecticut already on Daufuskie, cut pine logs to build an engineer wharf on the lower New River shore of Daufuskie and a wharf and causeway across Jones Island from Mud River to Venus Point. Many poles, or logs, were up to ten to fifteen feet long and averaged three to six inches in diameter, although some were a foot thick. The men carried them on their shoulders as far as two miles to the assembly point. Because of this heavy labor, "many of our best soldiers were ruptured or otherwise injured, and crept out of the service, maimed and ruined for life." Ten thousand poles had been cut by the fourth. The Daufuskie wharf was also completed on February 4. It extended into the New River to where the water was eight feet deep at low tide. That same day Sherman gave Gillmore the final orders for the construction of the battery on Jones Island, adding if he could complete the battery in one night it would "do you eternal honor."[3]

Gillmore described Jones Island:

> the substratum being a semi-fluid mud, which is agitated like jelly by the falling of even small bodies upon it, like the jumping of men or the ramming of earth. Men walking over it are partially sustained by the roots of the reeds and grass and sink in only 4 or 5 inches. When this top support gives way or is broken through they go down 2 to 2 1/2 feet and in some places much further.[4]

Everyone described Jones Island as a mass of mud, the consistency of "jelly" which varied from four to twelve feet deep. Although covered with matted sea grass and reeds, men sank to their knees at almost every step.[5] Private Alonzo Williams of the 3rd Rhode Island Artillery, was on Jones Island and recalled:

> It is soft unctuous mud, free from sand and of the elasticity of gelatine. A pole can be forced into it ten or twelve feet with ease, and the resistance diminishes with increase of penetration. Even in the most elevated parts the crust is but four or five inches in depth, and the substratum is a semi-fluid mud, which is agitated like jelly by the movement of bodies over it. A person is partially sustained by the roots of the grass and sinks only a few inches, but when this tip gives way, he goes down suddenly several feet and unless rescued at once is in imminent peril.[6]

During February 5 and 6, the engineer force on Daufuskie Island continued to cut poles and fill sand bags. Logs not used for the Daufuskie wharf were fastened into rafts and floated to Jones Island. Men of the 7th Connecticut, 48th New York, and engineers rowed boats full of sand bags and planks, and towed rafts of poles four miles through the channels to Jones Island. A pole and sandbag wharf was begun on the Mud River shore of Jones Island; it was 100 square feet and corduroyed with logs. A corduroy road began across the island but ended after 300 yards, and a wheelbarrow track, planks laid end to end, continued across the island to Venus Point. On the sixth, Gillmore spotted three Confederates on the island, and he ordered Captain Sears to cut a "wide zigzag through the reeds and grass" on the island to provide a fire break if the Rebels ignited the island grasses after discovering the Federal battery.[7]

On February 7 and 8, the engineers completed the Jones Island wharf. Across the island engineers staked out the battery site. Infantrymen carried several hundred heavy sandbags, planks, and other material 1,300 yards across the island and prepared the battery platform. Extra engineering materials that might be needed at Venus Point were loaded into lighters and brought near the Mud River wharf.[8]

On February 9, Rodgers planned to have his gunboats pass through Mud River. The *Mayflower* was to follow towing flats loaded with guns and supplies for the batteries. As the signal to begin was given, a driving storm arose, and the vessels could not move. The naval officers on the gunboats again expressed their customary reservations. They feared they might not be able to return by the Mud River and might be exposed to fire rafts and torpedoes from above. Gillmore feared that passage of the supplies without gunboat protection would be useless and decided to haul the guns across the island. On the tenth, the gunboats *Pembina* and *Unadilla* anchored in Wright River near Wall's Cut. The 4-gun screw steamer *Hale* made it up Mud River 200 yards east of the wharf.[9]

That same day Commodore Josiah Tattnall sailed down the Savannah River, examining the shore with his telescope. Infantrymen and engineers on the island crouched in the reeds and expected to be spotted and fired upon by the hovering steamer. Although he passed within 100 yards of the battery site, Tattnall did not see the nearly completed work behind its grass screen.[10]

During the night of February 10, Lieutenant O'Rorke, with a party of volunteer engineers, started the construction of gun platforms and a magazine at Venus Point. They began the platforms by raising the surface of the island six inches with sandbags. On the bags the volunteers laid thick planks closely parallel, but not touching, perpendicular to the line of the battery. On top of that a second layer of deck planks was laid perpendicularly, making a platform for each gun measuring nine by seventeen feet. The floor of the magazine rested on a base of sandbags 20 inches above the natural surface. The engineers directed the construction of sandbag transverses. On the morning of the eleventh, the men halted and concealed their work. They began a parapet of mud and slime. A member of the 48th New York recalled that "we persisted in shoveling it up on to the parapet and the mud as constantly persisted in slipping down." By morning they had thrown up a parapet eight feet wide, "somewhat shapeless broad at the base" but three to five feet high. The sun baked it hard, and they shovelled on more mud.[11]

Also, on February 10, Lieutenant Horace Porter floated six pieces of artillery aboard vessels from their anchorage in the New River off Daufuskie Island four miles to Jones Island. Sherman's chief of artillery, Captain John Hamilton, was sick and unable to command. Four flats containing three 30-pounder Parrott rifles, two 20-pounder Parrott rifles, and one 8-inch siege howitzer were pulled by row boat at 5:00 p.m. through Wall's Cut and up Mud River. They landed at the wharf on Jones Island three hours later. The last guns were ashore by 10:00 p.m. One 30-pounder Parrott and the howitzer were landed first and moved forward under the supervision of First Lieutenant Wilson. After the remaining guns, ammunition, and supplies were landed, First Lieutenant Horace Porter moved the remaining 30-pounder Parrotts forward; Major Oliver T. Beard then directed the movement of the two 20-pounder Parrotts. Wilson, Porter, and Beard each led a team of 35 men from the 48th New York. Because of a mistake of scheduling, all the initial infantry had been on duty, waist deep in water, for the previous 24 hours and were too exhausted to help much.[12]

Unloading and hauling the guns across Jones Island began the night of February 11. Problems arose immediately and were compounded by an incessant heavy rain, one of the most inclement nights of the entire winter. In the dark and rain, objects a short distance away were imperceptible. Jones Island is a low marsh and during spring tide is completely submerged. The roadway toward the battery had been well marked through the canes by the men carrying poles for the causeway, planks for the wheelbarrow path, and material for the batteries. By now the constant tramp had reduced the soft mud to the consistency of "oil" for a depth of several inches. Private James M. Green was with one group of the 48th New York. He recalled that "we had to work all night and keep out of sight during the day. It rained most of the time. We were out two nights and then relieved by others."[13]

Two fifteen-foot long pine planks, one foot wide and three inches thick, were laid on the marshy surface parallel to each other and spaced the distance between the wheels of the gun carriages. Three pairs of planks were used. The guns were moved forward in twos, and the extra pair of planks was available to be moved to the front. The guns would be moved along the first two pairs of planks, and the pair from behind was then taken up and brought to the front. Men would sink to their knees. The mud was especially slippery since it contained little sand; the guns frequently slid off the tracks and immediately sank to the wheel hub. With blocks, handspikes and great exertion, the gun was levered back onto the track before it could again be pulled forward.

Men tried pulling sandbags over their shoes and tying them at the knee to keep mud out; these served inadvertently as pontoons until the men had sunk a few times, and the bags became too heavy to drag and were abandoned. The planks soon became too slippery for the men to move, and ropes were attached so that they could be dragged forward through the mud. Williams recalled, "when the wheels struck the poles on which the planks were laid, the other end of the pole would fly up, striking the men in body or face and land them in the mud, if not seriously crippling them." Men tired quickly and many fell exhausted. The heavy rain of the winter storm complicated everything.[14] Some men slept in the rain on log rafts in the Mud River where small fires of fat pine smoked heavily while providing some warmth. At 2:00 a.m. on February 12, Gillmore suspended operations until the following night; the first two guns had been moved forward 400 yards, 80 fifteen-foot increments. The guns were masked with marsh grass.[15]

When darkness fell next evening, Wilson, Porter, and Beard resumed work with a fresh detail of men. Lieutenant Wilson had his two guns in the new battery by 2:00 a.m. on February 13; the remaining guns were in place shortly after 8:00 a.m. Captain Daniel C. Knowles recalled: "The work done, I threw myself on a plank covered with the softest of Carolina soil, myself a pillar of mud, my head softly resting on mud, and with a full South Carolina sun burning in my face, slept as sweetly as a babe in its mother's arms."[16]

Now that the battery commanded the river, two 24-pounder field howitzers, along with 50 rounds of ammunition for each gun, were sailed by way of Wright and Savannah rivers to the site. Extra ammunition for the guns was kept aboard a schooner at the Mud River wharf. Captain John H. Gould, 3rd Rhode Island Artillery, commanded the battery. The work completed, the men now cut away the canebreaks and "unmasked" the new battery—"Battery Vulcan."[17]

On February 11, Captain John Rodgers had six gunboats at Wall's Cut—the *Unadilla, Ottawa, Seneca, Pembina, E. B. Hale*, and the 3-gun screw steamer *Western World*. Now that Battery Vulcan was armed, these vessels tried to enter the Savannah River using Mud River, which varied from 18 inches at low tide up to seven to eight feet at high tide. Commander John B. Marchand had arrived at low tide to visit Rodgers and found:

> The six-foot draft *Hale* was a quarter of a mile up Mud River and the *Pembina*, nine foot draft, a hundred yards up so deeply in the mud that the bow of my boat could with difficulty get to the gangway. They were waiting for the highest of the flood tide to worry their way through Mud Creek. The *Ottawa* was at the mouth of Mud Creek astern of the *Unadilla* and also aground. The remaining gunboats were afloat in the creek astern.

Although Rodgers told Marchand that he hoped to pass into the Savannah River that night, Marchand thought it "utterly impossible" since the vessels must pass one and a half miles. Rodgers later confided to Marchand that although he and his gunboat captains were doubtful of success, since he had suggested the plan to DuPont he "could not avoid trying to carry it out."[18]

After Rodgers failed to pass Mud Creek, DuPont ordered him to return to Port Royal Harbor with all his gunboats except the *Unadilla*. The *E. B. Hale* and *Western World* were left to help protect the battery and assist in any firing. The two boats were moored in Mud River while the *Hale* wallowed crossways in the channel 200 yards east of the wharf with three of her guns bearing up the Savannah River. *Western World*, moored parallel to the central channel, covered the right flank of the Venus Point battery. Both vessels were aground in the river bottom except when briefly floating free, about two hours each day at each high tide. A hulk at the lower end of Wall's Cut, at the Wright River, provided sleeping quarters for the three companies of the 7th Connecticut when they were not guarding the batteries.[19]

On February 13, the unsuspecting *Ida* steamed down by Venus Point. The battery fired nine times without hitting the *Ida*, which continued unharmed down the south channel to the fort. The tide was down and the body of the *Ida* was not easily visible to the men in the battery. Except for one 30-pounder Parrott, every gun recoiled off its platform. The next day the Federals enlarged the platforms to eighteen by seventeen and one-half feet, twice their original size. The *Winfield Scott* transported some of the necessary lumber; the remainder was obtained by pulling down houses on Daufuskie Island.[20]

Also on the fourteenth, Tattnall again came down the Savannah River with four gun boats to help the *Ida* return. The Federals saw the long plumes of black smoke rising over the Savannah River and knew he was coming. Tattnall fired on the Federal battery at 3:00 p.m. After an hour's exchange, in which the *E. B. Hale* and *Western World* participated, Tattnall withdrew. The damaged flag steamer *Savannah* was taken in tow. The *Ida* failed to get away from Fort Pulaski but returned to the shelter of the fort. Two days later, February 16, aided by an unusually high tide, Captain Circopeley guided the *Ida* over the sand bars of the south channel and through Lazaretto Creek to return to Savannah. Sherman realized if the *Ida* could reach Savannah by this route, Confederate gunboats could "take our batteries in Savannah River in reverse." He wanted to block Lazaretto Creek, and DuPont provided two hulks (part of the stone fleet) which had been in Wassaw Sound since December.[21]

On February 12, Federal rowboats took soundings in the mouth of Wright's River and marked a passage. Although the passage was of sufficient depth at high tide it was within range of Fort Pulaski's guns. To reinforce the point, Pulaski fired on the rowboat without effect as the men finished their work. The navy, however, feared using the passage because a ship grounded would be stuck and most likely be destroyed by the fort before the next high tide.[22]

Lee was concerned about the Jones Island battery. He wrote Olmstead on February 17 suggesting that Olmstead shift some barbette guns to the gorge, the rear face of the fort. Further, Lee recommended that guns be placed in the casemate at the northwest angle so that they could fire up the river. He also ordered that the parapets of the mortar batteries located outside the fort be extended all around to protect their rear from fire from up the river as well as from Tybee Island. For the present, Lee continued, communication with the fort must be by light boats over the marshes, or by Wilmington Narrows to Causton's Bluff.[23] Major resupply of the fort was now impossible.

Sherman planned to build a second island battery on Long Island, although the ground initially had been found unsuitable. Battery Vulcan, across the north channel of the Savannah River, provided cover for the construction of a second battery. Since Long Island was unsuitable, Sherman and Gillmore chose upstream Bird Island. The upper end of Bird Island, opposite Battery Vulcan, offered an "uninterrupted command of the south channel of the river." A second battery could close the south channel and might reach the mouth of Saint Augustine Creek two and one-half miles to the northeast. On February 18, flats were loaded with guns for the second Federal battery; crews from the 48th New York manned the rowboats. At 5:00 p.m. on the twentieth, six flats containing an 8-inch siege howitzer, a 30-pounder Parrott gun, a 20-pounder Parrott gun, and three 24-pounder James rifles, along with ammunition and supplies, were towed up Mud River; they reached the Savannah River at midnight. Beard and Hamilton were in the advance boat and signaled to the trailing rowboats the proper direction and location to beach their flats. By 2:00 a.m. on the twenty-first, the Federals were on Bird Island. Lieutenant O'Rorke's engineers built a 100-yard causeway across the marsh and completed platforms and magazines during the remainder of the night; by daylight the 8-inch howitzer was in place. Captain James E. Bailey's Company E of the 3rd Rhode Island Artillery, Lieutenant Henry M. Dalrymple of the 1st New York Engineers, and Beard moved the guns into position. The other guns were positioned during the day and were ready to fire that afternoon. Fifty rounds for each gun were placed in the magazines, and the remainder kept aboard a schooner anchored nearby. Late in the day, the Rhode Island gunners got their ranges and fuse settings. The battery was named "Battery Hamilton" after

Sherman's chief of artillery.[24] On February 21, the river between Fort Pulaski and Savannah was closed.

Life on Bird Island was wet because rising tides frequently flooded the islands. Alligators living in the mud were an even bigger problem. They sank from sight in the ebb tide, but the firing of the guns brought them to the surface. Artillerymen frequently killed them for meat. The absence of drinkable water was another problem. At high tide, the river water mixed with the ocean and tasted like "Epsom salts"; at low tide, it was muddy with organic debris from the marshes. Washing clothes in the river merely exchanged fresh silt for that already dried into the items being "washed."[25] Martin Emmons, of the 6th Connecticut, who later served on the island, recalled Bird Island as "one of the worst playses [sic] I ever saw it [is] mud 6 inches deep and when the tide is in the water is from 8 to 10 inches deep we have to put our tents up on logs, about a foot from ground."[26]

On February 21, the first ordnance for the siege of Fort Pulaski arrived at Tybee Island. The following day, two companies of the 46th New York Volunteers, under Captain Anton C. Hinckel, with a battery of two field pieces and a 30-pounder Parrott gun were stationed on Descent Island (a westward extension of lower Tybee Island); they would subsequently be moved to an old hulk in Lazaretto Creek about 2 1/4 miles southwest of Fort Pulaski. This battery, joined by a small gunboat armed with a navy 6-pounder, in the same creek, along with the batteries on Venus Point and Bird Island, isolated Fort Pulaski. The blockade was now complete and the fort could not be resupplied. Starvation would force the fort to surrender when its provisions were exhausted. The Confederates, however, paid islanders to run mail between the fort and Savannah. They slipped through once or twice a week until the April bombardment.[27]

In early March, reconnaissance parties searched for Confederate forces on Wilmington Island. On March 4, Captain George A. Mercer, son of and assistant adjutant general to General Mercer, reported seeing large columns of smoke from the island. He "suppose[d] the enemy had gone up Wilmington River & set fire to the houses on the Island." During the next few nights, Major Beard made yet another nighttime reconnaissance, this one to McQueen's Island and removed a 300-foot segment of telegraph wire.[28]

Sherman told McClellan on February 23 of the two island batteries just completed. He characterized them as "in the *river*" considering the marshy nature of the islands. The day before, Sherman's men had captured three Savannah citizens taking mail to Fort Pulaski. They said Savannah could have been easily taken a month before, confirming Sherman's opinion, which he had "endeavored to carry out—but failed in consequence of the unwillingness of the navy to do it, though at first they appeared to." He added that the navy hoped to start for Fernandina soon, and that, while the expedition was gone, he would build the batteries on Tybee Island.[29]

Port Royal was the only Federal port south of Hampton Roads. It was a half day sail for ships blockading Charleston and Savannah. The lower Georgia and northern Florida coasts were open. Blockade runners could enter the many Florida inlets and travel the inland waterways to transport their cargos north to rail lines at Brunswick, Georgia, and Fernandina and Jacksonville, Florida, each of which had a deep port. The center of this activity was Fernandina, at the terminal of the Florida Railroad, which joined the Florida Atlantic and Gulf Central Railroad at Baldwin to the east. Fernandina as a Federal port would help with the blockade.

As the batteries on Jones and Bird Islands were built, events continued at a desultory pace elsewhere along the north Georgia coast. On the tenth, General Wright disembarked with part of his brigade on Wassaw Island, south of Tybee Island across Wassaw Sound. Separated from Skidaway Island by Romerly Marsh and tidal creeks, Wright could see the Confederate battery on Skidaway. Three days later, Federals in the mouth of Wright River pulled five linked torpedoes from the Savannah River. One was detonated by the 15-gun sidewheel steamer *Susquehanna*'s launch, towing an ammunition barge in Wright River, without doing any damage. Sailors also learned that a similar line of "infernal machines" stretched across the Savannah River.[30]

On February 15, Sherman requested an additional brigadier general for his command. Viele was occupied on Daufuskie Island and with the batteries on the Savannah River; Wright, with his brigade in Wassaw Sound, was waiting for the navy to sail to Fernandina; and Stevens and his brigade were on Port Royal Island. Hilton Head Island was without a commander and no one was available to coordinate, should the opportunity arise, any inland movement. Sherman was adamant that his newly appointed chief engineer, General Gillmore, was not available since he was "attached to my staff."[31]

On February 17, Commander John P. Gillis, of the *Seminole*, received yet another Confederate deserter, James Glenn, of Company C (City Light Guard), 1st Volunteer Regiment of Georgia, who had been assigned to the battery on Skidaway Island. Glenn reported that the batteries on Skidaway and Thunderbolt were being strengthened. Further, he said a five-gun masked battery was being built on the north shore of the Savannah River. He accurately said that the battery at Skidaway had ten guns served by 300 soldiers. Glenn finished with news that the *Fingal* was being converted into a nine-gun gunboat for Tattnall's fleet.[32]

Washington's Birthday dawned on Federal vessels with pennants streaming in Tybee Roads. The batteries on Tybee and the guns on the ships celebrated with 30-gun salutes, which were answered from Daufuskie Island and the two Savannah River batteries. The firing began at noon and lasted over an hour. Although Fort Pulaski remained quiet, three Confederate gunboats came down the river to "celebrate the day" by firing 30 rounds at Batteries Hamilton and Vulcan before returning to Savannah. Early the next afternoon, the *Ida* and *Leesburg* came down from Savannah and "threw several shells" at the battery on Jones Island, but were too far away to cause damage. Battery Vulcan answered with a single shot.[33]

* * * * * * *

Lee felt that Fort Pulaski's walls could never be breached by guns on Tybee Island. Other officers expressed the same opinion and this inspired confidence in the garrison. Substantial masonry walls, like those at the fort, had never been breached before by siege artillery at such distances. Rifled artillery with its elongated shot and shells did not enter Confederate calculations.[34]

Fort Pulaski's garrison consisted of 24 officers and 365 men. Colonel Olmstead was in command. Five companies were present: Captain John H. Stegin's German Volunteers; Captain John McMahon's Washington Volunteers; Captain M. J. McMullen's Wise Guards; Captain Thomas W. Sims' Oglethorpe Light Infantry, Company B; and Captain Lawrence J. Guilmartin's Montgomery Guards. All were part of the First Volunteer Regiment of Georgia except the Wise Guards, which was part of the 25th Regiment of Georgia Infantry. The fort was armed with five 10-inch and nine 8-inch columbiads, three 42-pounder and twenty 32-pounder guns, two 24-pounder Blakeley rifled guns, one 24-pounder iron howitzer, two 12-pounder bronze howitzers, two 12-inch sea coast mortars, three 10-inch sea coast mortars, and one 6-pounder gun, for a total of 48 pieces. Only twenty of them could be brought to bear on Tybee Island, five 10-inch columbiads, five 8-inch columbiads, four 32-pounders, one Blakely, two 12-inch mortars and three 10-inch mortars.[35]

On February 19, Lee wrote Ripley in Charleston and restated his November defensive plan, namely, that all exposed points within reach of the Federal gunboats be abandoned and interior positions be held from which mobile Confederate infantry could meet the enemy on more equal terms. All efforts, Lee added, were to be directed to that end.[36]

Throughout the latter part of February, Lee continued worrying about Savannah's defenses and the inner line he was developing with Fort Jackson at its center. On February 19, he wrote Brigadier General James H. Trapier, commander of the district of Florida, giving him the same plan. He explained that Trapier must use the men and guns in his state and "prepare to concentrate your force at the point liable to be attacked, & make every arrangement to secure the troops, guns, & munitions of war, at such points as you may deem proper to relinquish." Like Ripley, Trapier was to concentrate mobile forces away from the coast and maneuver rapidly.[37]

On February 23, Lee shared his concerns with his wife. From Savannah he observed, "here the enemy is progressing slowly in his designs, & does not seem prepared, or to have determined when or where to make his attack." He mentioned the Federal exploration of the intersecting waterways south and north of the Savannah River. Lee added that the newly built river batteries had caused no damage to Tattnall's steamers. Lee concluded that he was "engaged in constructing a line of defence at Fort Jackson which, if time permits & guns can be obtained, I hope will keep them out."[38]

Near the end of February, Lee and Tattnall conferred about relieving Fort Pulaski. They agreed that the only way was to capture the Federal island batteries, beginning with that on Bird Island. But they felt that it would be impossible because Federal gunboats and supporting troops were too close. Further, both knew a failed assault would open the way to Savannah. They abandoned the idea.[39]

During February and March, Fort Pulaski's garrison was on its own. Drill could not be held since the parade was cut with ditches to trap plunging shot and shell. The garrison realized it was permanently isolated.[40]

* * * * * * *

On February 28, Wright's Florida expedition finally sailed from Wassaw Sound. The South evacuated Amelia Island, near Fernandina, in the first four days of March, and Wright occupied the island and the city. On March 12, Federal forces took Jacksonville. Sherman had planned to accompany DuPont, but changed his mind at the last minute. Sherman, misled by Southern deserters, erroneously believed that he now faced up to 65,000 men near Savannah.[41]

As February ended, Sherman learned that his threats to Savannah and the lower Georgia coast had caused the Rebels to abandon Brunswick and Saint Simon's Island. At least twenty large caliber guns had been moved to the Savannah defenses. Sherman still felt that if Savannah itself were to be taken, the expedition would have to approach from the south, up the Vernon River and overland by Montgomery. He contemptuously dismissed the navy's cooperation, since they "could not assist us last month when no guns had been put up on the river except those at Fort Jackson, it certainly cannot now [assist infantry forces], when the enemy have completed so many of them." Sherman viewed the lower Georgia coast as but a "cobweb" to be penetrated with ease. Federal light draught gunboats darted easily through the passages between the Georgia coastal islands. Sherman wrote his superiors in Washington on February 27 that the "Savannah River is closed as tight as a bottle between Savannah and Pulaski, and we are pushing preparations at Tybee for bombardment as rapidly as the weather will allow." The first ordnance supplies had arrived at Tybee the week before.[42]

On March 6, Fox wrote DuPont that he had met with McClellan and Meigs. Fox stated that the government placed little importance on Savannah "beyond the possession of Pulaski."[43] Fox added:

> The people expected Sherman to march at once upon Savannah or Charleston, which was ridiculous, and impossible, though I think he could have cut the railroad. He and his compeers, expected the gun boats to go directly into the Savannah river [*sic*], and dash up to the city, which was impossible, so that a month ago he seemed to be waiting for the Navy to go South. In the meantime there is an immense force and the sickly season almost upon us. I look forward to it with dire apprehension.[44]

By the end of February, Sherman's command had been reinforced by a few regiments and the siege supplies that he had been requesting. Colonel Richard White's 55th Pennsylvania joined Viele's First Brigade. Colonel Henry R. Guss' 97th Pennsylvania was assigned to Wright's Third Brigade. Three further regiments of infantry, Colonel William Montieth's 28th Massachusetts, Colonel Thomas Welsh's 45th Pennsylvania, and Colonel John M. Power's 76th Pennsylvania, had arrived but were not brigaded. Earlier in February, Sherman had received his often requested regiment of cavalry, the 1st Massachusetts, commanded by Colonel Robert Williams, and the 1st Connecticut Battery under Captain Alfred P. Rockwell.[45]

Sherman now had men scattered along the South Carolina and Georgia coasts. Viele's 1st Brigade headquarters was on Daufuskie Island; the 48th New York was stationed here, with a total of over 800 men. Stationed along the "Savannah River" was the 3rd United States Artillery, Battery E, which consisted of about 60 men present for active duty, a mere half of the total on the rolls. Engaged in the developing siege works on Tybee Island were the 7th Connecticut and 46th New York comprising 1,400 men on active duty; health was good and only about 100 men were sick. General Wright's 3rd Brigade, destined for Florida, consisted of the 6th Connecticut, 9th Maine, 4th New Hampshire and 97th Pennsylvania, almost 3,400 men. On February 28, General Viele ordered Captain John E. Bryant of the 8th Maine to direct transportation from Daufuskie Island to Battery Vulcan and Battery Hamilton. All boats, flats, and scows were under his orders—a force of 70 boatmen and a fleet of twenty boats and a steamer.[46]

On March 10, Lieutenant Colonel John H. Jackson of the 3rd New Hampshire, Major George F. Gardiner of the 7th Connecticut, and Captain Joseph H. Liebenau of Viele's staff, left on a reconnaissance in several small boats manned by members of the 3rd New Hampshire. They pulled upstream from Bird Island for Elba Island in the Savannah River, across from the mouth of the Saint Augustine Creek. They landed on the eastern tip of Elba Island opposite the mouth of Mud River. The Confederates had earlier burned the grass cover on Elba; so when Jackson left the boats and most of the men under the command of Captain Josiah Plimpton (3rd New Hampshire), he instructed them to row for Mud River at the first sign of smoke from a Confederate vessel. At 1:00 p.m., Jackson sent Major John Bedal, of the 3rd New Hampshire, along with six men, to move up the south side of the island to the upper end. Meanwhile, the three officers, along with six men, ascended the north side. They planned to meet opposite the mouth of Saint Augustine Creek. They saw forces at the mouth of the Saint Augustine Creek and four steamers and two schooners. They spotted Confederate soldiers working on a battery near the mouth of the creek. Bedal observed five pickets near the upper end of Elba Island. The reunited Federals returned to their boats and rowed uneventfully to Daufuskie Island.[47]

Although Fort Pulaski had been isolated by the batteries on Bird and Jones Islands and in Lazaretto Creek, and busy preparations were well under way on Tybee Island, Viele was actively trying to get a 30-day leave without jeopardizing his career. He needed to be in New York "because of his private interests and for those of my children." Sherman was looking for an increase, not depletion, of his staff, and had already denied Viele's request. Viele turned to Hiram Birney, prominent Republican and Lincoln's appointee as Custom Collector for the Port of New York, to contact Stanton and try to obtain the leave for him.[48]

On March 20, First Lieutenant Henry W. Robinson, 48th New York, arrived at Daufuskie Island from the battery on Bird Island and brought with him two more Confederate deserters—Charlie Brown and William Gleaman of the German Volunteers—from Fort Pulaski. One was a German and the other a New Yorker. They had gone oystering and landed on Long Island. Both said they had been "pressed" into Confederate service. They reported that 500 men were in the fort and that a third of them had Northern sympathies. The deserters also reported that an ironclad was being prepared in Savannah to attack the island batteries. Robinson sent the men to Lieutenant Napoleon Collins of the *Unadilla*, and reported that communication between Savannah and the fort was still occurring every two to three days. The deserters repeated their story to Captain James L. Larnder, commander of the naval forces at Port Royal, that an ironclad was under construction and that it, along with eight flat-bottomed 400-man scows, would be towed down the Savannah River to take the island batteries. Lieutenant Henry Jackson, a member of Viele's staff, had previously seen the ironclad opposite Fort Jackson from atop a house on Daufuskie Island.[49]

Having regained its strength on Hilton Head, the 6th Connecticut was sent to Daufuskie on March 20.[50] Throughout March and April, two companies of the 48th New York, one company of the 6th Connecticut, one company of the 8th Maine, and three companies of the 3rd Rhode Island Artillery worked on the Jones and Bird island batteries.[51] The corduroy road was completed across Jones Island to Battery Vulcan. The Connecticut men sank in mud, slept in mud, and pitched and banked their tents in mud. One recalled being awakened one night with water "surging" into his ears and having to stand in the mud until the tide receded. Both batteries were elevated further and made level until work could be done at high tide. Like the men on Bird Island, the men on Jones Island used the brackish river water for cooking and drinking.[52]

By the end of February, the parapet at Battery Vulcan was more than 1,000 feet long, six to ten feet thick, and three to four feet high. The hot sun baked the mud hard, and each day the soldiers poured on yet another layer. Later, Battery Vulcan was enlarged to nine guns. Its magazine was covered with a five-foot thick layer of earth and sandbags. Plank roads connected the gun platforms.[53]

* * * * * *

After February 27, Confederate Brigadier General Hugh W. Mercer and his staff were headquartered on Skidaway Island at the home of Captain William R. Pritchard. His "Skidaway District, Department of Georgia" included the island and adjacent mainland to Genesis Point on the Ogeechee River. Two companies of the Savannah Volunteer Guards manned the ten gun Green Island battery. Colonel David J. Bailey's 30th Georgia Regiment was stationed near Isle of Hope. The Chatham Artillery and two companies of cavalry (Bullock [Georgia Cavalry, 2nd Battalion, Company C] and Screven Troops [Georgia Cavalry, 2nd Battalion, Company B])—under Lieutenant Colonel Montgomery Cumming, were also on Isle of Hope. Company B of the Georgia Huzzars, Major John McEnery's 4th Louisiana Battalion, and Colonel William H. Stiles' 4th Georgia Battalion—3,000 men—were on Skidaway Island. Three companies under the command of Captain William R. Pritchard, Lieutenant Colonel George W. Lee's 38th Georgia Regiment (formerly Wright's Legions), and Colonel [?William] Phillips' 27th Georgia Regiment were stationed around 10-gun Fort Bartow at Causton Bluff.[54]

Lee continued to wrestle with the problems of Savannah's defense. On March 2, he wrote, "I presume they will endeavour to reduce the fort & thus open the way for their heavier vessels up the river. But we have an interior line they must force before reaching the city. It is on this line we are working, slowly to my anxious mind, but as fast as I can drive them."[55]

On the evening of March 3, Lee received a letter from President Davis, "If circumstances will, in your judgement, warrant your leaving, I wish to see you here with the least delay." Lee responded that he would leave the next morning and immediately began giving directions to his staff officers. Concerned about the Savannah defenses, he detailed for Brigadier General Alexander R. Lawton those measures which remained and places which needed fortifying. Lee urged Lawton to commence the three gun battery on the right bank of the Savannah River to unite with that on Hutchinson Island. He emphasized completion of the raft and a two gun battery, with rifle loopholes, to protect it. Feeling Sherman would approach the city by the Savannah River, Lee urged Lawton to remove the guns from Green and Skidaway Islands. Regardless of Northern moves, Lee felt that abandoning those positions was desirable. He urged Lawton to reinforce the battery at Thunderbolt and at Beulah and reserve the heavy guns for use on the Savannah River. Finally, Lee told Lawton to station scouts on Elba Island and both banks of the river to alert the defenders at the first sign of a Federal move so it could be halted in the early stages. Major Armistead L. Long would remain to finish arming the new batteries in the vicinity of Fort Jackson. Captain Joseph C. Ives would complete the batteries and obstructions on or near Saint Augustine Creek. Marine Captain John R. F. Tattnall, son of the Commodore and aide to Lee, would finish gathering boats for use on the rivers. Lee concluded his business sooner than expected and departed for Richmond that same night to serve as President Davis' military advisor; he never returned to Savannah during the war.[56]

On the night of March 8, Lawton ordered the dismantling of batteries on Skidaway and Green islands. Mercer planned to try moving the guns from Skidaway that same night. Mercer knew he must be careful since the batteries were clearly visible to the Federal vessels. By the following day, he had dismounted five guns and taken four to Thunderbolt. Wooden "guns" rested in the positions of those removed. On March 10, the last five guns were dismounted, and all had been removed to Thunderbolt. That same night, the men at the Green Island battery began to dismount their guns and the Phillips' Regiment baggage train started for Savannah. During the day of March 10, three large Federal steamers entered the sound, joining the three already there, but the sailors failed to see that the batteries were being dismantled. By March 14, the Southerners had removed all of the guns and valuable supplies from both sites. One officer noted, "Dummies, covered with canvas, occupy the place of the guns; the sentinels pace the ramparts, . . . and the gun boats in the sound seem perfectly unsuspicious."[57] By March 17, the Confederates felt they had secured the river approaches to Savannah against a sudden Northern dash.[58]

It was not until late March that the Federals discovered that Skidaway had been abandoned. A small boat came within 200 to 300 yards of Skidaway Battery and an officer "examined the Batteries with a glass." Southern cavalry pickets fired at them and they left "doubtless fully aware that the guns have been removed." On March 25, gunboats again approached the batteries on Skidaway, fired a few shells, and landed 200 men. As the cavalry pickets quietly observed, the Northerners burned the "wood works" of the battery and placed the United States flag on the roof of "Miller's old house." After the Federals left, Captain E. I. Dawson, a volunteer aide on Mercer's staff, took down the flag and burned the house. Two days later, DuPont, just returned from the Florida coast, learned that the batteries on Green Island and Skidaway Island had been abandoned. He realized that this gave the navy control of Wassaw and Ossabaw Sounds and the mouths of the Vernon and Wilmington Rivers.[59]

Major General John C. Pemberton was Lee's successor as commander of the Department of South Carolina and Georgia. Brigadier General Trapier now was in command of the Department of Middle and Eastern Florida. On March 21, Pemberton redivided the military districts in South Carolina; however, Drayton retained the same territory, although now titled the Sixth Military District.[60]

On March 15, two fishermen left Wilmington Island and brought fresh meat to the fort. That same day, the guns on the hulk in Lazaretto Creek fired at the fort, but the shells passed over and caused no damage.[61]

On March 17, Mercer and his staff left Skidaway for the Isle of Hope. Twenty-one cavalry pickets, of Colonel Phillips' Regiment remained at Beaulieu. Colonel Lamar's Battalion was located at Bethesda. On March 23, Wright's Legion moved to Savannah. Two days later, Tattnall was ordered to Norfolk to take command of the ironclad *Virginia*, relieving the wounded Franklin Buchanan.[62]

* * * * * * *

On March 20, Viele was concerned about the possibility of Confederate assaults on his two island batteries, and Lieutenant Napoleon Collins sent the 2-gun sidewheel steamer *O. M. Pettit* and two launches from the *Susquehanna* to help him. Three days later, Sherman returned from the Florida coast and, learning of Viele's fears, urged the navy to supply him with gunboats to protect the island batteries from enemy approaches from the Savannah and New Rivers.[63]

On the twenty-third, part of the 6th Connecticut made a reconnaissance up the New River and found no threatening enemy activity. A second reconnaissance, two days later, revealed no change. Major Beard led yet another reconnaissance up the Savannah River on March 28 that discovered several steamers off Fort Jackson, and also an ironclad vessel built like the C.S.S. *Virginia*. Both Sherman and Viele were concerned about an impending attack. Viele suggested placing schooners armed with rifled guns and howitzers and occupied by infantry, in Mud, Wright, and Cooper Rivers, and at the mouth of the New River. DuPont had little confidence or trust in Viele since first working with him in 1861 and regarded him as showing "panic" and "disingenuousness." DuPont responded bruskly to Sherman, offering to be of any assistance but adding, "I never expected that a naval force could be required to protect the batteries on Venus Point and Bird Island after they were completed." DuPont had learned that his gunboats lay grounded in the mud nearly all the time and felt it his duty to "withdraw every one of them." The next day, he added that some of his officers at Wall's Cut had seen the ironclad off Fort Jackson. He added sarcastically that the gunboats mired in the channels were not the blockading fleet, which was in Tybee Roads. DuPont sent Rodgers ashore to "attend all this and see the General [Sherman]. The truth is everybody is demoralized, I don't say it injuriously, since the *Merrimack* affair."[64]

Sherman's chief of artillery, Captain John Hamilton, who had been working with the island batteries, went to DuPont on March 29 to ask that hulks be sunk and that the armed steam tugs *Mercury* and *O. M. Pettit* be sent as additional protection for the batteries. DuPont mused, "Two poor tugs against Tattnall's fleet, whether there be an ironclad or not. . . . [Hamilton] said the life had been taken out of them by the iron boat." The following day, Hamilton, along with Lieutenant Collins of the *Unadilla* in Wright River, had changed their minds. Both men felt the battery on Bird Island was better protection for Battery Vulcan than the *Hale* and *Western World* wallowing in the mud. DuPont exclaimed "all these annoyances would vanish if the bombardment of Pulaski could commence."[65]

As work continued on Tybee Island, Sherman continued active inspection of all other aspects of the coming siege of Fort Pulaski. In early March he visited the batteries at Venus Point and Bird Island. Sherman found everything in order on Bird Island. He felt, however, that Battery Vulcan was "not in that advanced state that it should be," given the length of time it had been occupied and the number men at Viele's disposal. The light draught steamer *Pettit* was anchored at Venus Point and a similar vessel, the transport *Mayflower*, was by Battery Hamilton. Each was anchored and rarely moved; Sherman was concerned about their inactivity. He felt the *Pettit* should be able to rapidly move around to the north of Jones Island to help protect against Confederate assaults from the New River. Sherman wanted both vessels to actively patrol the Savannah River, be ready to assist the batteries, and to be seen by the Confederates at unpredictable times at unexpected places.[66]

* * * * * * *

Colonel Edward W. Serrell, senior engineer on Sherman's staff before Gillmore's promotion, left Hilton Head headquarters on March 8 for Washington, D.C. Six days later, he visited the new Secretary of War, Edwin M. Stanton, who asked him about conditions in Sherman's command. Serrell was happy to answer. He reviewed the progress made against Fort Pulaski on Tybee Island (to be discussed in the next chapter). Although a three-gun battery had been established on the west end of Tybee Island at Goat Point, Serrell erroneously believed it was to be abandoned and a new line of batteries established near the newly repaired Martello tower. Serrell reported that as of the eighth, thirteen mortars were on Tybee Island, including two of the large 13-inch mortars. He also reported that a hulk placed in Lazaretto Creek had closed Confederate routes to Fort Pulaski from the south. Confederate forces, he continued, remained in great strength near Bonaventure and northward toward Fort Jackson. Serrell confirmed that the channel at Wall's Cut was only seven feet deep at high tide, preventing all but the most shallow draft vessels from using this passageway out of the fort's range.[67]

Stanton asked the cooperative engineer what would be necessary "to produce a successful and speedy result." Serrell gladly offered that the "most essential requisite" was the presence of an "intelligent, vigorous, energetic general, in whom the Army would have entire confidence, who would counsel with his principal officers, and act promptly upon any decision he might form, and who, having orders, would concentrate his efforts on some particular object and accomplish it."[68]

Serrell's report must have been the last straw in the pile of concerns in Stanton's mind regarding Sherman's seeming lack of progress. The following day, March 15, Stanton reorganized the area currently under Sherman's administrative control in South Carolina, Georgia, and Florida, as the Department of the South and placed it under the command of Major General David Hunter.[69]

On March 26, a disappointed and bitter Sherman acknowledged the orders relieving him of command and answered his superiors, pointing out that since mid-December he had wanted to take both Savannah and reduce Fort Pulaski. He reminded the War Department that he had the opportunity to take Savannah by a *coup de main* but had failed for "want of co-operation of the Navy, the particulars of which the Department has already been appraised of."[70]

Sherman also reminded Stanton that preparations for the bombardment of the fort were going rapidly. All of the mortar and columbiad batteries on Tybee Island had been constructed, the mortars all mounted, and shot and shell accumulated. The batteries on the mud flats of the Savannah River, he added, "work like a charm, and, what is remarkable, our men there are in perfect health." He concluded with his hope that once operations against Fort Pulaski were concluded, the seasons would still be early enough to assemble a force to move on the more valuable Charleston.[71]

The following day, Sherman summarized conditions in his entire department for Stanton. His forces held the southeastern coast from North Edisto, South Carolina to Saint Augustine, Florida. The Savannah River had been blocked and preparations were well under way for the reduction of Fort Pulaski. General Wright, with three regiments and two sections of light artillery, occupied Fernandina, Jacksonville, and Saint Augustine. Lacking light-draught steamers, boats, and wagons, Sherman added that he had not been able to occupy any more of the Georgia or South Carolina mainland. Indeed, his forces were so scattered that more troops would be required to accomplish anything significant.[72]

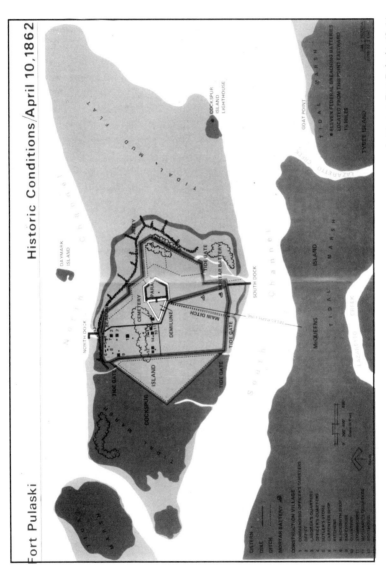

Lattimore, Fort Pulaski, 43-44

Map of Cockspur Island on April 10, 1862, showing Fort Pulaski, the two mortar batteries south of the fort, and the offices, quarters, storehouses and shops (1-14) to the northwest of the fort.

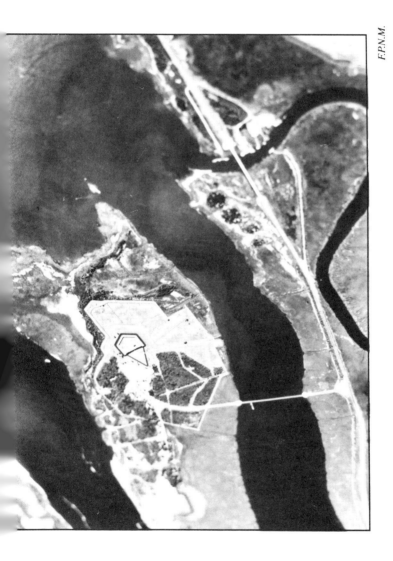

F.P.N.M.

Aerial view of Fort Pulaski today, showing the fort, moat system, and tidal canals. Silting has enlarged the island westward. Southeast of the fort, Lazaretto Creek winds its way to the Savannah River. The land in the lower right corner of the photograph is Tybee Island; construction of the highway destroyed the sites of the Federal batteries.

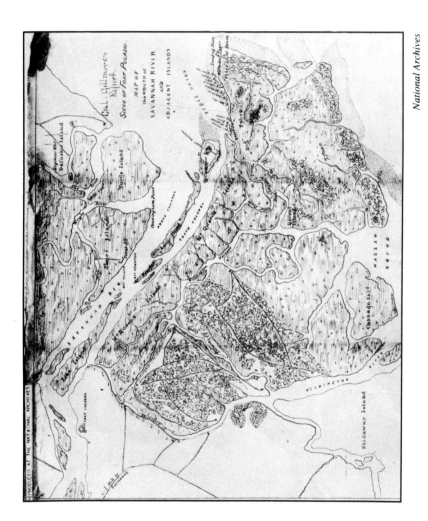

Original ink map which accompanied General Gillmore's report of the siege of Fort Pulaski. The misspelled "Rivir" was perpetuated in the engraved version included in his book.

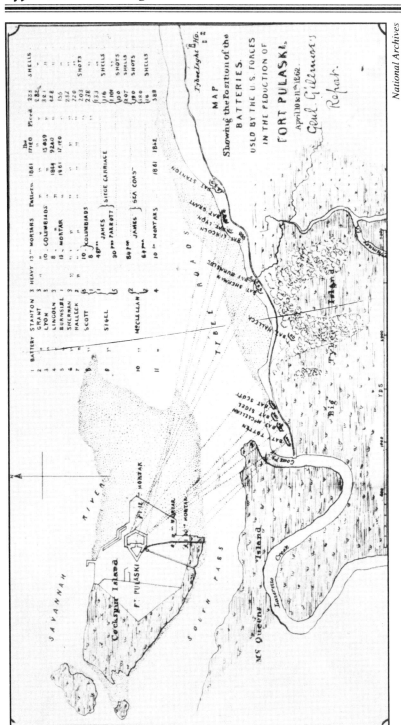

Original ink map showing the location of the Federal batteries on Tybee Island which accompanied General Gillmore's report of the siege and reduction of Fort Pulaski.

Chapter 5

<hr/>

"We are now at work in earnest"

Gillmore arrived on Tybee Island to direct siege preparations on February 19. Two days later, the first vessel carrying ordnance supplies arrived. From the arrival of that ordnance until the beginning of the bombardment seven weeks later the troops stationed on the island toiled continuously. Colonel Rudolph Rosa's 46th New York had initially occupied Tybee; they were joined by Colonel Alfred H. Terry's 7th Connecticut, and later by two companies of the New York Volunteer Engineers, five companies of the 8th Maine, two companies of the 3rd Rhode Island Artillery, and a small detachment of Company A, Corps of Engineers (First Lieutenant James H. Wilson). Before Gillmore's arrival, Terry commanded the Tybee force. Terry expressed optimism from the outset: "Pulaski is almost entirely cut off from communications & works are in progress which it is hoped will compel its surrender."[1]

Men were constantly landing and hauling heavy guns, stores, and construction materials; making roads and fascines; and building individual batteries and the associated magazines and bombproofs. The infantrymen also drilled in their artillery duties.[2]

Like the other coastal islands around Fort Pulaski, Tybee is largely a tidal marsh. On the east and north shores there were several areas of higher ground; the siege batteries would be built on the north shore. The distance from the landing near the Martello tower to the future site of the most western of the batteries was two and one-half miles. The last mile, to be the location of the seven batteries closest to the fort, was low and marshy and would be crossed by a road corduroyed with brushwood and fascines and in full view of the fort's guns. Construction of the batteries, gun platforms, magazines, and splinter-proof shelters; hauling supplies; and mounting the guns and mortars was all done at night, frequently in driving rain. The men covered all work with brush before daylight to conceal it from Fort Pulaski. Gillmore allowed the appearance of the brush screening the batteries to change gradually every night but forbade abrupt changes in the outline of the land. Once a safe parapet was complete, work could continue behind it with more freedom. Parties of men did mechanical tasks during the day; they arrived before daylight and returned to camp after dark. By the end of February, First Lieutenant Thomas B. Brooks, 1st New York Volunteer Engineers, was directing the two engineer companies preparing Tybee's row of batteries. "Most of the work for a short time to come will have to be done in the night," he wrote, "as the low sand ridge does not afford concealment or protection." He added, "we have not been fired on yet and I hope not discerned." On February 27, Sherman gave Gillmore command of all the troops on Tybee Island.[3]

U.S.A.M.H.I.

Thomas B. Brooks

First Lieutenant Horace Porter supervised the landing of guns and supplies and their transport across Tybee. After completing the sand fort near the lighthouse, he reported to General Viele at Port Royal Sound on February 22, then returned to Tybee two days later to continue arming the batteries.

Porter began by directing the unloading of the heavy gun barrels that weighed up to 17,000 pounds. Strong decking was built across gunwales of lighters, and the guns were lowered onto them. At high tide, rowboats towed them ashore. On the shore, soldiers pulled ropes from the gun-laden lighters until they tipped and the gun rolled off in to the water. At low tide, the men dragged the guns across the sand above the high water mark, often by lantern light. Lieutenant Colonel Joseph R. Hawley described the March 2 mortar landing. At 7:00 p.m. the surf was high and 50 men went to tip a lighter and dump it. Low tide came at midnight, and a large part of the regiment used one and one-half hours hauling the gun above the high water mark.[4]

Tipping the iron gun carriages from the boats onto the hard sand damaged several bolts. The carriages were among the last part of the armament to arrive, and there was no time to replace the bolts until after the bombardment had begun. Although several bolts broke from the force of the firing, once replaced, the guns served until the bombardment ended.[5]

Fitting the north shore batteries began on February 21, when members of the 7th Connecticut spent a fatiguing rain-soaked night drawing mortar carriages west toward future battery sites. They spent the following day "shoveling a road to get to the mortar batteries on the west side of the fort." During the next five days, additional mortar carriages and barrels were dragged above the highwater mark and pulled westward.[6]

Once an 8 1/2 ton mortar barrel was ashore, it was placed on a pair of skids made of two 20-foot long foot-square timbers, and held together by three smaller

13-inch mortar

cross pieces. The forward end of the skids was then raised and lashed to the front axle of a large sling-cart with the hind end dragging on the ground. Soldiers then pulled the mortar onto the middle portion of the skids. The rear of the skids was then raised and attached to a second sling-cart, thereby forming a four-wheel wagon with skids and mortar suspended beneath the axles. It took as many as 250 men to drag these wagons across the island to the battery sites. As on Jones Island, the wheels of the sling-carts frequently sank five feet to their hubs in the marshy soil, even on the prepared road. The wheels had then to be laboriously extricated with levers and brute force. Sometimes the men had to cut a mortar barrel from the cart and roll it along planks to firmer ground. The men worked at night, often in heavy rain, and whispered so the men in Fort Pulaski would not discover their labor. Officers blew whistles to give directions. Hawley wrote his wife that "it is too much to hope that this will all keep out of the papers for 4 weeks. If Pulaski knew it we should suffer."[7]

Mounting the heavy mortars in their batteries was a further problem. The combined weight of gun and carriage cracked the previously constructed wooden platforms, and the wheels sank through the deck. Gillmore installed flat iron tracks, five feet long and four and one-half inches wide, partially countersunk into the gun platforms, which solved the problem while allowing the wheels to roll freely.[8]

* * * * * * *

U.S.A.M.H.I.

10-inch mortar

U.S.A.M.H.I.

8-inch columbiad

During February and March, the fort's garrison saw an occasional Union soldier walking on the Tybee beach but no other activity was visible. At night, however, pickets on the south wharf of Cockspur Island heard noises near Lazaretto Creek. When daylight came, they saw nothing. Olmstead did not fire, since "it seemed to me a waste of ammunition that could not possibly be replaced."[9]

* * * * * * *

It was time to complete plans for the placement of the batteries by late February. Porter wrote his family that his duties on Tybee were "to put up the armament for the reduction of Fort Pulaski. We are now at work in earnest and every night's work begins to tell. . . . The enemy have not yet learned the true nature of our work, and seldom fire." He appreciated his assignment. "The taking of this work will be the great act of this campaign, and I take a natural pride in the prominent position that has been assigned me." He offered his family an account of the placing of the batteries.

I may say to you, if to no one else, that six batteries were being constructed when I arrived, but in what I considered a very disadvantageous place. On my recommendation Gen. Gillmore changed them. First he placed two in the position I proposed, then two more, and yesterday he consented to remove all.[10]

After the war, Brigadier General Henry W. Benham, who did not arrive until April and intensely disliked Gillmore, recalled what he had heard of the same gun replacement incident:

The original intention of Captain Gillmore, appeared to have been, to arrange the batteries on the *farther* half of the shore line, and nearest the Tybee Light House; the line thus selected, being between 2600 and 3500 yards distant from the Fort. But a request of Lt. Porter to be relieved in such case, as I am told was witnessed by Genl. [then Colonel] Terry;--(as Lt. P. stated he would as soon bombard the fort from Long Island, N.Y.) with Porter's recommendation for the nearer position at Goat Point, at 1600 yards distance, caused the directions the next day; from Capt. Gillmore for the placing of five batteries in advance, and beyond a broad open space (most dangerous for communication, it is true, as was found) but still in the only position from which any effective battering of the fort took place. It is not certain indeed that *any* important injury was done to the Fort or its garrison from the 6 batteries beyond 2600 yards.[11]

Major Charles G. Halpine, Hunter's adjutant general and also present only in April, was outspoken in his recollection of Gillmore's role in the siege. He wrote:

Had his [Gillmore's] original plans been carried out, we might have been firing ten-inch solid shot from columbiads, and thirteen-inch shell from mortars, from the day the bombardment commenced until now, without having caused any serious discomfort to the men and officers of

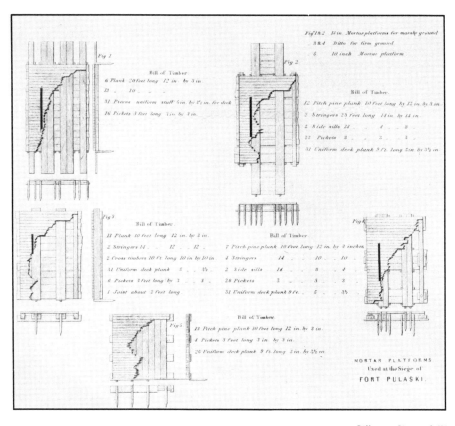

Gillmore, Siege, pl. IV

Details of mortar platform plans used in the Federal batteries on Tybee Island.

the opposing garrison. Gillmore's original plan only contemplated a bombardment from the upper sand-hills of Tybee Island, with columbiads and mortars--his nearest batteries being about 2,600 yards, and his farthest batteries fully 3,700 yards, from the work to be assailed.

Out of this ineffectual scheme, he was reluctantly but effectually derided and argued—but chiefly derided—by Lieutenant Horace Porter, . . . Lieutenant J. H. Wilson, . . . and Lieut. Patrick J. O'Rorke. . . . They laughed at the fears which Gillmore expressed, that ordnance and ordnance stores in any sufficient quantity could not be moved across the open place on Tybee Island called "the jaws of death,"—a place clearly under the fire of, and without any protection from Fort Pulaski's barbette guns; and having at last obtained the doubting Captain's [Gillmore's] consent to this experiment, it was by the inspiration and under the guidance of these young officers that the lower, and only effective, batteries of the siege were erected.

It was, we say, by the request, and still more by the ridicule, of these young officers, that the then Captain Gillmore was compelled—sorely against his own judgment and protest—to consent to the erection of batteries at Goat's Point, on Tybee Island, distant only 1,700 yards from Fort Pulaski; and to the armament of these, under the direction of the then Lieut. Horace Porter, of the Ordnance Corps, with 30-pounder Parrott guns, and some 8-inch columbiads throwing James projectiles. All know the result.[12]

Captain Alfred B. Ely, Benham's assistant adjutant general, arrived with his superior on the first day of April and met Gillmore on an inspection of Tybee. Ely viewed himself as a "novice" on the subject of sieges and artillery and closely questioned Gillmore to learn his "expectations and reasons for them." Gillmore told him that his "main reliance was upon the thirteen-inch mortars and eleven-inch columbiads." When Ely asked him what he expected these to accomplish, Gillmore told him that the shells should strike the terreplein (the flat part of the wall on which the guns are placed) of the fort and crash through into the casemates. Ely then asked what would be the role of the two batteries of James and Parrott guns. Ely reports that Gillmore said that he "did not rely much upon them, they were an experiment; it was the big mortars and columbiads that were to do the business." Ely was concerned about the effectiveness of plunging mortar fire, since the earth-covered casemate arches, beneath the terreplein, were built to withstand it. Ely claimed he was more optimistic about the rifled shells chipping the brick facade, given enough time.[13]

U.S.A.M.H.I.

Charles G. Halpine

Opinions differ over who sited the batteries. Location was vitally important because rifled, as well as smooth-bore, guns placed too distant would be ineffective. Although the accounts of Benham, Halpine, and Ely may be questioned as based on "hearsay," Porter's contemporaneous letter written to his family at the beginning of preparations for the siege proves that others, not Gillmore, deserve credit for the proper placing of the rifled guns. Lending additional support to Gillmore's experimental use of the rifled guns is the heavy preponderance of mortars and smooth-bore columbiads he would install in the batteries.

The slow work of building batteries and hauling guns continued throughout March. On the third, Lieutenant Colonel Hawley wrote his wife about the pace of work at Tybee Island. He wondered if he "should ever see or hear of these magnificent spectacles and thunder of siege and battle of which I had so often dreamed." Although the fort had been quiet for days, Hawley reported hearing daily "the sublime bass of some heavy gun—Wassaw Sound or the rebel Skidaway battery, or our batteries on the river just above Pulaski, or the rebels at Fort Jackson and thereabouts."[14]

Hawley realized that preparations for the bombardment of Fort Pulaski would not be completed for at least another four weeks. The 7th Connecticut had about 700 men available to work and 100 on the sick list. Most of those not on the sick list suffered from colds or diarrhea and were not fit for "severe" work. Hawley himself was plagued by chronic dysentery during most of his stay on Tybee. By mid-March the soldiers had installed charcoal filters that had "improved the drinking water."[15]

On March 7, the 7th Connecticut pulled more mortars a "little ways" toward the batteries. Three days later, they pulled mortars and carriages onto the beds in the newly constructed batteries. Sherman and his staff visited the sites. The next day, the men "drawed a mortar up to the casemate battery and tipped it off and brought the [sling-cart] wheels back." The teams continued hauling shells up to the batteries. During the nights of March 12 and 13, they pulled more mortars to the batteries.[16]

Tedium was relieved in early March when the 46th New York regiment accidently set its camp afire. The Germans had earlier "built a little summer house in front of each tent of poles, and covered them with palmetto leaves." The southern sun quickly dried the vegetation into tinder. On the night of March 8, one end of a street caught fire "and away they went." It was not until the fire destroyed an entire company's tents that it was put out. Ammunition exploded and loaded guns discharged, wounding one soldier in the side and head.[17]

The next day, March 10, Connecticut Private Milton Woodford wrote a friend, describing the labor that continued day and night,

> We have got a lot of mortars here. The *largest ever used*. They throw *200-lb* shell. It is rather slow work getting them to their places as we have to draw them nearly two miles and *17,000 lbs* is quite a load you know. There are a number of ten inch columbiads to get up to the batteries, more batteries to build, over *10,000 shells* to get ashore, and cart up there, and various other things to do too numerous to mention and only the N.Y. 46th and part of our Rgt to do it all.

As an afterthought, he mentioned that the Federals were preparing a chain to stretch across the Savannah river above the fort to stop Confederate fire rafts.[18]

That same day, Private Henry L. Glines wrote his parents that his Connecticut regiment had thus far unloaded twelve mortars and carriages. Like everyone else, he reported that the work was slow and difficult, comparing the mortars to five foot-long hogsheads. He had measured the iron at the muzzle to be fifteen inches thick, and he estimated that at the breech was three inches thicker. He was unable to lift the shells, not surprising, since each weighed about 200 pounds. Glines noted that five batteries faced west toward the fort and that construction of batteries had begun at Goat Point.

> We had to make a road in the night time as it is in full view of the Fort. Last Friday night we started with a mortar to draw·up to Goat Island, before we started our Col'n gave us a few words of caution. We were not to speak a loud word or make any noise as the Rebels have a look out in the light house by the Fort, as it would cost many lives and probably the undertaking. So that officers should not speak, the orders were to be give with a whistle, one whistle was to pull, two was to stop, and three whistles was to slack up the ropes. Well we started and went about fifty rods from the Casemate Battery when the hind wheels began to sink and before we had gone ten feet they were in up to the Hub. We pulled and pulled until we broke an inch and a quarter rope three times we found we could not pull it out, so we rolled the Mortar off, quick as it struck the ground it began to sink and before we would get some planks to put under it had got most half covered up after a while we got it up on to a hard spot and covered brush over it so the Rebels could not tell what it was and left it. I believe they are going to try some other way to get them up.

Glines contemptuously added that "the Engineers that are here don't know anything, they put the Mortars in one place and then move them to an other and so on, they set three mortar beds took them up and now have to put them back again, it will take till the first of May to get the batteries done and take the Fort."[19]

By March 13, Hawley still felt that at least two weeks would be necessary before the preparations were completed. He was happy that the three companies of the 7th Connecticut, which had been at Daufuskie Island, had rejoined the main part of the regiment. Two nights later, members of the 7th Connecticut were again busy pulling three carriages and one mortar up to the batteries. On the eighteenth, they drew up two more mortars; on the nineteenth, a 42-pounder rifle to the casemate battery and a 10-inch columbiad to another battery.[20]

Adrian Terry had learned of the behavior of Major Gardiner, commander of the three Connecticut companies recently arrived from Daufuskie. The entire regiment had come to view Gardiner as "the little beast of a major. . . . It will be long enough before he get another separate command. He is in every way *contemptible*."[21]

Terry noted that his brother, Alfred, "is busily employed . . . [with] preparations for the bombardment of Fort Pulaski which are now proceeding with great

Harper's Weekly

Federal infantrymen hauling a mortar with a sling cart at night across Tybee Island; Fort Pulaski is on the horizon to the right of the cart.

energy and rapidity." Adrian estimated that at least two more weeks were needed to complete the works. He then hoped to "astonish the inmates of that place with a shower that they can have no conception of." April 12 was the anniversary of Fort Sumter's fall, and Adrian Terry noted that the date "has been fixed upon by the Charlestonians for a great celebration. We expect to celebrate the day inside of Fort Pulaski, and thus render their celebration rather an unsatisfactory one." The fort was "completely cut off from all succor" and deserters claimed a $35,000 reward awaited anyone who could "effect the removal of the garrison."[22]

On March 20, an exhausted Porter reported his responsibilities to his mother. Besides Gillmore, he was the only regular officer on the island and felt he was "made a pack horse of." He wrote, "I have to instruct volunteers in the use of the guns as fast as we put them up, superintend the preparation of the immense stores of ammunition, &c." Although the army would construct eleven batteries, everything had thus far been kept secret from the Confederates, a fact he attributed to banning all newspaper reporters from the island. Porter viewed them as "the curse of an army."[23]

That same day, Hawley wrote his wife of the "terrible preoccupation of our entire thoughts, day and night, by the siege that we are engaged upon." The entire 46th New York and 7th Connecticut, along with two companies each from the 3rd Rhode Island Artillery and the 1st New York State Volunteer Engineers, were laboring on the preparations. It had taken 200 men two hours to drag one mortar from the beach to above the high water mark. Sometimes 300 men could not pull the sling cart through the sand and mud. "A columbiad weighs from 13,000 to 15,000 pounds [and] it has been no light job to drag them up there, the wheels sometimes sinking to the axle and the tugging procession sneaking along an open beach within 1,600 to 2,000 yards of the scores of guns in Pulaski and nothing but a placid bay between." Of the 32 pieces then ashore and mounted, about 20 could not be approached during daylight hours. Hawley added that magazines made of heavy timber, covered with 20 feet of sand, supported the batteries. The innermost chamber held the powder; rooms for filling the shells adjoined. Over a thousand tons of mortar shells were stored ashore. Shot and shell for the rifled guns and columbiads— enough for eight days and nights—had also been landed.

Hawley calculated that "the twelve big mortars will each fire five times an hour (it is a slow job to clean, load and aim them) making 60 shells an hour. Each mortar gives two reports—the firing of the mortar and the bursting of the shell." Hawley figured that with the mortars and other guns firing at their expected rate, there would be 250 reports, from the guns and exploding shells, every hour. He expected Confederate fire to be heavy, especially against the closest batteries. Hawley had seen the men in Fort Pulaski piling up sand bag traverses and preparing to resist. Although the Federal preparations were not visible, if "they had any shrewdness they must have known" what was occurring. "If Gen. Sherman and his drunken ordnance officer [Lieutenant Francis J. Shunk][24] have not made some serious omissions (of which there are grave suspicions) in the articles sent for, we shall be ready to open fire by the 1st of April. Hawley knew by now that his regiment would work at least eight of the mortars and perhaps more, since his regiment was half the men on the island. "The mortars are the safest to work, for they are behind high banks and are aimed by stakes and lines the whole concern being out of sight of the enemy."[25]

On March 21, the Federals fired six shots from a Parrott gun in the fort by the lighthouse. The Confederates answered with 10-inch columbiads and exploded several shells near the sand fort and over the road along which 200 men of the 7th Connecticut were tugging a columbiad to the batteries. There were no casualties. The next night, members of the 7th Connecticut pulled a columbiad to another battery.[26]

Also on the twenty-first, Horace Porter and an assistant crept along Goat Point with a telescope to inspect the fort. A casemate gun in Fort Pulaski fired and Porter rolled behind the bank just as he felt the woosh of a 42-pounder shot flying over his head. The shell struck the marsh 100 yards behind.[27]

* * * * * * *

During March, pickets at the shore of Cockspur Island could hear the Federals across the river at Kings Landing on Tybee, but they still could see no activity; the sand ridge on Tybee remained unchanged to the observers. Except for the three men who appeared on the beach on December 29, Confederates had seen no Federal soldiers.[28] On March 19, the *Savannah Republican* reported that the Federals had "one rifle cannon on an old hulk near Decent Island, 2 1/2 miles south of Fort Pulaski, one on the Martello Tower, and a battery of Dahlgrens and Columbiads on the point of Tybee; and a battery on Dafuskie Island, apparently of four guns."[29]

During the night of March 22, Second Lieutenant Christopher Hussey of the Montgomery Guards, with two of his men, slipped over to Kings Landing on Tybee and "discovered a Battery the yankees were erecting." At 10:00 p.m., Fort Pulaski opened on Kings Landing, but in the darkness damage could not be evaluated.[30] The Confederates now knew for sure what they had previously only suspected: the Federals were building batteries on Tybee.

* * * * * *

On March 24, the 7th Connecticut continued working with the mortars. During the previous night, a group of forty men had pulled another gun carriage to Goat Point. They then returned to help unload shells from a boat. Three nights later, the Connecticut men stuck brush in front of the Goat Point battery to allow work to continue during the day.[31]

That same day, Adrian Terry wrote his wife, "I suppose it is no longer a secret in the North that the bombardment of Pulaski is at hand and that the strong fort must soon fall under the overwhelming fire which we shall be able to land upon it." While the 7th Connecticut would work the mortars the "nineteen pieces of heavy cannon will be worked by the artillery companies of the 3rd Rhode Island and the 46th New York Regiments for battering down the walls." By March 30, all of the mortars and carriages had been landed on Tybee. Some columbiads still awaited carriages.[32]

On March 30, an armed boat with men of the 46th New York from the hulk in Lazaretto Creek reconnoitered the Wilmington Narrows. They encountered Captain J. Terrell Crawford and three companies of the 13th Georgia who killed one New Yorker and captured eighteen others. The Germans badly wounded one Confederate. The prisoners "made little resistance & seem perfectly well satisfied to be captives." The Federal captives complained of poor food and harsh treatment by their officers while on Tybee Island. Several prisoners described the batteries, as well as their armaments, for the anticipated bombardment of the fort. The Savannah *Republican* published the information the next day and it soon reached Fort Pulaski's garrison.[33]

Colonel Rosa unsuccessfully searched for his missing men on Whitemarsh and Wilmington Islands as far as Thunderbolt and Saint Augustine Creeks. The following day, he reported the patrol missing. A second patrol of seventeen men, previously believed captured, belatedly returned to the hulk on April 3.[34]

On April 1, men of the 13th Georgia captured two more Yankees on Whitemarsh Island. Both from the 46th New York, they confirmed that the force on Tybee Island consisted of 1,000 to 1,200 men. This information, too, appeared in Savannah's newspapers.[35]

The capture of the New Yorkers increased Gillmore's worry about the lack of security of his western batteries at Goat Point. He recommended that men from the

Bird Island battery picket McQueen's Island. Gillmore could then place a large battery, screened from view of the fort, to cover Lazaretto Creek.[36]

During the night of March 30, Captain Daniel C. Rodman of Company B, 7th Connecticut, slipped over to Cockspur Island and discovered mortars south of the fort. He planned to repeat his nighttime visit and spike the guns.[37]

As time passed, following the fire in the 46th New York's camp, the 7th Connecticut began to ignore their instructions not to build shelters from the sun using tree limbs and palmetto fronds. On March 31, the officers ordered that "all the things around the tents that were combustible to be taken down." One Connecticut soldier noted, "Our tents came close together so that if a fire should break out it would be hard stopping it until a whole street should burn up."[38]

* * * * * * *

In Fort Pulaski at the end of March, Lieutenant Theodorick W. Montfort commented on the increasing army of winged allies:

> The position occupied by the Yankees between this & Savannah is right in a marsh & I am told by those acquainted with those points that no man can live there through the summer, for mosquitos, sand flies, & sickness. . . . I look to Providence, sand flies, mosquitos, & sickness relieving us than to any one else.[39]

By April 2, the Confederates realized that an attack was coming because they saw lights at Kings Landing in the night. The Oglethorpe Light Infantry and Wise Guards spent the day widening ditches on the parade and piling more dirt against the blindage in front of the mess rooms.[40]

Chapter 6

"Untiring and scientific exertions"

In late March, Lieutenant Colonel Joseph R. Hawley wrote a friend that discussions in the officer's mess did not ascribe to Sherman much "generalship." "Dyspeptic domineering uneasy fault finding," the general had exhibited "a certain efficient energy" but "not much fixed purpose and none of the high qualities that mark a real leader." Hawley regarded Gillmore as the "head of the force we have here." "Gen. Sherman, in his love of despotic authority—(he loves it strongly; he does *not* know how to use it) proclaimed Gillmore a Brig. Gen. much to G.'s disgust and embarassment." Hawley, anyway, believed the sincerity of Gillmore's reticence about the promotion. A partisan of Gillmore, Hawley regarded him as "a dear man, a good officer & a good fellow." He regarded First Lieutenant Horace Porter, busily overseeing everything for Gillmore, as "a splendid young officer with twice the genius of Sherman & more brilliancy than Gillmore." "He is a treasure & if Sherman will keep away we shall get along." Hawley assessed Fort Pulaski's Colonel Charles H. Olmstead correctly as "an able and spunky officer" without having yet seen the substance of his character.[1]

Another officer of the 7th Connecticut, Captain Charles Palmer, shared Hawley's opinion of Sherman. Palmer lamented that had "Old Timothy" shown enterprise such as Brigadier General Ambrose E. Burnside had recently exhibited in eastern North Carolina, Savannah and Charleston would already be occupied. Sherman's inaction "had concentrated a rebel army of 60,000 in the vicinity, and rendering Savannah almost impregnable." Bitterly, he added, "We have already lost more soldiers by exposure on 'fatigue' than would have been killed in taking Savannah. And all the weather lost, hot weather coming on & *nothing* accomplished." The captain had little better to say about the navy, which had failed to exploit the opening of Wall's Cut. He condemned DuPont, who "had nightmares of fire rafts and infernal machines & torpedoes, till he backed square out and acknowledged he dare not go."[2]

U.S.A.M.H.I.

David Hunter

When the news came at the end of March that Sherman had been relieved, the 7th Connecticut's Adrian Terry wrote that it was "very much to the satisfaction of the whole division, as Sherman is very unpopular." However, many felt that criticism of Sherman in the Northern newspapers had been "unjust as he has been hampered and harassed in a number of ways that are not generally known. He certainly has not had it in his power to accomplish one half the deeds that he is blamed for not doing."[3]

Sherman's replacement, Major General David Hunter, had graduated from the United States Military Academy in 1822 in the middle of his class. He served in the army for fourteen years, resigned, and later returned to serve as paymaster in the Mexican War. Lincoln had invited Hunter, who was politically active and an abolitionist, to accompany the presidential party to the District of Columbia for the inauguration. Seriously wounded at First Manassas, Hunter was appointed major general in August, 1861, and spent four months in Missouri as a replacement for Major General John Charles Fremont. There he brought relative order to the chaos of Fremont's regime.

Brigadier General Henry W. Benham accompanied Hunter. Benham had graduated first in the class of 1837 at the United States Military Academy. An engineer officer, he had made a career in the army. He had served in West Virginia with Brigadier General William S. Rosecrans before his assignment to Hunter's command. Although highly regarded as an engineer, he had not distinguished himself before this assignment to Hunter and the Department of the South.

On March 24, Hunter ordered Benham, then in New England, to report to the Department of the South and upon arrival to take charge of the division composed of the brigades of Wright, Stevens, and Viele. Hunter, Benham, and their staffs met in New York City and together steamed to Fort Monroe, Virginia, aboard the *Adelaide*. On March 26, they de-

U.S.A.M.H.I.

Henry W. Benham

parted on the steamer *Atlantic* for Hilton Head Island. Leaving Hampton Roads, they saw the fleet transporting McClellan's Army of the Potomac to the Virginia Peninsula.[4]

Hunter and Benham arrived at Port Royal Sound on March 31. Hunter had begun to consider his priorities, especially in South Carolina, before landing on Hilton Head and had anticipated needing 25,000 more men. Sherman briefed Hunter on the progress against Fort Pulaski. Twenty-four guns—twelve 13-inch seacoast mortars, four 10-inch columbiads, three 8-inch columbiads, and five large rifled guns—were already in place on Tybee Island. The Savannah River had been closed since February 11. Finally, Sherman told Hunter his sad story of how his plans to take Savannah in late January had been thwarted by an uncooperative navy.[5]

Hunter promptly began by reorganizing his department into three districts. The Northern District covered the states of South Carolina, Georgia, and some of northern Florida, essentially Sherman's old command. The Southern District covered southern Florida, and the Western District included the western Florida to the Georgia state line. Benham received the Northern District and immediately asked Sherman to turn over "all charts, maps, plans, reports, moneys, &c. . . . appertaining to the expeditionary command in this district." Hunter officially thanked Sherman and expressed his "full appreciation of the amount and importance of the services rendered" and shortly after that Sherman left for assignment in the west with the Army of the Tennessee. Hunter expected to begin the "attack and storming" of Fort Pulaski within five days "just as soon as the heavy siege guns brought with us can be put in position in the works already extant."[6]

Although many of Sherman's officers had been discontent with him as a commander, some who had worked with him felt genuine regret over his departure and bitterness at how he had been replaced. DuPont felt there was no justice in relieving Sherman of command.

> Poor fellow, a more onerous, difficult, responsible, but thankless piece of work no officer ever had to do, and none ever brought to such a task more complete self-sacrificing devotion—he ploughed, harrowed, sowed, and it does seem hard that when the crop was about being harvested he is not even allowed to participate in a *secondary* position. . . . I never knew until he told me the other day how shamefully his requisitions have been neglected.[7]

DuPont was correct when he told Fox that Sherman's "position was never understood by the Government or the people—he was required to make bricks without straw." Since Benham's geographic area of responsibility covered exactly that of General Sherman, DuPont felt this gave "more point to the recall, or rather *making* it [a] recall which was unnecessary if not unjust; I believe *both*, and I think it came from the influence of *extreme* men."[8]

Reviewing his six-month relationship with Sherman, DuPont wrote his wife, "He ever deferred to me, we never had a single difficulty; a passing suspicion or misgiving, when something seemed to elicit it, was sure to give way at our next meeting—and a more thorough, devoted public servant, self-denying and unostentatious, never lived." DuPont later contrasted the old regime with the new: "General Hunter and General Benham came on board yesterday, with a staff that had no end, like bobs on a kite. What a contrast to poor Sherman, and his check shirt and collar awry!"[9]

Porter also felt that Sherman had been "badly treated by the Administration." He believed that Sherman had no transportation to move inland and that the navy had failed him constantly. "Though he accomplished more than they required the *people* expected more still, and the Administration as if they had not laid down his line of conduct dismissed Sherman." Porter concluded, "Personally he was a very disagreeable man, and I am not sorry the change has been made, but always let the 'Devil have his due.'"[10]

On April 4, Sherman left the Department of the South aboard the *Atlantic*. DuPont had instructed her captain, Joshua H. Eldridge, to sail by the *Wabash* where DuPont had assembled the entire crew in the rigging to give the departing Sherman "three hearty cheers."[11]

* * * * * *

Benham immediately reviewed the plans for the bombardment of Fort Pulaski. Gillmore was to remain as Benham's chief engineer; Porter, his chief of ordnance. On April 1, Benham visited Tybee Island and inspected the different camps and gun positions and "pressed the work of these batteries . . . by all the means in [his] power." Gillmore proudly noted that Benham "suggested no modifications of any of the siege works on Tybee Island or the manner of conducting the bombardment." Benham was concerned that Gillmore and Sherman had neglected concentric fire against the fort from opposite quarters. To correct that deficiency, Benham told Viele that he wished to discuss building additional mortar batteries, perhaps on the lower part of Long Island, to be better able to take in reverse the south, southeast, and northeast faces of the fort. Benham ordered an immediate reconnaissance.[12]

That same day, Benham also disapproved Gillmore's idea of preparing a large scow as a floating battery, bringing it through Wall's Cut, beaching it in a predetermined position and then converting it into a land battery. Benham had earlier disapproved of a similar plan to float a scow battery up Lazaretto Creek. He believed such a battery would add little to the existing Tybee Island batteries to the angle of fire against the walls of the fort. Benham felt that for such a battery to be effective it must be farther up the south channel where its concealment would be difficult.[13]

In the meantime, Gillmore, ever conscious of status and rank, expressed concern about possibly losing control of the bombardment of Fort Pulaski after all his planning and work. Benham reassured him that should additional troops be sent, even if a senior officer such as Wright was sent, both Hunter and Benham had already agreed that they both would see "the fullest justice done to your labors and efforts."[14]

On April 1, Lieutenant James H. Wilson reported to Gillmore and immediately began helping in artillery instruction. Also that day, members of the 7th Connecticut helped unload two more boats of shot for 10-inch columbiads. Private

Henry C. Glines noted, "I threw out twenty[;] they were about as much as I wanted to handle."[15]

On April 2, preparation of the batteries continued as members of the 7th Connecticut dragged four 10-inch mortar carriages onto their beds in the batteries and built a traverse in a columbiad battery. That night they hauled a 10-inch columbiad to Battery Scott on Goat Point. Horace Porter assessed the situation: "we have been getting along slowly but surely." He added that if all of the requested material had been sent sooner, the bombardment could have begun in mid-March. "This, however, is a remarkably rapid erection of a siege armament."[16]

* * * * * * *

On April 4, Fort Pulaski received Savannah newspapers telling about the soldiers captured on Wilmington Island and the batteries at Kings Landing. The garrison continued moving earth from the parade and placing it against the north and west blindages. Construction of traverses to protect the rear of the rampart guns began.[17]

The mail arrived the following day. The Confederates in Fort Pulaski expected an attack from seven batteries, which they knew were present on Tybee Island, and from the guns on "innumerial" boats. Men scattered sand on the casemate floors to soak up blood. They removed all combustible materials.[18]

April 6, the garrison pulled down the colonade in front of the officers' quarters and mess rooms. They deepened further the trenches on the parade. Now the Confederates could see men working on the western batteries on Tybee Island. It was also apparent to the Southerners that the batteries on Tybee were within 1,900 yards from the fort. Inside the fort, Lieutenant Theodorick W. Montfort put his trust "in God, ourselves, the mosquitoes & sand flies."[19]

* * * * * * *

Benham had been concerned—correctly it turned out—that the Confederates would learn of Federal preparations. Savannah newspapers arrived in Fort Pulaski on April 4 with news of the batteries at Kings Landing. Because of the capture of the New Yorkers, Gillmore believed he needed a gunboat to guard the creek, and he requested one from Commander Sylvanus W. Godon, commander of the 6-gun screw steamer *Mohican*, then in charge of vessels in Wilmington Narrows off Gibson Point, the northeast end of Whitemarsh Island at the confluence of Turner's and Richardson's Creeks. Godon took the 5-gun screw steamer *Norwich* (Lieutenant James M. Duncan) up Shad Creek, a tidal stream in eastern Wilmington Island, within two miles of Fort Pulaski and found no Confederates. Godon explored the area where the New Yorkers had been captured, but again saw no Rebels. Four days earlier, the hulk *Montezuma* had been sunk in Lazaretto Creek to serve as a gun platform. Gillmore requested a small gun boat to protect it. He worried that if the hulk was overpowered, "our batteries against Fort Pulaski would be exposed to a very annoying fire from her." Godon left the *Norwich* to guard the hulk and Wilmington Narrows, although he felt she was unsatisfactory for this purpose.[20]

Benham appealed to DuPont for official sanction of the cooperation between Godon's gunboats and Gillmore's force at the hulk. Benham had two concerns. First, he feared that the Confederates would learn more about preparations on Tybee Island, thus forcing the Federals to act prematurely. To prevent that, he ordered Viele, commander of the two river batteries above Pulaski, to see that there was no communication between the fort and Savannah. He also wanted men passed across the river to McQueens Island to secure that island and the south channel. Benham worried that the Confederates were concentrating on Wilmington Island and from there might try to relieve or reinforce the fort.[21]

On April 3, DuPont acted on Benham's concerns and ordered Godon to take his *Mohican*, armed with two 11-inch guns and a rifle, up the Wilmington River to locate the best site for obstructing the waterway with pilings or hulks. The Wilmington River, joined to Saint Augustine Creek and hence the Savannah River, was the last link between Savannah and the Atlantic. When closed, DuPont could withdraw all but one gunboat from Wassaw Sound.[22]

That same day, DuPont wrote Fox about renewed rumors of an iron-clad ram being prepared under the guns of Fort Jackson. DuPont chaffed over the "greatly exercised" army commanders who kept him from sending away his light draft vessels to help his own people elsewhere. DuPont's resistance on this matter was the subject of "very sharp criticism" by many army officers.[23]

By April 5, Benham told DuPont he feared a concentration near Wilmington Island would try to relieve or reinforce the Fort Pulaski garrison. Benham and Hunter conferred and requested that DuPont increase his presence in the Wilmington River, Wilmington Narrows, and the Tybee River. DuPont forwarded the 20-gun sloop of war *Vandalia* from Tybee Roads to Wassaw Sound and the mouth of the Wilmington River, where she joined the *Mohican*. DuPont also dispatched a sailing corvette, bringing the total force to four vessels, three of which were steamers.[24]

Benham also moved infantry to strengthen the rear of the Tybee batteries. On April 4, five companies of the 8th Maine, under Colonel John D. Rust, arrived at Tybee Island aboard the *Cahawha*. The remainder of the regiment was on Daufuskie, Bird, and Jones Islands, "where they have been on fatigue duty for a couple of months past." Two days later, more men from the 8th Maine arrived to guard the rear of Goat Point from a possible Confederate attack from Little Tybee and Wilmington Islands. Their position on the western island was visible from

U.S.A.M.H.I.

John D. Rust

the parapet of the fort. Brush covered this part of the island, and during the night the men shoveled up "a sort of sand earthen breastwork" which they covered with bushes. The Confederates never noticed the change on the island. At sunrise, the men lay down behind their cover and tried to hold themselves "in readiness to protect the batteries from an expected attack."[25]

On April 4, Dr. George Andrew had returned to Tybee accompanied by G. W. Smalley, correspondent for the New York *Tribune*. There they met another correspondent who was serving as a volunteer aide, with the rank of first lieutenant, to Gillmore: Adam Badeau of the New York *Evening Express*. Badeau was short, well dressed, bright in appearance, and had "eyes to see everything and somewhat lax ideas of political morality."[26]

Three days into his new command, Hunter reported to the War Department the disposition of his forces. In preparation for the bombardment he had 2,200 men on Tybee Island, 1,600 on Daufuskie Island, 300 at the battery on Bird Island, and another 300 on Jones Island. The remainder of his 17,000 men was scattered from Saint Augustine, Florida, to the North Edisto River, south of Charleston harbor. Hunter now echoed his predecessor Sherman about being "retarded by the non-arrival of the necessary guns, ammunition, &c." He had confidence in Gillmore, who he felt "deserves great credit for his untiring and scientific exertions" and added that the engineer officer "is now ready." Following the capture of Fort Pulaski, Hunter, like Sherman, planned to direct his attention against Charleston.[27]

Benham remained concerned about the lack of encircling batteries north of the fort. On April 2, he had agained raised the issue with Viele. First Lieutenant James H. Wilson had told Benham that Turtle Island, two miles from Fort Pulaski and immediately east of Jones Island and south of Daufuskie Island, had an elevated ridge that might be a suitable battery site. Benham had two 10-inch mortars and two 8-inch columbiads at Hilton Head available for Viele's use and offered to ship them immediately. Hearing nothing from Viele, he reproved him the next day for the two days it had taken to answer.[28]

Viele finally responded, enclosing the reports of the two officers who had made the reconnaissances, and adding his own "rapid conclusions." He felt that two flat-boats, one with the two mortars and one with two rifled guns and an 8-inch howitzer, could serve effectively at the lower end of Long Island. These guns were to fire at the gorge, but were of such caliber that they could serve only as a diversion. Although the Turtle Island site was attractive, the seven to ten days necessary to prepare a battery and move two 10-inch columbiads would prevent completion before the bombardment of Fort Pulaski began and, therefore, would render Viele's effort "inoperative under the circumstances." Although ordered to Turtle Island on April 9, the columbiads arrived too late to take part in the bombardment.[29]

Benham visited Viele on Daufuskie Island on April 6 with his adjutant Captain Alfred B. Ely, and his senior aide Captain E. F. Hawes. Benham told Viele to build the battery on Long Island by April 6 to "attack the gorge of the fort on the west." In the early morning darkness of April 9, the Long Island battery was "thrown up."[30]

On the afternoon of April 9, Confederate Second Lieutenant Christopher Hussey, Montgomery Guards, left Fort Pulaski on a reconnaissance to Long Island where he discovered the mortar battery one and one-half miles from the fort. He brought away six shovels and a barrel of fuses. He soon returned to the mortar battery with fifteen men in two boats and removed two barrels and five kegs of powder, twenty-five shells, screened lanterns, and aiming and firing tools. Unable to remove the mortar, he spiked it with a 10-penny nail.[31]

On April 6, Viele wrote Benham that a Black had escaped the previous night from Fort Pulaski, made his way to Daufuskie, and reported that Colonel Olmstead had read to his garrison a letter from the commanding general in Savannah that stated they would be relieved in a few days by a force of up to 30,000 men. As the relief force approached, the fort would simultaneously open on the Tybee Island batteries. Hunter's staff concluded the letter was two days old and that if relief was planned, it was coming soon. Meanwhile Viele worried about the withdrawal of naval assistance from Batteries Vulcan and Hamilton. DuPont had strengthened the armed vessels at Wall's Cut by sending the armed steam tug *Mercury*. DuPont now had five vessels guarding the island batteries and four in Wassaw Sound "protecting soldiers."[32]

On April 7, the *E. B. Hale*, freed from guarding Battery Vulcan, and accompanied by the *Mercury*, ascended the Wright River beyond Wall's Cut. They found no enemy vessels and only a few Confederate soldiers building earthworks.[33]

That same day, members of the 7th Connecticut practiced the drill on their mortars; the next day, they unloaded yet more 13-inch mortar shells.[34]

Benham and his staff arrived at Tybee on the afternoon of April 8 aboard the *McClellan*. That same afternoon, Hunter, Benham, Gillmore, and Halpine, along with staff officers, made a final inspection of the batteries and an examination of Fort Pulaski. Major Halpine said he could "count the buttons on the coats of the men moving round the ramparts." He felt the outcome of a Federal attack "doubtful" because of the strength of the fort. Halpine and Hunter were concerned that the longer the bombardment lasted, the greater the risk that the Confederate ironclad might pass the batteries on Bird and Jones Islands. Halpine sensed jealousy by DuPont and the other navy officers. He noted the Confederate earthwork batteries outside Fort Pulaski that could prevent the landing of "our men after our guns in Lazaretto Creek shall have breached the walls in the rear where they are weakest."[35]

Later that same day, Hunter told DuPont that he planned to begin bombarding Fort Pulaski the following morning; yet he postponed it, perhaps because of the "rain in torrents" which fell all day. Although the batteries on Tybee Island were not in perfect condition, Hunter felt that delays were of more service to the Confederates than to his besieging forces. He planned to remain aboard a ship opposite Fort Pulaski so he could observe the effect of the artillery.[36]

Before the bombardment began, Hunter wrote Brigadier General James W. Ripley, Chief of Ordnance in Washington, D.C., requesting that the ordnance officer he had inherited from Sherman's staff, First Lieutenant Francis J. Shunk, be replaced with "some competent officer of correct and regular habits." Several observers had delicately referred to Shunk's problem during the campaign. Even Porter observed to his sister, "Frank Shunk came down to see me the other day. He is now but a poor *drunken simpleton*, and the surgeons say beyond all redemption. Unless he stops liquor at once he cannot live a year."[37]

So rushed now were preparations to begin the bombardment that there was not time to await the arrival of all the ordnance supplies expected from the North. Bags for the powder for the 13-inch mortars did not arrive in time for the siege; the men would have to measure the powder with empty vegetable cans, pour it loose into the guns, and the crew had to adjust it in the chamber before firing. That practice was dangerous but caused no problems during the bombardment. Columbiad shells were bound to rough wooden sabots with strips of tent canvas. The night before the bombardment, April 9, the Federals discovered there were no fuse plugs for their 10-inch mortar shells. Men of the 7th Connecticut whittled a full supply. After the exertions of hauling guns and building batteries, the men were content to sit and whittle.[38]

Recalling the eve of the bombardment, Private Milton Woodford, 7th Connecticut, wrote:

> The rebels were not entirely ignorant of our doings, but thought it was kind of "fient" to draw their attention from the *gunboats*, from which they expected the *hotest* fire. . . . Goat Point is nearly a mile from the fort, and the guard can see it plainly with the naked eyes. Our boys used to hear the guard call "all's well" nights when we were at work.[39]

Colonel Terry made his last inspection during the evening of April 9. Men detailed to work the batteries were all in place and orders given to show no light anywhere. Terry, accompanied by Dr. Andrew, rode along the entire line and found everything in perfect order until coming to Goat Point and the splinter-proof occupied by the Germans of the 46th New York, a regiment "recruited in New York City, and largely composed of toughs." Terry ordered the men in the first shelter to extinguish the three candles that were burning, and they promptly complied. In the second splinter-proof, four men were playing cards by the light of a candle. They met Terry's order to blow it out with a blank stare. He repeated the order in English; other Germans present, sensing trouble, translated the order. The card players replied "nix vershta" and Terry promptly leveled his revolver at the group and "uttered the only oath charged against him." The card game ceased in darkness.[40]

By April 10, the Northerners on Tybee Island had constructed eleven batteries containing 36 artillery pieces. Benham later remarked that Gillmore had named the batteries for "the persons most prominent *or most likely to be so*, in political or military service." The batteries, their armament, and distance from Fort Pulaski follow listed below:

Battery	Armament	Distance to Pulaski, yds.
Stanton	3 heavy 13-inch mortars	3,400
Grant	3 heavy 13-inch mortars	3,200
Lyon	3 heavy 10-inch columbiads	3,100
Lincoln	3 heavy 8-inch mortars	3,045
Burnside	1 heavy 13-inch mortar	2,750

Sherman	3 heavy 13-inch mortars	2,650
Halleck	2 heavy 13-inch mortars	2,400
Scott	3 10-inch columbiads	1,740
	1 8-inch columbiad	
Sigel	5 30-pounder Parrotts	1,670
	1 48-pounder James rifles	
	(old 24-pounder)	
McClellan	2 84-pounder James rifles	1,650
	(old 42-pounder)	
	2 64-pounder James rifles	
	(old 32-pounder)	
Totten	4 10-inch siege mortars	1,650

The 7th Connecticut manned the mortars—Batteries Totten, Halleck, Sherman, Grant, and Stanton. Trained artillerymen of the recently arrived 3rd Rhode Island Artillery staffed Batteries McClellan, Scott, Lincoln, and Lyon. The 46th New York served Batteries Sigel at the onset of the bombardment but would be replaced the second day. Members of the newly arrived 8th Maine manned Battery Burnside.[41]

Close to each battery was a service magazine filled with sufficient powder for two days' firing. A depot magazine near the Martello tower and the landing pier had a capacity of 3,600 additional powder barrels.[42]

Traverses separated the guns within each battery. The sides of the traverses and epaulements had been revetted with marsh sod, other materials proving ineffective in preventing sand from sifting through. Each ordnance battery had splinter-proofs for the shifts of men not on duty. A bomb-proof surgery was located at Goat Point. Each battery had its own well. The advanced batteries were all connected by trenches for safe communication.[43]

Except for Batteries Lincoln and Totten, the magazines were placed near the center against the epaulement with an opening to the rear. Each had an attached ante-room for filling cartridge-bags. The magazines for Batteries Lincoln and Totten were in the rear of the platforms.[44]

Gillmore issued General Order Number 17 on the ninth, specifying the rate of fire and the objective of each battery. The eastern mortar batteries, and Battery Totten, were to drop their shells on the terreplein above the arches (north, south, and northeast walls), to explode after penetrating the earth cover and collapse the casemate arches. Columbiads in Batteries Lyon and Lincoln were to fire over the southeast wall and take the gorge and north face in reverse. Columbiads in Battery Scott were to help silence the barbette guns, then begin to breach the *pan coupé* between the south and southeast face. The rifled guns of Battery Sigel, after silencing the barbette guns, were to begin breaching the *pan coupé* between the south and southeast faces and the embrasures next to it on the southeast face. The rifled guns of Battery McClellan were to breach the *pan coupé* between the south and southeast face. Years later, Gillmore would add that the purpose of breaching the walls at the *pan coupé* of the south and southeast face was "with a double view of opening a practicable breach for assault and of exposing to a reverse fire the maga-zine in the opposite angle."[45] The second "objective," however, was not apparent until the fort had surrendered and, as will be seen, not considered at the time of the bombardment.

On the eve of the bombardment, Hunter and Benham sailed from Port Royal Sound to Tybee Island; Hunter anchored off the lighthouse early in the morning of April 10. Hunter had invited DuPont to watch the bombardment aboard the *McClellan*, but the commodore felt it was "an army affair," that he had no business there, and "had better be in my place." While Benham made his final inspection ashore, Hunter remained on board to prepare his summons for Olmstead's surren-der. Porter noted the arrival of those two new "stars" and observed that they were "as impatient for the fray as Roman ladies for the commencements of a gladiatorial combat." The two generals were accompanied by scores of divisional surgeons "with a broad grin on their faces at the idea of having a 'job.'"[46]

Chapter 7

"Pulaski is ours; Sumter is avenged!"

As light dawned on April 10, the Confederates in Fort Pulaski discovered that mounds of earth at the west end of Tybee had been leveled, brush cut away, and that four batteries were visible where dunes had stood before. The chimneys of the burnt houses at Goat Point were also down.[1]

Only part of Fort Pulaski's artillery—ten barbette guns, six casemate guns, and two mortars—could fire on Tybee. Only four barbette guns and three casemate guns could bear on Goat Point, site of the rifled artillery batteries. The garrison had returned to the casemates to clean up when a flag-of-truce boat appeared.[2]

At 5:30 a.m. Major General Hunter sent First Lieutenant James H. Wilson to demand the fort's surrender. Wilson climbed into a four-oared boat and sat in the stern; a crewman held aloft a white flag. Brigadier General Benham was on hand and called out, "Take your seat in the bow of the boat, Captain Wilson." Wilson did not move. "Take your seat in the bow of the boat, Major Wilson," Benham called out again. Wilson still did not move. "Take your seat in the bow of the boat, Lieutenant Colonel Wilson!" Benham yelled for a third time. Wilson finally realized the order was for him and replied, "All right, General, but you have my title all wrong. I am only a lieutenant." "Never mind, sir," Benham replied, "you shall have them all in due time. Meanwhile take your position in the bow of the boat so you can see better when you approach the island."[3]

The document Wilson brought from Hunter read:

I hereby demand of you the immediate surrender and restoration of Fort Pulaski to the authority and possession of the United States. This demand is made with a view of avoiding, if possible, the effusion of blood which must result from the bombardment and attack now in readiness to be opened.

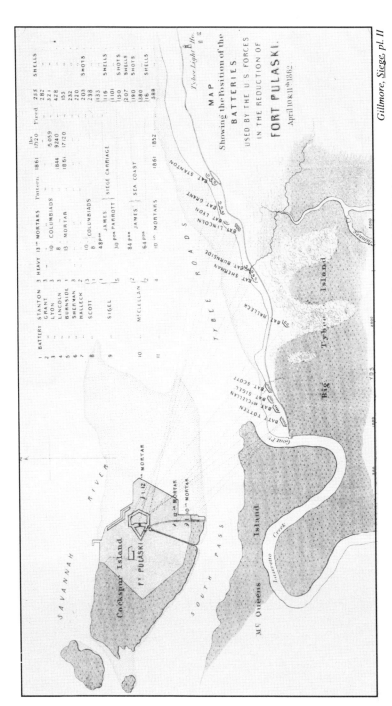

Gillmore, Siege, pl. II

Map showing the position of the Federal batteries on the north of Tybee Island.

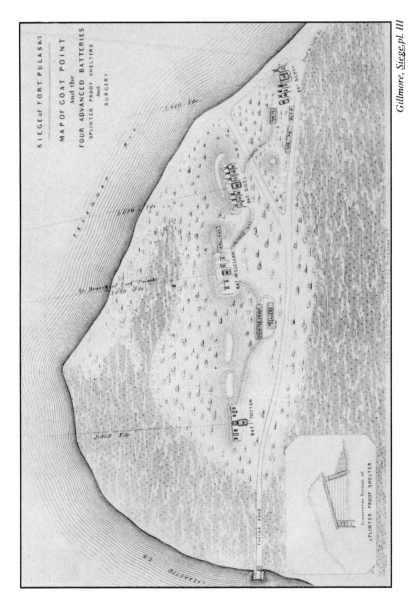

Gillmore, Siege.pl. III

Map showing the location of the four Federal batteries on Goat Point. Batteries McClellan and Sigel contained the rifled guns which successfully breached Fort Pulaski.

The number, caliber, and completeness of the batteries surrounding you leave no doubt as to what must result in case of your refusal; and as the defense, however obstinate, must eventually succumb to the assailing force at my disposal, it is hoped you may see fit to avert the useless waste of life.[4]

Wilson's orders allowed him to wait only thirty minutes for a reply. Lieutenant Thomas W. Sims, also with a flag of truce, politely received Wilson at the south wharf. Sims took the letter into the fort while Wilson waited at the wharf. Exactly thirty minutes later, Sims brought Wilson a sealed reply, and the boat rowed back to Tybee.[5]

With the Federal batteries unmasked, Colonel Olmstead knew the moment he had awaited for two months had arrived. He used his "thirty minutes" to assemble the men, post them to their guns, serve the ammunition, and prepare the hospital.[6]

Olmstead's message to Hunter was brief:

I have to acknowledge receipt of your communication of this date demanding the unconditional surrender of Fort Pulaski. In reply I can only say that I am here to defend the fort, not to surrender it. I have the honor to be, very respectfully your obedient servant,

Chas. H. Olmstead

Colonel, First Volunteer Regiment
of Georgia, commanding Post.[7]

After Wilson returned with Olmstead's reply, Hunter sent him to command the batteries at Goat Point. All of the Federal batteries had received Gillmore's instructions the day before. After Wilson returned with Olmstead's message, Hunter sent his aide O'Rorke to Porter with the message, "The General sends his compliments and desires you open the ball at once." At 8:15 a.m. Porter aimed and fired the first gun, a 13-inch mortar in Battery Halleck, signaling the onset of the Federal bombardment. Members of the 7th Connecticut had chalked on the side of the shell, "A nutmeg from Connecticut; can you furnish a grater?" Confederate First Lieutenant Henry Freeman of the Oglethorpe Light Infantry responded with a 32-pounder under his command. Initial firing on both sides was wild, but each soon learned the others' range. In less than an hour, Federal guns were firing three rounds a minute. The sound of nearly fifty cannons from both sides made the ground shake.[8]

After opening the bombardment, Porter ran to Battery Scott at Goat Point, racing across a hundred and fifty yards of unprotected space under the direct fire of the fort. Dashing across the open ground, Porter heard whizzing shells overhead. He later reflected that they always sounded nearer than they were.[9]

At Battery Scott, Porter found the three 10-inch columbiads had recoiled off their pintles at first firing, pintles being the iron pin that anchored the front of the carriage to the platform and allowed the rear to roll on a traverse track. Two guns in

Harper's Weekly

Mortar battery firing at Fort Pulaski.

Battery Lyon also were useless because of defects in pintles and because defective bolts weakened the wrought-iron chassis. The problem with the pintles was that the gun carriages were of a new iron pattern while the pintles and pintle-crosses belonged to the old wooden carriage system and were unsuitable. The hard landings damaged the bolts when the iron chassis were tipped out of the lighters before being dragged ashore. Porter worked all night making repairs, and the next morning all the guns resumed firing, chipping away the shattered surface of the fort.[10]

Benham told Colonel Edward W. Serrell how to correct the problem of the faulty pintles and ordered him to send a boat (keeping well out of range of the firing) to Viele with instructions telling how to fix the problem if it occurred. Late that same day, Benham found Serrell had never sent anyone to Viele. Instead he offered an elaborate explanation for his inaction. Benham cancelled the order but "made up my mind as to the value of this Engineer."[11]

Private Henry Glines was with his mortar battery when the firing began. His crew fired 101 shots before they were relieved at noon; he felt most of the rounds had struck the fort. Confederate rounds did not touch Glines' battery; however, an exploding shell wounded nine men in the 7th Connecticut camp. Private Milton Woodford was also working a mortar. He saw that the mortars fired once every 15 minutes, and that the rifled and big guns fired more rapidly. Woodford noted that the Goat Point batteries closest to the fort "seemed to occupy their [Fort Pulaski's] entire attention . . . and shot and shell came among us as fast as they could send them but *strange to say not one* of us were hurt." Woodford's battery kept a man on the lookout who would yell when a shell was to be approaching. Everyone would duck behind the parapet; it was "save our bacon." At Battery Scott, Porter wrote

N.Y.H.S.

Rudolph Rosa

U.S.A.M.H.I.

John Irwin

that the crew was "peppered from the fort. Shots flew around our heads as thick as flies on a hot day." Almost from the first, clouds of ruddy brick dust over Pulaski showed that shells were hitting the wall.[12]

During the morning of the first day, Benham lamented that his artillery fire seemed to be making little impression upon the fort. Even the heavier guns in the more distant batteries were having little effect.[13]

Colonel Rosa's "German" regiment manned Battery Sigel, five Parrott guns and a single 24-pounder James rifle. Rosa disregarded his firing instructions and, mounting a flank parapet, drew his sword, and directed his six guns to fire in one volley. In his enthusiasm he failed to open the embrasures of his sand parapet with consequent ricocheting of the projectiles. The New Yorkers continued firing in salvos; at each discharge the men raised loud cheers. Unfortunately, what the infantrymen possessed in enthusiasm they lacked in accuracy. Colonel Rosa could not control his men, ignored his orders, and generally "was making bad work of it" when Gillmore "lost all patience and ordered him away." The Germans refused to work the guns without their colonel and they, too, were "packed off." Benham directed Gillmore to replace them on the morning of the eleventh. A detachment of the 8th Maine under Captain William M. McArthur was sent to serve two of the guns; Captain John W. Turner and Lieutenant Wilson had instructed them. Lieutenant John Irwin and a naval detachment of 100 men from the *Wabash* served the four remaining guns. Gillmore later observed that "their skill and experience were applied with telling effect."[14]

Shortly before noon on the first day of bombardment, Hunter came ashore and, accompanied by his staff, walked to a small knoll protected by a sand ridge between Batteries Lincoln and Burnside. Although he conferred several times with Benham, who was busily moving from battery to battery, Hunter issued no orders.

Hunter remained three hours before leaving for a champagne lunch at the lighthouse. He then boarded the *McClellan*, anchored opposite the lighthouse and out of sight of the fort. He would not disembark again until he visited the captured fort on April 12.[15]

Shortly before noon on the day of the bombardment, the fort's blasted flag pole fell down. Thinking the fort had surrendered, Federal soldiers mounted the parapets and cheered their victory. Inside the fort, Second Lieutenant Christopher Hussey and Private John Latham removed the tangled flag from the parapet and remounted it in the northeast angle of the fort on a temporary staff. A volley from the fort sent the Federals scampering into their batteries and Union fire immediately resumed.[16]

The fort's shells, directed against the middle batteries, frequently fell short into the river. The marshes behind the breaching batteries at Goat Point caught many Confederate mortar shells that sank before exploding.[17]

By the end of the first day, Gillmore saw "the beginning of a breach in the easterly half of the *pan coupé* connecting the south and southeast faces." He also saw that the breach extended across the southeast face for the width of two casemates. The plunging mortar fire not having the desired effect, Gillmore feared that the Federals must depend "upon breaching alone ending perhaps in an assault," to reduce the fort. Other observers reported little damage to the angle of the fort in the twilight at the end of the first day. After the surrender, however, Gillmore would claim that "the breach had been ordered in this portion of the scarp so as to take in reverse through the opening the magazine located in the angle joined by the gorge and north face."[18]

* * * * * * *

A detachment of the 3rd Rhode Island Artillery under Lieutenants Peter J. Turner and Ferdinand Tisdale manned Viele's newly built Long Island mortar battery. The Federals repaired the damage caused by the Confederates on Long Island and although the mortar fired more than fifty times, none of its shells reached the fort. Viele later claimed his Long Island battery had received "the most constant and heaviest fire from the fort of all the batteries erected." He further believed that had he had time to move additional heavy guns into position before the bombardment, he could have done a "great deal of execution."[19]

Gillmore would disgustedly note that anyone able to use a reference table for 10-inch mortars could have foretold Viele's failure. Like Gillmore, Benham believed Viele's battery provided only a "slight distracting fire, with little or no effectiveness" against Fort Pulaski. He felt Viele had not made an "earnest or proper effort . . . to do any effective service in that way." Benham learned later from a close relative that Viele had told Captain C. Raymond P. Rodgers: "Oh, we don't want to do anything about it [strengthening Long Island], unless we can do the whole."[20]

The other batteries Viele was to have built would have been closer than some of Gillmore's guns and would have denied shelter to the barbette gunners.

Although Benham provided the guns, Viele did not place them in time for the bombardment. Benham blamed Gillmore for never having tried to coordinate the bombardment with Viele.[21]

* * * * * *

Inside the fort, one shot came through an embrasure early in the firing, dismounting a gun and severely wounding one man. The James shells flaked off brick in every direction. After two to three hours, one of the barbette guns was useless because piles of masonry blocked its fire. "Thirteen inch mortar shells, columbiad shells, Parrott shells, and rifle shots were shrieking through the air in every direction, while the ear was deafened by the tremendous explosions that followed each other without cessation." After three hours of firing, three casemate guns lay dismounted. Barbette artillery crews served four hours and then went below to the casemates for rest.[22]

Olmstead soon noted that "the effect upon the fortification was becoming disastrous." A shot from one columbiad at Goat Point "struck the wall beneath an embrasure while it was still intact and bulged the bricks on the inside, a significant fact that left little doubt of what the ultimate result would be." Most of the Confederate guns were on the sea faces and lay dismounted by the end of the first day. That night, Olmstead went out to inspect the fort.

> It was worse than disheartening, the pan-coupe at the south-east angle was entirely breached while above, on the rampart, the parapet had been shot away and an 8-inch gun, the muzzle of which was gone, hung trembling over the verge. The two adjacent casemates were rapidly approaching the same ruined condition; masses of broken masonry nearly filled the moat, as was the interior of the three casemates where the dismounted guns lay like logs among the bricks.[23]

To his wife, Olmstead wrote that the angle opposite the Goat Point batteries was shattered and that he knew "that another day would breach it entirely."[24]

During the morning of April 10, residents of Savannah distinctly heard the onset of the bombardment to the east. Around noon, the wind changed direction and all rumbling of artillery ceased, but the explosions over the fort were visible from the streets. Steeples and roofs were good observation points for both the fort and batteries. Before darkness, the direction of the wind again shifted and the sound of the guns and explosion of shells was clear. Late in the afternoon heavy squalls with shifting winds began; they would continue throughout the next twenty-four hours.[25]

From his camp near Savannah, Lieutenant Cornelius R. Hanleiter saw the drifting clouds of smoke and the traces of shells above the tree tops. From another island battery Captain George A. Mercer observed the bombardment and could "distinctly see the heavy columns of white smoke shooting up from the mortars on Tybee, and then see the immense shells bursting over the Fort. The enemy fired four and five times every minute, while the Fort replied more slowly.[26]

* * * * * * *

From Daufuskie Island on April 10, soldiers of the 48th New York saw little effect from the first day's bombardment. One observer reported that "when several [cannon] are discharged together they fairly shake the ground *under us*." During the early night it was quiet, but after midnight the guns "kept a steady fire" until the next day.[27]

* * * * * * *

Benham and Gillmore agreed that one of them should supervise the batteries during the night. Benham wanted firing continued throughout the night to prevent the Confederates from repairing damage. He spent the night at the "central main battery" until 1:00 a.m. on the eleventh, when he returned to the lighthouse, and Gillmore took his turn in the batteries. During the night, only four guns fired and these at 15 to 20 minute intervals. They were two 13-inch mortars (Batteries Burnside and Halleck), a 10-inch mortar (Battery Totten), and a 30-pounder Parrott (Battery Sigel). Confederate Captain George Mercer, east of Savannah, observed, "At night the sight was grand. The tongue of flame was seen to leap from the mortars and then the flash of the bursting shell appeared just above the Fort.[28]

* * * * * * *

At dawn on the morning of April 11, the Confederates began "heavy and well directed fire." Only three parapet guns bearing on Tybee were usable, and of these, only the 24-pounder Blakely bore on the batteries at Goat Point.[29]

At day light in Savannah, residents thought the bombardment resumed with redoubled fury. Guns fired ten to fifteen times a minute. Heavy firing continued until 10:00 a.m. and at times it seemed as "rapid as musketry." The concussions shook windows and vibrated houses in the city. Around noon, amid the sound of desultory firing, someone brought a report that the fort had silenced all but two of the Federal batteries and had sunk one of the ships in Tybee Roads. As the bombardment continued, Confederate infantry returned to abandoned batteries on Skidaway Island to watch and listen. On the second day at noon, the wind shifted again and the bombardment could not be heard.[30]

When the Union batteries resumed firing on the morning of the eleventh, Benham concentrated "carefully against the *pan-coupé* of one gun on the South East angle." From his observation point Benham and his staff could see the growing pile of rubble overflowing into the moat. Shells continued to penetrate deeper and deeper; by 10 to 11:00 a.m. "we saw that the thinnest wall, (of the recess arch) at the angle, was entirely thrown down, and within an hour or so, the recess wall of the next gun north, went down also, when portions of the mask and parapet wall above, began to fall." Gillmore observed that "at the end of 3 hours the entire casemate next to the *pan coupé* had been opened, and by 11:00 o'clock, the one adjacent to it was in similar condition." Gillmore ordered the batteries to concentrate on the adjacent casemate. As the brick face crumbled, Benham saw "a portion of the work I may say I had witnessed the building of as an assistant to Lt. Mansfield, 25 years before." Benham, Gillmore, Halpine, and a few other staff members, were standing on a slight sand-hill in the rear of Battery Lyon observing the progress with a large tripod telescope. Confederates saw the sun's reflection off the telescope and fired at it; Benham later confirmed his impression that Confederates aimed their Blakelys at individuals rather than guns in the batteries.[31]

* * * * * * * *

Benham knew that Fort Pulaski's garrison of 360 to 380 men allowed only one man to each linear foot of wall on the southeast face of the fort. He reasoned that

the whole fire of the batteries should be directed (as their position was suitable) at the *rear edge* of the mask wall of that face, at its junction with the casemates and their piers, expecting to *peel this whole wall* from that face; the debris of which would form a good ramp in the ditch, (as was the fact, at the angles) so that if it should prove necessary, the whole front could be stormed at once, with a large force, as I proposed; knowing that but a single line of men could oppose them. And at about 12 to 1 o'clock, while examining that fact through a large tripod telescope, with Captain Gillmore, I directed him to have scaling ladders of 12 to 19 feet in length prepared, for a storm of the work, if it should be deemed advisable as I thought possible by the next night.[32]

Benham's plan was to peel off as much of the face as possible, fill the ditch with rubble, and on the night of April 12 assault through a breach larger than could be successfully defended by the garrison. Benham agreed to let Halpine lead the assault. Halpine said there were two Irish companies on Tybee and that he would like to lead the column; Benham agreed. Preparations for the assault were under way when the fort surrendered.[33]

Years later Gillmore wrote: "It was clear that for the reduction of the work we should have to depend on breaching alone, ending, perhaps, in an assault. An assault was impracticable, owing to a lack of boats to carry the troops, although these could have been procured from the navy after considerable delay."[34]

* * * * * * *

From the mortar batteries on Tybee, Lieutenant Colonel Joseph R. Hawley intently watched the fire directed at the *pan coupé* from the rifled cannon and heavy columbiads. Each shot that solidly struck the wall, raised "a cloud of brick dust" and "a cart-load of brick [would] fall into the ditch." The second day's bombardment knocked great masses of brick, loosened the previous day, into the moat. Once the first hole became visible, Tybee Island rang with "cheer after cheer." "And what a scream ran down the line when the first hole appeared! Every shot that enlarged it was hailed with another yell."[35]

Leslie's Weekly

The bombardment of Fort Pulaski, viewed from Daufuskie Island, during the morning of the second day.

Adrian Terry saw that "soon a huge opening appeared in the wall through which a two horse wagon might have been driven. This was hailed with cheer after cheer by all upon on Tybee, and the excited gunners redoubled the rapidity of their fire while it seemed as if even the solid earth shook with the long thunder peal."[36]

Captain Theodore Bacon of the 7th Connecticut, watching with Hawley, said that he "had never so enjoyed a 4th of July." From the lighthouse, Dr. Andrew saw that the James percussion shells "would cover the face of the Fort with dust and show the broken bricks tumbling down by the wagon-load."[37]

During mid-morning, Porter was going to Battery McClellan when a shell burst near a gun and mortally wounded Private Thomas Campbell, Company H, of the 3rd Rhode Island Artillery. "His face was burned perfectly black, his left side torn away and his left leg taken off. He lived three hours, spoke about his wife and family, seized hold of his captain's hand and died." Campbell was the only Federal fatality of the bombardment.[38]

From Daufuskie Island on the second day of the bombardment, members of the 48th New York saw clouds of dust rising from the southwest angle of the fort "indicating that progress was being made." One observer recalled that "brown brick-dust told where huge ragged rents were being made in the wall of the fort." Excited soldiers lined the shore, many climbing into trees to obtain an unobstructed view of the bombardment. Members of the 6th Connecticut on Daufuskie and Jones Islands also saw "clouds of brick dust" fill the air.[39]

* * * * * * *

In the fort on the second day, after shells passed through the breach in Fort Pulaski, Olmstead realized "it was simply a question of a few hours as to whether we should yield or be blown into perdition by our own powder." By now, seven barbette guns were disabled, the traverses were "giving way," the west side of the fort was a wreck, and the southeast angle was badly breached, allowing "free access of every shot to our magazine." Olmstead conferred with his officers and "they united in advising me to surrender," a conclusion Olmstead had already reached. Olmstead's men lessened his pain; they crowded around him and "endeavored by every means in their power to show me that they were willing to share whatever fate may be in store for me. . . . I was unprepared for this manifestation."[40]

The breach widened during the second day's bombardment. Soon shot and shell were passing across the parade and hitting the opposite angle, site of the north magazine. The magazine entrance was protected by a large traverse; however, between 1:00 and 2:00 p.m. a shell passed through the top of the traverse and exploded in the entrance way. The magazine filled with light and smoke but did not explode. Olmstead knew that the next such shot could blow up the fort beneath them. He now realized that "we had reached the end. We were absolutely, beyond any possibility of help from the Confederate Authorities, and I did not feel warranted in exposing the garrison to the hazard of the blowing up of our main magazine. . . . There are times when a soldier must hold his position 'to the last extremity,' which means *extermination*, but this was not one of them, there was no end to be gained by continued resistance." After the surrender, a shell from the battery in Lazaretto Creek was found in the bricked-up ventilation air hole into the southwest magazine.[41]

* * * * * * *

When the second day's bombardment opened, Brigadier General Alexander R. Lawton in Savannah wanted news from the fort. He sent a signalman with Corporal Charles Law of the Phoenix Rifles, then on Thunderbolt Island, to Fort Pulaski in a small boat. Law had previously reached the fort after the river passage was cut. The men reached the fort at 6:00 a.m. on the eleventh. Confederate fire ceased at 2:00 p.m., the colors struck, and both men escaped and reached Savannah at 8:00 p.m. When they left, all the barbette guns were disabled but three— the columbiads "Jeff Davis" and "Beauregard" and a Blakely gun. The breach was wide enough to "drive a four-horse team through"; and seven casemates "in succession, was nearly all knocked down."[42]

At the time of surrender, others reported that all but two of the barbette guns and two of the casemate guns bearing on Tybee Island had been dismounted. The outer wall covering two casemates had been destroyed and that of the adjoining casemate on either side was crumbling.[43]

After the surrender, Olmstead submitted a report to Lawton, stating that when the firing ceased about 7:00 p.m. the first day, he went outside to inspect the exterior of the fort. He found that wall "was flaked away to a depth of four feet, while here and there shot had made its way clear through. The parapet above this point was leveled and both columbiads there were disabled. By noon on the second day "clouds of brick and mortar" filled the casemates. By 1:00 p.m. the wall in front of two casemates had fallen into the moat, and the breach was widening continually. "The west-side of the Fort was a perfect wreck of timbers and masonry. Six of the barbette guns dismounted or useless, and many of our traverses much shattered. . . . A new danger that sprang upon us, the breach in our wall gave free access to the projectiles that had made it directly to our north magazine, the brick work covering the magazine door was struck five or six times in succession and it was evident that it was only a question of two or three hours whether the lives of the whole garrison would be destroyed by the explosion of the magazine, for this result was inevitable." Three Confederates—A. Shaw and Isaac Ames of the Oglethorpe Light Infantry and Pvt. T.J. Moullon of the Washington Guard—were seriously wounded. Olmstead's assessment of Gillmore's James rifles was that "masonry yielded like wood before the projectiles from these guns."[44]

George Mercer described what he learned of the condition of Fort Pulaski at the end of the bombardment: "The hot shot furnace in the yard was knocked to pieces. Every barbette gun was dismounted & useless; every casemate gun, except one, bearing on the enemy's batteries, was also dismounted by their tremendous fire."[45]

* * * * * * *

Hawley noted that although the Federals had fired over five thousand projectiles, the fort had returned only one-third as many. Allowing for shells that failed to explode, Hawley felt there must have been over 400 shots exchanged each hour, nearly seven every minute. Sometimes there would be a pause for up to half a minute then the "whole earth would tremble as the fire ran down the line, and the smoke would drift by, obscuring the fort for a moment."[46]

* * * * * * *

About 2:00 p.m., the flag over the fort began to waver. For quarter of an hour it rose and fell, progressively coming down, until at last it was at half mast. The Confederates then abruptly hauled down and ceased firing. After the previous days' experience with the falling flag, General Benham doubted Confederate intentions and continued firing. Soon, however, "a very curious white (scarcely white) flag was thrown up" and Benham ordered firing to cease. Fearing a trick, he moved to the front and ordered the cheering men off the parapets. Lieutenant Colonel James F. Hall, Serrell's second in command, rode up and offered Benham his horse. Benham declined, but ordered Hall to gallop with orders to all batteries to cease firing. Benham then took Porter's hand in both of his and thanked him for his services. "Then arose a shout that seemed even louder than the tremendous roar which it succeeded," Adrian Terry recalled, "and it passed from one regiment to another until it reached the other extremity of the island conveying to all the welcome tidings of the surrender." Porter exclaimed: "Pulaski is ours; Sumter is avenged!"[47]

"Surrender of Fort Pulaski—Lieutenant Colonel [James F.] Hall of Serrell's [1st N.Y.] Volunteer Engineers announcing the surrender and carrying the order to National batteries to cease firing."

Benham and members of his staff went to Lazaretto Creek to find a boat to take them over to the fort. Finding one, he called for a crew among the infantrymen and directed his adjutant, Captain Alfred B. Ely, to cross over and receive the surrender of the fort. Benham wanted to send Gillmore, then at his lighthouse head-quarters three miles away, erroneously believed to be having dinner. As the boat was about to leave, Major Halpine rode up and joined Ely to receive the Confederate capitulation. The terms were those proposed in Hunter's original surrender demand, requiring "the surrender of the garrison, and all the armament and weapons; no other modification to be allowed than they should have as favorable terms as are given by our Government in this war."[48]

Dr. Andrew had been on the beach near the Martello tower watching the bombardment. Because of the shifting winds of the storm during the last phase of the bombardment, he "heard no sound of the tremendous cannonading, although we could see that it was still going on." Andrew saw the firing cease and then saw the white flag above the fort. He walked a few hundred yards to the lighthouse where Gillmore was pacing the porch of his headquarters, unaware that the bombardment had ceased. Andrew told him the news and Gillmore instantly mounted his horse and, racing toward the batteries, met his aide, Captain Adam Badeau, who was bringing the surrender news from the batteries. Andrew reflected that the wind was high and although it seemed scarcely sufficient to explain the silence, the fact was there. . . . Thirty-six guns were attacking and forty-seven were defending:—the smoke of discharges was plainly seen from our point of observation, but no sound but the rushing of the gale from the sea across the Island. It had something of the uncanny about it, but interest in the bombardment as to its results was so intense that the fact scarcely excited comment at the time. Though unheard at headquarters or Tybee, the roaring was said to have been continuous at Beaufort some 13 miles away in a straight line.[49]

The "tremendous gale," which had been raging for the previous 24 hours, prevented Halpine's party from rowing out of Lazaretto Creek and across the channel to Cockspur Island. During the 15 to 20 minute delay, Gillmore galloped up, anxious to go to the fort. Benham gave him permission, assuming that he would accompany Halpine's party which was waiting for the storm to pass. Instead, Gillmore found another boat and crewed it with *Wabashers* who had served in Battery Sigel. Understanding currents and tides, they quickly brought Gillmore to the south wharf of the island, where he disembarked. Hurrying to the fort, he crossed the drawbridge to the demilune and then over the moat into the fort. Once inside, he ordered the massive doors swung shut. Gillmore met with Olmstead for almost an hour and arranged the terms of surrender. When Halpine's party finally arrived, they were forced to wait outside the fort until Gillmore opened the doors and emerged with the surrender document.[50] Its terms were as follows:

ARTICLE 1. The fort, armament, and garrison to be surrendered at once to the forces of the United States.

ART. 2. The officers and men of the garrison to be allowed to take with them all their private effects, such as clothing, bedding, books, &c.; this not to include private weapons.

ART. 3. The sick and wounded, under charge of the hospital steward of the garrison, to be sent up under a flag of truce to the Confederate lines, and at the same time the men to be allowed to send up any letters they may desire, subject to the inspection of a Federal officer.

Signed this the 11th day of April, 1862, at Fort Pulaski, Cockspur Island, Ga.

CHAS. H. OLMSTEAD,

Colonel First Vol. Regt. of Georgia, Comdg Fort Pulaski

Q. A. GILLMORE,

Brig. Gen. Vols., Comdg. U.S. Forces, Tybee Island, Ga.[51]

Halpine, Ely, and Irwin then passed in to take charge of the fort and received the surrender of swords and flags.[52]

Twenty-six year old Olmstead handled the surrender gracefully. After the garrison had been assembled to stack arms, he asked if he might be spared ordering his men to disarm. Halpine gave the necessary orders. Next, the officers surrendered their swords and sidearms. Olmstead stepped forward first, placed his sword on the table, and said, "I yield my sword, but I trust I have not disgraced it." The other officers came forward according to rank and lay their swords on a table, "most of them making a slight inclination of the head and showing good bearing." A few sullenly threw their swords down. One said, "I hope to be able to resume it to fight for the same cause." Another officer claimed to have no sword and offered to surrender his sash, which was refused. After this ceremony was completed, the officers adjourned to the mess room where food and wine were served. Feelings of awkwardness lifted, and during the informal conversation one Confederate officer joked, "Why you are only four and we three hundred and fifty; I think we ought to take you." Another Confederate officer sarcastically asked a Connecticut officer about wooden nutmegs. Pointing to a 10-inch columbiad shot, the Northerner answered "we don't make them of wood any longer."[53] Benham reported 361 prisoners, of whom 24 were officers; 18 prisoners were sick.[54]

The New York *Times* correspondent wrote: "Colonel Olmstead strikes all who come in contact with him as a man of superior character. . . . reflective countenance, and mild and gentlemanly manners. In him the fire-eater finds no type. As a body the officers I have seen are men of very gentlemanly manners, but thoroughly rebellious in their feelings."[55]

Olmstead wrote his wife after the surrender that the Federal officers were "most courteous and gentlemanly." "I feel I have done my duty, my whole duty, that I have been forced to yield and only then to superior [illegible] of metal. Guns such as have never before been brought to bear against *any* fortification, have overpowered me, but I trust to history to keep my name untarnished."[56]

Halpine's party had come over without a national flag; it was not until the next morning that the stars and stripes again flew over the fort. The raised flag set off yet another round of cheering on Tybee Island. Adrian Terry noted that "all previous cheers seemed insignificant in comparison with the tremendous cheer that hailed the glorious old flag and the men danced & sung & hugged each other until one who knew not the cause would have imagined himself in an army of maniacs."[57]

While Halpine was receiving the capitulation, Gillmore, accompanied by Lieutenant Colonel Hall, returned to the lighthouse to present Benham with the terms of surrender. Benham sent the document to Hunter on the morning of the twelfth. Benham regretted that the terms did not call for the exchange of the Confederate sick for the 46th New Yorkers captured days earlier on Wilmington Island. On the twelfth Benham and his staff went up the Savannah River to the north wharf on Cockspur Island "to examine the work, inspect our garrison there, and receive the prisoners."[58]

In his official report, Benham says when Gillmore arrived to receive the surrender, he did so at Benham's behest. Benham did not mention Gillmore's separate trip. Both Benham and Hunter praised Gillmore's work and recommended that he be confirmed as a brigadier general, which he was on April 28.[59]

Benham ordered the 7th Connecticut to occupy the fort. Private Seth Reynolds wrote a friend that on April 11, "we marched into the fort and stationed guards over them; their arms, and the ramparts they had defended so gallantly—all praise is due them, they fought bravely, and it was only when the magazine was in danger that they struck their colors."[60]

Seven companies of the 7th Connecticut were quartered in the fort and the other three pitched their tents outside. The garrison of the 7th Connecticut would be augmented by the 1st New York Volunteer Engineers (Colonel Serrell and Lieutenant Colonel Hall). Along with the national flag, the flags of those two regiments were flown above the fort.[61]

The men stationed in the fort found the casemates much cooler than the tents outside. Private Carroll E. Kingsley, Company G, 7th Connecticut, marveled to his mother that "it seems almost impossible that an engagement could last so long with so little of loss of lives, but it is so. We lost but one man & one wounded the rebels losses was small. There is fifteen [sick and wounded] prisoners in the fort at the present time. They are to be sent up to Savannah in a few days."[62]

Another 7th Connecticut soldier, Private William H. Harrison, arrived in Fort Pulaski after the prisoners had been sent north. He found the fifteen sick in the hospital under the care of Confederate hospital steward First Sergeant L. Wilson Landershine, a "fine specimen of a real Southerner." Harrison reported that Landershine said " 'you have the advantage of us just now but if you think we shall give up this contest you are very much mistaken.' " Harrison added that the Confederates had not expected the fort to capitulate. When the " 'cart hubs' [James rifle projectiles] began to come in they knew the *end was near*. Several of their parapet guns were dismounted. Piles of brick scattered in every direction. The flag was twice shot away and in many places the wall on the parapet was torn away—still the Rebels *stuck to* it, not one of their number was killed."[63]

A Connecticut soldier wrote to his family, giving his impression of a slave's account of the bombardment, in his version of the dialect:

When you get do great big hole in de wall, we raise de white flag but you no stop firing. Den de men say de *damn Yankees get mad* and dey going to kill us all, and de men da run around and say *O dear* what shall we do? de Yankee is got mad de Yankees got mad an going to kill us all. Den da think of de oder flag and de Col says *pull down de flag pull down de flag* den da run and pull it down, but it git fast, and da tear it all to pieces and get it down. Den de Yankees stop firing. But we *taught* you was going to kill us all sure.[64]

On the twelfth, Porter went into the fort to inventory the captured ordnance. Besides the forty-eight guns he found 400 barrels of powder and an abundance of shot and shells. The Ordnance Sergeant gave Porter his record books "with a very good grace and said he would be glad to do anything for me while he remained."[65]

DuPont was grateful that the siege was over. The surrender of Fort Pulaski was "a thorn out of our flesh," and its possession would give secure control of the Savannah River and the waterways leading into Wassaw. His vessels would at last be free for blockading duty. DuPont felt it was now time to move overland and take Savannah, but he knew that a "timid" army command would "want us to go up with gunboats."[66]

The Commodore also recalled the former Department commander, Sherman, now that Fort Pulaski had fallen:

> One man in a million will know and feel and perhaps say, "Why, it was hard to take away General Sherman when he was so nearly ready."The masses, however, will see it in another light—and will see what a new man has done. General Hunter has not been a week hardly before he took Pulaski. Nearly three months of heavy toil produced the result.[67]

After talking with Olmstead and his staff officers on April 12, DuPont realized that the Confederates had expected a naval assault. Olmstead said that Fort Pulaski's guns were arranged to cover the channel and "they were prepared to give the *Navy* gentlemen a very warm reception—but had no idea of such an attack from Tybee." DuPont felt vindicated that his advice to Sherman had been correct, namely, light draft gunboats would have failed while a land-based bombardment must succeed. The fort's barbette guns did all the work, DuPont felt, while the casemate guns contributed little.[68]

Years after the fall of Fort Pulaski, Sherman wrote his view of the operation delayed because many mortars and shells had to be cast before being sent. He had two objects in the "besiegement," the "certain reduction" of the work and the learning of the effect of rifled artillery.[69]

The effectiveness of rifled guns stunned the Confederates; Captain George A. Mercer's reaction was typical, "Their steel pointed shot bored through the brick walls as if they were so much paper." He believed nothing could withstand them. Siege warfare was revolutionized and masonry forts were now obsolete. "We must have *iron forts* and *iron clad ships*." Fort Pulaski was the first victim of the new siege techniques. Both citizens and soldiers were "sadly depressed" by the loss of Fort Pulaski. Mercer added that all the senior departmental officers—Lawton, Pemberton, Wright—were sadly deceived about the potential effectiveness of the Tybee Island batteries. "The science of war has leaped a century forward and all are behind the age."[70]

The fall of Fort Pulaski "threw Savannah into consternation" and caused the Confederate authorities to begin constructing a fleet that could properly defend the city. A correspondent for the Richmond *Dispatch* said that "women are leaving, and property of all kinds is being sent off."[71]

On April 11, at 11:40 p.m., General Pemberton, now in Savannah, wrote Lee, then in Richmond, about the surrender of the fort. Pemberton had left Savannah at 5:30 p.m. for his Pocotaligo headquarters, believing everything was all right. He telegraphed Lee that he had later learned the fort had surrendered at 2:00 p.m. after "seven breaches in the wall; all barbette guns dismounted, and three shots had entered the magazine."[72]

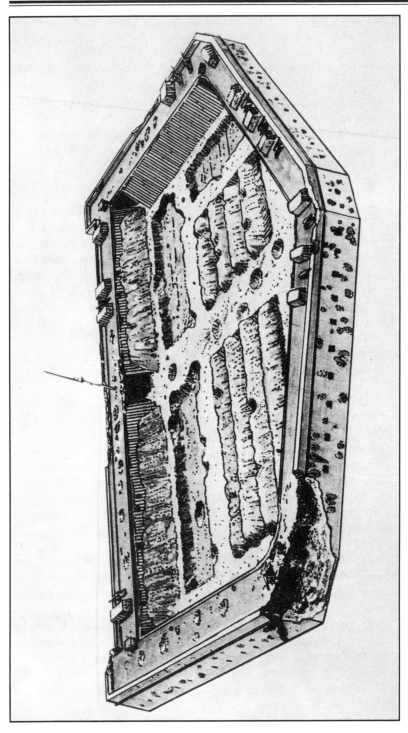

F.P.N.M.

Sketch of aerial view of Fort Pulaski at the time on its surrender on April 11, 1862.

Fort Pulaski after its surrender. The breached *pan coupé* viewed from the south of the fort.

U.S.A.M.H.I.

Exterior of Fort Pulaski after its surrender. Damage to the *pan coupé* is visible and one of the casemate arches exposed. Note the damage to the adjacent southern wall, which is also seen on the photograph of the present day fort (p. 147).

F.P.N.M.

Fort Pulaski after its surrender. View of the breached *pan coupé* with the moat filled with rubble.

U.S.A.M.H.I.

Exterior of Fort Pulaski after its surrender. View of the southeastern wall with the breached *pan coupé* on the left. Rubble nearly fills the moat at the point of the breach. It was across this rubble and through the breached wall and case-mates that the Federals plan-ned to assault the fort before its precipitate surrender.

U.S.A.M.H.I.

Interior of one of the ruined casemates after the surrender of Fort Pulaski. The rare chips in the brick piers suggest that few projectiles entered the breach.

U.S.A.M.H.I.

Interior of Fort Pulaski after its surrender. The mortar and one columbiad are damaged. Note the traverses between some of the barbette guns.

F.P.N.M.

F.P.N.M.

Interior of Fort Pulaski after its surrender. The cascabel of this barbette columbiad bears the name "Beauregard." Note the sandbag traverse to the right of the gun to protect the gunners from explosions at adjacent guns.

U.S.A.M.H.I.

Fort Pulaski after its surrender. The Blakeley gun sits on the brick-strewn barbette.

One of the dismounted mortars, inside Fort Pulaski.

U.S.A.M.H.I.

U.S.A.M.H.I.

View of Fort Pulaski after its surrender, taken from the northwest of the fort.

Fort Pulaski after its surrender.
View from the northern wall
toward the southern end of
the western wall. The earth-
covered blindage is visible. A
gun and adjacent traverse are
present on the parapet. A tower-
like structure covers the stairwell in the southern corner of
the fort.

F.P.N.M.

F.P.N.M.

Fort Pulaski after its surrender. View across the parade from the southeastern wall
toward the entrance in the western wall. The ditches in the parade are in the foreground.
The timber blindage, with earth piled against it, protects the quarters in the wall.

F.P.N.M.

Fort Pulaski after its surrender. View from the southern wall toward the northern half of the western wall. The earth-covered blindage is clearly visible. The powder magazine in the northwest corner is located below the wooden tower (arrow) covering the stairwell. These wooden towers in the northwest and southwest corners were later removed by the occupying Federal troops. Some feel the northwestern tower served as sighting target for the gunners on Tybee Island, since from the Federal battery sites it would help direct fire at the southeastern *pan coupé*. Such fire, if it penetrated the wall or descended over it, would then hit the exterior of the northwest magazine.

F.P.N.M.

Interior of Fort Pulaski after its surrender. The blindage is still intact; Federal soldiers are drying their laundry in the sun. Ditches in the parade are visible in the foreground.

One of the two Confederate mortar batteries on Cockspur Island south of the fort.

F.P.N.M.

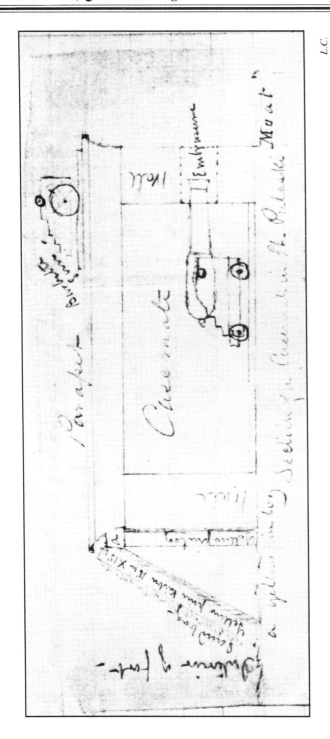

C. N. Schoonmaker's sketch of "Section of a Casemate in Ft. Pulaski." The blindage was built of pine timbers placed vertically against the wall and casemate doors. Against these, at a 20 to 30 degree angle, were placed "yellow pine timber 15 x 15 in." which were, in turn, covered with sand bags and earth.

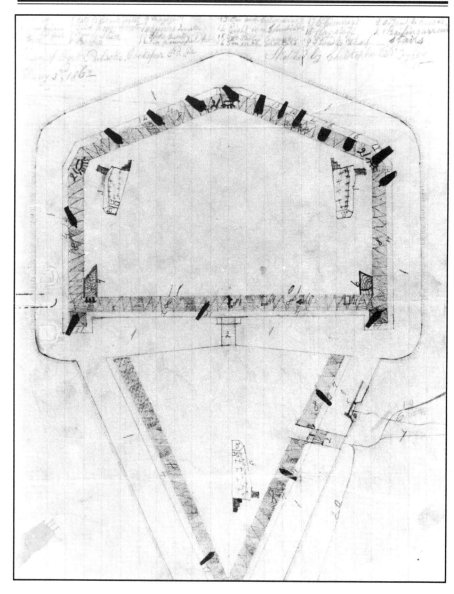

C.S.L.

Plan of Fort Pulaski sketched by Christopher D'Oley on May 3, 1862. The numerical key is: 1-moat, 2-draw bridge, 3-hot shot heaters, 4-wall, 5-gate to let out water, 6-ditch to carry out water, 7-board of sluice, 8-parapet, 9-magazines, 10-officers' quarters, 11-ranks' quarters, 12-five-pound field pieces, 13-ten inch columbiads, 14-eight-inch columbiad, 15-two-rifled cannon, 16-ten-inch mortars, 17-chimneys, 18-flag staff, 19-road to wharf, 20-road to houses, 21-railing around stairs.

Chapter 8

"$\mathcal{T}$he result of this bombardment must cause, I am convinced, a change in the construction of fortifications as radical as that foreshadowed in naval architecture by the conflict between the *Monitor* and *Merrimac*. No work of stone or brick can resist the impact of rifled artillery of heavy caliber."

In his official report, Gillmore said that 4,079 shells and 914 shot were fired at the fort. In an article written over twenty years later, he said that his 20 guns fired 3,543 projectiles and his 16 mortars fired 1,732 shells for a total of 5,275, representing 20 percent of the available supply. The following tabular summary of each battery provides yet another total and shows that more than five thousand projectiles were hurled at Fort Pulaski:

Gun	Shot		Shell		Total
13-inch mortar			1,144		
10-inch mortar			588		1,732 mortar
10-inch columbiad	203		321		
8-inch columbiad	298		428		1250 columbiad
42-pdr James	190		209		
32-pdr James	380		16		
24-pdr James	113		116		1024 James
30-pdr Parrott	210		1101		1311 Parrott
	1394	shot	3923	shells	5317[1]

129

Gillmore inspected the walls of the fort after the bombardment to learn the depth of penetration of the various projectiles. The 84-pound solid James projectile, fired by a rifled old 42-pounder gun from 1,650 yards at 4 1/2 degree elevation with an eight-pound charge, had penetrated 26 inches. A 64-pound solid James shot, fired by a rifled old 32-pounder gun from the same distance at a 4 degree elevation with a six-pound charge, had penetrated twenty inches. A 48-pounder James solid shot, fired by a rifled old 24-pounder gun from 1,670 yards, at a 4 1/2 degree elevation with a five-pound charge, had penetrated nineteen inches. The 30-pound Parrott solid shot, fired from 1,670 yards at a 4 1/2 degree elevation with a 3 1/2-pound charge, had penetrated eighteen inches. A 128-pound solid round shot fired from a 10-inch columbiad at a 4 1/2 degree elevation with a twenty-pound charge, penetrated or shattered to a depth of thirteen inches. Finally, a 68-pound solid shot fired by an 8-inch columbiad at a 5 degree elevation with a ten-pound charge, penetrated eleven inches. The lateral effect of the solid shot from the columbiads was little greater than that of the James rifle shot; the latter guns, however, had much greater penetrating effect and "performed their true office in crushing out the immense masses of masonry."[2]

The two 42-pounder and two 32-pounder James rifles in Battery McClellan were responsible for the breaching. Projectiles from one of the 32-pounders tended to turn end over end. The James shells penetrated at least eighteen inches before exploding, causing lateral shattering. The 42-pounder shot penetrated the earthen traverses between the barbette guns up to twelve feet.[3]

The rifling of the James guns easily fouled with powder residue, although a special scraper kept the tube clean. Failure to clean the grooves resulted in poor firing. Although the James projectiles were wrapped with greased canvas, Gillmore had each projectile greased again before firing.[4]

The accurate firing of the James guns was the direct result of cleaning the rifling with its scraper. Gillmore claimed he developed the tool to clean the fouled rifling grooves of the tubes. Several strips of steel, equal to the number of grooves, were attached to the end of a rammer head. The ends of the strips were bent outward at right angles. A removable metal ring was placed around the base of the strips and held them against the rammer head. The head was inserted down the tube into the breech, the ring removed, and the strips would spring against the grooves in the tube, enabling the scraper to abrade the fouled powder and clean the grooves. Using the scraper after every five or six firings assured consistently good performance of the James rifles. Parrott projectiles relied on a wrought-iron or brass ring at the base to engage the rifling and no special precautions or cleaning was necessary.[5]

Sherman wrote that General James himself previously developed a similar device to prevent wobbling and short-falling of his rifle projectiles, a problem that he had observed earlier. Sherman, an artilleryman himself, recorded that James had corrected the problem by keeping the grooves cleaned with "a pronged instrument, manufactured for the purpose, inserted in the bore occasionally so as to sweep the grooves clean throughout their length."[6] Since Sherman claims the scrapers had already been invented, perhaps they were absent from Gillmore's supplies and he might have had to fabricate them during the bombardment.

The five 30-pounder Parrott guns in Battery Sigel were smaller in caliber and less effective than the James rifles. Their projectiles were 4.3 inches in diameter and weighed from 25 pounds (shell) to 30 pounds (solid shot). Many of the Parrott projectiles turned end over end and many wobbled; those that did hit properly, penetrated up to eighteen inches, although they did little damage by lateral shattering.[7]

Gillmore reviewed the effectiveness of rifled shells compared to solid roundshot. Data gathered from several sieges in Spain during the Peninsular Campaign showed that 24-pounder smoothbores at 500 yards distance required 254,000 pounds of metal for every 100 feet of breach of an earth-backed rubble wall. To attempt a comparison, even if imperfect, with what was accomplished at Fort Pulaski, Gillmore first subtracted the projectiles used against the barbette guns, 10 percent of the Parrott projectiles which tumbled end-over-end, and half of the 64-pound James shot because one of the 32-pounder guns had been bored 1/4 inch too large and fired poorly. After these deductions, the batteries had fired 110,643 pounds of metal at the breach. Further complicating the calculations was the fact that although the actual breach was 30 feet wide, the adjacent scarp wall was severely damaged across three adjacent casemates and, had they not been backed by arches but by earth, the breach would have been at least 45 to 50 feet wider. For a 45-foot breach, the metal thrown was 2,485 pounds/linear foot as compared to 2,544 pounds of metal/linear foot with smoothbores in Spain. Gillmore believed that had the fort held out for a few more hours, the difference would have been greater since much of the badly shattered scarp would have collapsed for 25 to 30 feet on either side of the breach. After the surrender of Fort Pulaski, the Connecticut men and New Yorkers rebuilt 100 feet of scarp. Gillmore's rifled guns had knocked down the wall in less than eighteen hours of continuous firing.[8]

Rifled guns fired only 58 percent of the breaching metal; the 8- and 10-inch columbiads in Battery Scott fired the remainder. The smoothbores did their damage from a distance of almost 1,700 yards as compared to 500 yards, previously thought to be the maximum effective distance of smoothbores. Further, brick masonry set in mortar 7 1/2 feet thick with heavy arch and pier backing was much more durable than a rubble wall backed with earth.[9]

Gillmore further felt that had he used more James percussion shells in addition to James solid shot, the shattering effect of the former would have equaled the 10-inch solid shot fired by the columbiads. This was important because James rifles were easier to handle than the large columbiads.[10]

Gillmore drew several conclusions about the use of guns in operations against Fort Pulaski. First, closer than 700 yards, heavy smoothbore guns would be satisfactory for breaching. Second, at 700 yards, light smoothbore guns would be satisfactory for breaching, but rifled guns firing projectiles of the same weight would be better. Third, beyond 700 yards, rifled guns were much superior for breaching to any combination of rifles and heavy or light smoothbores. Fourth, beyond 1,000 yards, smoothbores should not be included in breaching batteries because they required so much manual labor to handle them and their ammunition, and the results achieved were poor compared to the rifled guns. Fifth, whenever rifled guns were used against brick walls, half of the projectiles should be percussion shells.[11]

Gillmore believed that "good rifled guns, properly served, can breach rapidly at 1,650 yards distance. A few heavy round shot, to bring down the masses loosened by the rifled projectiles, are of good service." This is what happened at Fort Pulaski. Gillmore concluded that with the proper guns he could cause the same effect at 2,000 yards distance, slightly greater than one mile.[12]

Gillmore believed that the 42-pounder James rifle, with clean rifling, was best suited for removing the brick scarp from a fort. He postulated that 30-pounder Parrotts would be effective. Smoothbore guns, such as the 8- and 10-inch columbiads were effective in shattering the scarp, especially at close range or if it had been previously fractured. For batteries farther than 1,000 yards, however, Gillmore recommended the sole use of rifled guns, simply because they were easier to move and their lighter ammunition was easier to handle. Had Gillmore known how effective the rifled guns would be, the eight weeks of laborious preparation could have been shortened to one week, since he would have omitted the heavy mortars and columbiads and eliminated the long-distance batteries.[13]

Before the bombardment, artillerymen and engineers had placed great faith in the destructive effect of the mortars. During the two days of firing on Fort Pulaski, the wind blowing in from the sea made mortar firing unfavorable. More important, the mortar crews were completely inexperienced, having only drilled for ten days and having never fired their pieces. The nearest 13-inch mortar, firing at a 45 degree angle, was 2,400 yards and the farthest 3,400 yards from the fort, which Porter felt was much too far for successful vertical fire against the small area of the fort. The 10-inch mortars, one battery of which was closer, dropped more than half of their shells outside the fort. Many mortar fuses were those captured on Hilton Head from the Confederate stores and frequently failed to explode the shells. The whittled fuses made by the 7th Connecticut were little better. The navy supplied some quality paper fuses.[14]

Gillmore concluded that the 13-inch mortars were valueless. Less than 10 percent of their shells fell within the fort. The few that hit the terreplein caused no damage to the casemate arches. Contrary to previous doctrine, he concluded that mortars had no role in the reduction of good casemated works of small area, like most of the American seacoast fortifications.[15] Given the crudeness of aiming of such guns and the complete lack of information from within the fort, Gillmore was correct in this conclusion. The inexperience of the crews and the winds contributed to the poor showing of the mortars.

Observing the bombardment from the lighthouse, Dr. George Andrew saw many mortar shells go beyond the fort and explode in the mud, sometimes throwing up earth "in such quantity that we could see it two miles away." From within the fort, First Sergeant L. Wilson Landershine also noted that most of the mortar shells exploded "way beyond the fort." Although they did not crack the casemate roofs, the mortars played a role in silencing the barbette guns and igniting the wooden, combustible buildings.[16]

Gillmore saw that the "success so fully demonstrated the power and effectiveness of rifled cannon for breaching at long distances—at distances, indeed, hither to untried and considered altogether impracticable, thus opening a new era in the use of this most valuable and comparatively unknown arm of service."[17]

First Lieutenant James H. Wilson believed that the 42-pounder James rifles and the 10-inch columbiads, fired mainly on the second day, did most of the work in breaching the walls of Fort Pulaski. He concluded that the 30-pounder Parrotts were too light for much effect. The 13-inch mortars accomplished little, "but demonstrated satisfactorily the fact that they cannot be used against circumscribed spaces of small area. Their legitimate use is for the bombardment of cities." Wilson concluded that ordinary brick fortifications could not resist heavy rifles and 10-inch columbiads closer than 2,500 yards. Despite the advantage of the new technology, Wilson believed that "the old fashioned works will answer admirably the primary purpose of delaying the enemy. Fort Pulaski has kept us out of Savannah for four months and we are not there yet and probably will not be soon."[18]

After the war, Southern Colonel Charles C. Jones concluded that 3,000 shot and shell from the mortars and columbiads caused little damage and had they been the sole Federal guns, "probability is that the structure would have preserved its integrity, and would have held out for an indefinite period." Jones agreed completely with Gillmore's conclusions that the power of the rifled guns made the others unnecessary to the siege.[19]

Sherman was not so quick to declare mortars and columbiads obsolete for use as siege guns. He noted that although Fort Pulaski was reduced by rifled projectiles in thirty-six hours, it did not mean the mortars and columbiads were ineffective. Sherman believed that, "thirty-six hours were hardly sufficient time for raw cannoneers, working upon an arm utterly strange to them, to get their range at that distance (from one to two miles)." He added that "Pulaski would have fallen in five to six days with the 13-inch mortars and Columbiads alone manned by raw volunteers—and probably in much less time—if manned by old and experienced artillerists. Because our heavy rifles succeeded so well—even beyond general expectation—it must not be admitted at once—at a jump—that 13-inch mortars are of no effect—even upon so small an area as Pulaski." Sherman recognized that the siege was a "lesson in Engineering and Artillery" for posterity, "overthrowing past results and establishing the James and Parrott systems as unique for breaching purposes at distances before unheard of."[20]

Hunter best summarized the significance of what happened at Fort Pulaski. "The result of this bombardment must cause, I am convinced, a change in the construction of fortifications as radical as that foreshadowed in naval architecture by the conflict between the *Monitor* and *Merrimac*. No works of stone or brick can resist the impact of rifled artillery of heavy caliber."[21]

* * * * * * *

During the days immediately following Fort Pulaski's fall, the army inspected the fort. Benham found that 100 feet of brick facing had collapsed into the moat, completely filling the ditch and providing "a fine ramp for an assault." Three recess arches were completely exposed. Benham further noted that shells passed "without obstruction, through these casemates, diagonally across the passage, to the magazine on its north west angle, at the north end of the gorge, where the inner wall of this magazine was being seriously injured." Gillmore claimed later this was his intention and that fears of an exploding magazine were "the main cause of the so early surrender."[22]

The double timber blindage had provided little protection for the casemates behind. Sergeant Edwin J. Merriam of the occupying Connecticut regiment noted the ineffectiveness of the blindage; he found that balls "went through six feet of earth and timber 15 inches square." Other balls had buried themselves in the brick wall. Like other observers, Merriam felt that the James projectiles caused the most destruction. He also saw one of the mortar shells blasting a seven feet deep hole in the ground. Lieutenant Schoonmaker, visiting the fort twelve days after its fall, also described the breached wall, smashed embrasures, tumbled barbette guns, and damaged pine blindage.[23]

Chapter 9

"Fort Pulaski is the first work that has ever been exposed to the fire of the newly invented rifled cannon and the results have proved that brick and mortar cannot stand before them."

On April 12, the first full day of occupation, a Confederate in the fort observed that "Yankees are all over the fort," some talking with the prisoners while "others are sneaking around our quarters to see what they can pocket."[1]

The Fort Pulaski garrison had consisted of 413 men; however, thirty were detached at the time of the bombardment. Twenty-four officers and 359 men surrendered. The prisoners embarked on steamers for the North on April 12 and 13. Almost all the men were well enough to be transported; the few sick and wounded remained in the fort with the Hospital Steward. Hunter declined to ratify the surrender article regarding the wounded and decreed that the entire garrison must be sent as prisoners to the forts in New York harbor.[2]

Olmstead wrote his wife that he and his men left the fort on April 13 aboard the *Ben DeFord* , anchored for the night in Skull Creek, and the following day landed on Hilton Head. He disembarked around noon the following day. Thus far he had experienced "nothing but kindness" from his captors. Hunter returned to him his sword. Olmstead told his wife he "fear[ed] my reputation should suffer from the disastrous result of our fight, before I have an opportunity of defending myself." He recounted that after the wall of two casemates had been knocked down and projectiles were hitting the traverse protecting the magazine door, it was only a matter of time before the fort was blown up. "Fort Pulaski is the first work that has ever been exposed to the fire of the newly invented rifled cannon and the result have proved that brick and mortar cannot stand before them."[3]

On April 18, Olmstead and 179 other prisoners boarded the *Oriental* for their voyage north. Many expressed surprise at their kind treatment. Some Confederates could not resist "cheering for Jeff Davis & Confederacy." Many Germans and Irishmen viewed leaving the fort, even as prisoners, as "liberty." The garrison of Fort Pulaski was sent to Governor's Island, New York; the officers were confined in Fort Columbus and the men in Castle Williams. They began arriving by April 17.[4]

On April 13, Hunter declared "all persons of color" held in involuntary service in Fort Pulaski to be "hereby confiscated and declared free." He reported to Secretary of War Stanton that Fort Pulaski had surrendered when the wall was breached after thirty hours of continuous fire. Hunter added that he was about to storm the work when the Confederates surrendered. He related that he had captured forty-seven guns, seven thousand shot and shell, forty thousand pounds of powder, a supply of provisions, and three hundred "sickly" prisoners. This at the cost of one killed and one wounded.[5]

The cleanup of the fort began immediately. Men of the 7th Connecticut cleaned out the cool casemates and began moving into them. Hawley described his quarters in the fort for his wife. "Our office is a large parlor; . . . through folding doors is the bedroom of Col. Terry & myself with iron frame cots, mattresses, good frames & mosquito nets, &c. Col. Olmstead (rebel) gave Col. Terry his good cow & we have milk enough for coffee and tea." In early May, Hawley sent his wife "*the white flag that was hoisted on Pulaski.*"[6]

During the cleanup of late afternoon of April 14, a group of five Rhode Island artillerymen was gathering to empty unexploded shells. One man tapped a James shell on a granite traverse and it exploded, killing two of his comrades immediately, mortally wounding two, and maiming the fifth.[7] Sergeant Edwin J. Merriam was outside the fort in the kitchen when he heard an explosion and saw shell fragments flying.

> I went immediately onto the parapet and saw the most horrid sight
> I ever saw 5 men all mangled and blown to pieces 1 was killed instantly
> and one died in five minutes one poor fellow was so broken to pieces he
> could not be moved without falling to pieces, and lived 5 hours another
> died just as they got ready to take his legs off the other has had his leg
> amputated and was alive this morning [April 15].[8]

* * * * * * * *

After the surrender, Benham asked Gillmore to submit his report and, after the men had rested, to gather up the ordnance on Tybee and send part to the fort and the remainder back to Hilton Head for use against Charleston. Helped by Porter and Wilson, Gillmore directed the gathering of siege material. Some Tybee guns were dismounted and placed in the fort. The mortars were being "quietly loaded on board vessels"; members of the 7th Connecticut speculated the guns would next be used against Charleston.[9]

DuPont was at Hilton Head for the April 12 arrival of the *McClellan* with Hunter and Benham, and Rodgers and the *Wabashers* who had served the guns of Battery Sigel. DuPont sent his sailors aloft to cheer the army commanders and then went himself aboard to congratulate them and thank them for allowing the navy a role in the bombardment.[10]

Upon his return, Hunter detained all steamers going north until the official reports could be prepared. Benham had written his brief report aboard the *McClellan* and submitted it to Hunter to be included with his own. Hunter held up the mail steamer until April 14 while Benham repeatedly asked Gillmore for his report. Gillmore delayed his report, dated April 12, until just after the mail steamer had left for the North.[11] Benham later recounted:

> much to our amusement or surprise, at the "rebound,"—or return of the steamer from New York, we found that about one full page *each* of *three* principal New York daily papers were filled with the most detailed reports and orders of the captain, as they must have been printed, from his *triplicate* manuscripts only. For with the many reporters he had about him, he well knew that these papers would only publish matter as *original*, from such manuscripts only, a fact I was afterwards informed of. And fuller reports and returns were thus sent to these newspapers, than were ever made to his commanding generals, and in the body of his main report, as eventually rendered, no mention at all is made *even of the names* of those two generals. So that I told Capt. Gillmore "that General Hunter and myself would probably have to get certificates that we had been present at the bombardment and capture of Fort Pulaski." While *I* had done *him* justice, from what I had personally witnessed there, where was under fire, as much or more, than he was, to ask Genl. Hunter to urge the President to confirm him in the rank of Brig. General, that General Sherman had assumed to appoint him to.[12]

Gillmore's report appeared in the April 19 issue of the New York *Times*, in a "Supplement to the New York *Times*"; Benham's and Hunter's reports were published in the April 20 issue.

Halpine later wrote that for Gillmore to assume all of the credit for the successful siege would be like "the Chief Engineer on the staff of General Grant, have suppressed General Grant's name altogether, and only given his own, in reporting the sieges and surrender of Fort Donelson and Vicksburgh."[13]

* * * * * * * *

On April 16, Adrian Terry told his wife that he had finally spent his first night in the fort, having been involved with moving the gear of the 7th Connecticut into the fort for the past three days. The next day, Horace Porter wrote that "the fort is knocked to pieces. Our guns worked beautifully, and our firing was much better than that of the Rebels."[14]

Lieutenant Wilson later recalled that after the surrender no real effort was made to move inland. General Stevens made an ineffectual demonstration toward Pocotaligo, but nothing more. Many officers went home on leave. Wilson added in a letter to his friend McPherson, on Halleck's staff, that they all felt Hunter had been "shuffled" to the South Carolina coast to get him out of the way. The often promised reinforcements never arrived. Wilson "strongly suspect Hunter of senility and Benham of being a conceited ass. The latter is certainly a most absurd compound of impudence folly and imbecility I ever met. When such men are made generals it is not strange that the national arms should suffer disgrace."[15]

Wilson continued to McPherson that Gillmore had to "contend with the fears, doubts, adverse opinions and remonstrances of old fogies as well as natural obstacles of no insignificant character." Wilson recalled General Totten's remark that "Fort Pulaski could not be breached in any length of time with any number of guns of a manageable calibre." General Wright had also stated that the fort "might be buried in iron but could not be reduced if properly defended." Wilson recalled that others feared the guns of the Goat Point batteries would be lost. Despite all the concerns, Gillmore "hung out, carried out his plans and attacked the fort, with what success you know." Wilson had worked with Porter; he felt Porter had "contributed more than any one man to our success."[16]

Maneuvering behind the scenes continued. Captain Alfred Ely, Benham's Assistant Adjutant General, wrote to Senator Charles Sumner for a favor. As a mere captain, Ely found himself "ranked" by every other captain serving as adjutant to the other generals in Benham's district. To achieve "efficiency in the office,...for the sake of the service as well as of myself," and adding for good measure "the position of asst adj. gen is not of my seeking," Ely requested Sumner to intervene with the War Department and have him appointed major.[17]

* * * * * *

U.S.A.M.H.I.

Willliam M. Fenton

On April 16, the 8th Michigan landed on Whitemarsh Island for a reconnaissance. Seven companies, under Colonel William M. Fenton accompanied Lieutenant James H. Wilson on the expedition. General Gillmore authorized the reconnaissance without "consultation with or any authority" from his superior, General Benham. Benham later speculated that Gillmore did so "by the advice of urgency" by Lieutenant Wilson. Gillmore later claimed he had ordered the move to confirm Colonel Rudolph Rosa's previous observations of the firm ground and streams of the island and to discover if the Confederates were preparing a boat expedition against the hulk in Lazaretto Creek.[18]

The Michigan men left Goat Point on Tybee Island at 8:00 a.m. aboard the *Honduras*; accompanying them was a small detachment, with one gun, of the 3rd Rhode Island Artillery. Passing along the Tybee River, they entered Wilmington Narrows. They first stopped at Screvens' plantation, and Captain Gilbert E. Pratt with 115 men of Companies B and G disembarked; they were to skirt "Turner's Creek on the right, so as to cover the boat party, which was to follow that stream to the Wilmington River." Continuing to the junction of Oatland and Turner's Creek, the balance of the five companies, about 300 men, landed at Gibson's plantation, at the eastern-most tip of Whitemarsh Island.[19]

The first two companies ashore at Gibson's moved to the southwest end of Whitemarsh Island, "skirting Turner's Creek" opposite Pratt's party and left a small picket at the road intersection from Gibson's and Oatland to Turner's until they were relieved. Another company advanced on the road to the ferry at Causton's Bluff to protect the boat party in Oatland Creek. The remaining two companies remained at Gibson's plantation. Unable to land their 6-pounder, Lieutenant Augustus W. Colwell and the Rhode Islanders remained on the steamer. After the first company landed at Gibson's, Lieutenant Wilson continued in a boat along Turner's Creek.[20] Once the company of Federals encountered the Confederates on Whitemarsh and fell back, Fenton recalled his men to the Gibson house.[21]

Confederate Colonel Marcellus Douglass was headquartered at Causton's Bluff, on the Saint Augustine Creek. Across the creek to the east was Oatland Island, largely a marshy point to the south of McQueen's Island and bounded north and east by Saint Augustine Creek and south by the narrow, shallow Oatland Creek (currently known as Richardson's Creek). Oatland Creek waterway separated Oatland Island from Whitemarsh Island. The latter island was much larger and had marsh only at its periphery. It had been Douglass' practice to keep pickets on Whitemarsh Island and on April 16 he had sent Lieutenant Thomas G. Medders and 45 men of Company H on scouting and picket duty. About 3:00 p.m. Douglass took Captain J. T. Crawford, Lieutenant R. T. Bowie, and 37 men of Company G to Oatland Island to cut trees to prevent the Northerners from secretly building batteries. While engaged in this labor, a scout brought news that Federals were landing on Whitemarsh next to the Wilmington Narrows at Mr. Gibson's place. The scout reported that a regiment-laden steamer was holding in the river 400 to 500 yards away from the landing site. Medders and his company had fallen back two miles to a crossroads from which they could observe the Northerners. Douglass immediately sent forward Crawford and his men to help Medders hold the crossroads, and to send pickets toward the Dr. Gibson's house landing site and west to Saint Augustine Creek to observe the approach to Skidaway Island. Telling Crawford to await him, Douglass returned to his camp and ordered Companies A, B, and C (Lieutenant E. L. Connally, Captains James McCally and John L. Moore, respectively) to take the steamer *Leesburg* and join Crawford. Douglass disembarked McCally across Saint Augustine Creek on Oatland Island; McCally was to cross the island and use a small boat to cross the creek and then join Medders and Crawford at the crossroads on Whitemarsh Island, and await Douglass, who was coming with the other reinforcements. Douglass then continued on Saint Augustine Creek, beached in Whitemarsh

Creek that penetrates the island from the west, disembarked around 5:30 p.m. and began his two-mile overland trek.

Before Douglass' arrival, McCally reached Crawford and Medders. Crawford had discovered 50 to 75 advancing Federals. Crawford's pickets fired on them and fell back to the crossroads. Believing they faced a small force, Crawford and McCally advanced on the Michigan front and left flank. Falling back to the Gibson house landing site, the Federals found cover behind a cedar hedgerow and began a briskly returning fire.[22]

Colonel Fenton's men had now reunited at Gibson's when Crawford's force attacked, between 4:00 and 5:00 p.m., "about 800 strong, and armed with Enfield rifles." After delivering the first volley, the 8th Michigan bugler sounded "The Charge." In the chaos of the regiment's first actual combat, the bugler immediately followed with "The Retreat." As Fenton later recalled, "The first line, mistaking the signal, fell back to the next cover."[23]

As the forward line fell back through an open space, the Confederates took advantage of the confusion by "pouring in . . . steady destructive fire." By this time Douglass' reinforcements had arrived and joined Crawford and McCally. Firing continued for an hour. Fenton and Wilson made "ineffectual efforts" for the hour to charge and drive back Douglass. They were then finally able to gain the flanks of the Rebel force and dislodge it. In the increasing darkness the Confederates fell back. Fenton now decided to reembark and return to Tybee. The five small boats could together ferry only fifty men to the *Honduras* every half hour and it was 10:00 p.m. before the embarkation was completed.[24]

By the time darkness fell and the Federals disembarked, the Confederates had only sixty men with cartridges who were "physically" able to fight. Douglass elected to cease fighting "knowing their overwhelming force of 800 men." The following day Douglass found:

[The 8th Michigan] had remained on the island only long enough to gather up their dead and wounded, as they had left knapsacks, cartridge boxes, canteens, haversacks, overcoats, blankets &c., and a number of guns, all of which we gathered up. I also saw the doors that they had taken from the houses there and on which they had borne off their killed and wounded. The doors were very bloody.[25]

In the early engagement of Confederate Captains Crawford and McCally, Georgia infantrymen had mortally wounded Lieutenant Frederick M. Badger. Badger told them they had faced 800 to 860 men, a clear exaggeration of the strength of the 8th Michigan. The entire Confederate force engaged at one time never exceeded 90 men, since many had been detailed to cover the flanks and guard the streams. Douglass lost four killed and fifteen wounded. Most of the losses were in Captain Crawford's Company G.[26]

The following day, April 17, a regiment of Georgia state troops arrived to reinforce Douglass at Causton Bluff. They bivouacked between the bluff and the causeway to Saint Augustine Creek and helped the engineer officer at the earth fort.[27]

The 8th Michigan returned to Tybee aboard the *Honduras*. A 7th Connecticut infantryman on a barge alongside the *Honduras* after her return, wrote, "the sigh that met my gaze wer something that I had not seen before in my life, their ley forty-one men upon her deck, eleven dead, some dying, others groaning with paines from their woundz their ley private's [and] officers suffering the same panes." Charles P. Lord, of the 8th Maine, and Lieutenant Schoonmaker both confirmed the losses.[28]

Engineer officer Gillmore accomplished little at the cost of ten killed and 35 wounded, 10 percent of the regiment's strength. Wilson was hit just below the knee by a musket ball, but the top of his heavy West Point boot deflected the ball. He had been able to sound Turner's Creek to Screven's plantation at ten feet at half tide. Wilson confirmed that a "well constructed barrier of piles and live-oak logs" was in place in the Wilmington Channel leading to Saint Augustine Creek. Although he did not explore Oatland Creek, he did not think it was navigable.[29]

With self-serving justification, Gillmore declared "the reconnaissance, so far as these points required it, was entirely successful." At Hilton Head, General Benham elected not to hold Gillmore "to severe account for this failure . . . on account of the recent good service," although the operation had been neither authorized nor approved.[30]

Hunter, too, chose to overlook Gillmore's action. Hunter proclaimed he did not doubt "that this reconnaissance has been ordered from your best motives and judgment." "Although presuming you had reasons for ordering that reconnaissance which are not stated in your report or otherwise known," Hunter felt the attack on the Confederates, "at least two regiments," was not necessary. In fact, Hunter had ordered Gillmore to send the 8th Michigan to Fort Pulaski on April 12, the day after its fall, to help in repairing the fort and to aid in dismantling the batteries on Tybee. Tybee was to have been left to the 46th New York alone, and any troops not on Cockspur Island were to have been sent to Viele on Daufuskie. Hunter concluded that the information gained from the reconnaissance was "not a compensation for the great loss to ourselves which has been suffered in the affair." Like Benham, Hunter recognized Gillmore's service in the bombardment and dropped any further reference to the reconnaissance.[31]

Within two weeks of the affair at Whitemarsh Island, Gillmore was pressing Benham and Hunter for permission to leave the Department. Benham still chaffed that he and Hunter had been mentioned only once in the published version of Gillmore's Fort Pulaski report ("10th of April, Genl Hunter and Benham arrived today."), both officers felt that "the work had been done, and well done, and we did not devote ourselves to obtaining all or even a part of the credit of it." Gillmore's appointment as brigadier general was confirmed seventeen days after Fort Pulaski surrendered.[32]

On May 3, Gillmore became ill with malaria and, on May 14, started for West Point, New York, on sick leave. He was found "unfit for duty" and still recuperating in late June; he would remain on sick leave until August 15, 1862.[33]

* * * * * * *

By late April, many officers had received furloughs. Hawley did not receive one since his superior, Terry, had been nominated to the grade of brigadier general, and upon confirmation he would leave "the whole care of the regiment" to Hawley.[34]

On April 29, Adrian Terry wrote his wife about his duties at the fort. As quartermaster, on that day, he had directed the transfer of 1,200 heavy cannon balls from the wharf into the fort, supervised the landing of a balloon and its appurtenances from a steamboat, supervised the unloading of 15,000 bricks to be used in repairs, and directed the unloading of an additional 1,500 heavy shot and shell from another steamboat.[35]

By the end of April, infantrymen, under the supervision of masons, were busily repairing the breach in the wall and other damage to the fort. The work was expected to be completed within a few days. On April 30, Private Henry Glines of the 7th Connecticut spent the morning unloading shells in the yard. The next two days he spent hauling the blindage out of the fort on a sling car. In late May, Porter was hard at work finishing the dismantling of the batteries on Tybee Island. "The fort is almost as good as ever, the repairs going on rapidly." Porter had been assigned Chief of Ordnance of the Northern District, Department of the South, and had three regiments helping him. "It is well they are not regulars," he added, "or the colonels would make a great cry against being put on such duty and under such orders."[36]

April 30 returns for the Department of the South document General Viele had 120 officers and 2,662 men on Daufuskie, Jones, and Bird Islands. Gillmore had 142 officers and 3,265 men on Tybee and Cockspur Islands and in Fort Pulaski. Hunter's department, extending along the coast of southeastern South Carolina, Georgia, and northeastern Florida, had a total of 16,000 men.[37]

Porter wrote his sister that "Gen. Gillmore presented me with a sword captured from a Rebel officer in the fort with a speech about as long as the sword about gallantry &c. which would have made a capital fourth of July oration." When Benham later presented Porter with another captured sword, he declined the second and suggested that Benham award it to another officer "who behaved well under fire and received none." Hunter presented Major Halpine with "a beautiful Damascus sword" surrendered by one of the officers of Fort Pulaski.[38]

The 48th New York was ordered to Fort Pulaski on May 23 and departed Daufuskie Island two days later; they relieved the 7th Connecticut. Seven companies of the 48th New York occupied the fort on the 25th; the remaining three companies joined the regiment later. They garrisoned the fort until May, 1863.[39]

* * * * * * *

By the time of the bombardment of Fort Pulaski, the batteries on Bird and Jones Islands had been enlarged to seventeen guns, along with substantial magazines and splinter proofs. After the fort's surrender, Colonel John L. Chatfield was ordered to have his 6th Connecticut dismantle Battery Vulcan on Jones Island. By a misunderstanding, the gunboats were withdrawn before the operation was complete. Chatfield had the last 10-inch columbiad transferred to a raft during the night of May 19 and floated down to the fort; he replaced it with a black log with a barrel nailed to the end. After the Federal evacuation, the Confederates "occupied" the battery site.[40]

* * * * * * *

On April 23, Mercer moved his headquarters to the house of Judge DeLyon on the mainland. Earlier, his troops had evacuated Isle of Hope. On April 22, thirty United States Marines made a reconnaissance to the Isle of Hope in 8-oared boats with howitzers in the bow. They questioned a Mr. Wait, whose house was only one-half mile from Mercer's headquarters, about Confederate activities and left.[41]

* * * * * * * *

Olmstead was exchanged in October, 1862, and soon after that reported to Mercer, commander of the military district of Georgia. Olmstead's regiment was divided among Fort Jackson, Fort Bartow, Fort McAllister on the Ogeechee River, and the lines around Savannah. He transferred to Charleston in July, 1863, and served in Battery Wagner and Fort Johnson. Olmstead returned to Savannah in the autumn of 1863. In the spring of 1864, he briefly commanded the Third Military District of the Department of South Carolina, based in Pocotaligo. After a few weeks, Olmstead turned his brigade over to Brigadier General Thomas Jordan and rejoined his regiment, then on its way to General Joseph E. Johnston in northwest Georgia. He served in Mercer's Brigade during the retreat to, and battles around, Atlanta. Too late for the battle at Franklin, Tennessee, he did take part in the fighting around Nashville. As part of the subsequent Confederate retreat, he was stationed in Alabama and Georgia before surrendering in Greensboro, North Carolina, in April, 1865. After the war, he returned to Savannah where he was a prominent member of society; he died in 1926.[42]

Gillmore launched his career with the surrender of Fort Pulaski. Following service in Kentucky, he was promoted to major general on July 10, 1863, and given command of the X Corps and the Department of the South. He conducted successful siege operations against Battery Wagner and shelled Charleston, but was unsuccessful in forcing the surrender of Fort Sumter. Transferred with his corps to join the Army of the James in May, 1864, he participated in the Bermuda Hundred Campaign under the direction of Major General Benjamin F. Butler. Relieved of command after an unsuccessful attempt on Petersburg the following month, Gillmore was transferred to the Washington, D.C. defenses, where he commanded two divisions of the XIX Corps in the pursuit of Jubal Early. Gillmore was severely injured by a fall from his horse on July 14, 1864; upon recovering in February, 1865, he was reassigned to command the Department of the South and his X Corps. He remained in the army after the war and served on many boards and commissions and published texts on various aspects of fortifications and the conduct of his wartime sieges. Gillmore remained on active duty until his death in 1888. Many officers who served with him found him difficult to work with. A year after the fall of Fort Pulaski, Brigadier General Alfred H. Terry was serving in the Department of the South. He wrote his friend Halpine, that Gillmore was "a man of most '*intense mediocrity*' just an engineer & nothing else. He has not a spark of genius or enthusiasm in his composition."[43]

Thomas W. Sherman's career never recovered following his dismissal from his command in South Carolina and Georgia. He was assigned to Halleck in Tennessee, but relieved of command during the approach on Corinth, Mississippi. He then held various commands in the Department of the Gulf and lost a leg in the fighting around Port Hudson. He remained in the army until 1870 and died nine years later.

*   *   *   *   *   *   *

Many factors contributed to the obsolescence of the impressive and costly masonry forts. Steam-powered vessels had maneuverability and independence that sail-powered ships lacked. Iron armor reduced their vulnerability to shore fire. Shore forts had an advantage over vessels in armament since the fort could concentrate its fire on one vessel while the rocking ship offered an unstable platform for accurate firing. The major factor in the obsolescence of the masonry forts, however, was the coming of rifled artillery.[44]

Rifled artillery allowed in-flight stability of elongated projectiles and thus opened advantages over the spherical projectiles fired by smoothbore cannons. An elongated projectile has more mass than a spherical projectile of the same diameter; and it does not encounter increased air resistance during flight. Rifled guns deliver more mass with more energy for greater impact than smoothbore guns. They were also effective at greater ranges and showed improved accuracy. The effect of shells on masonry fortifications was irreparable at the time; later, earth forts and sandbags proved far more effective and easily reparable. More than any other event, the use of rifled artillery "spelled the end of the style of fortification of which Pulaski is an example."[45] The successful use of rifled artillery against masonry Fort Pulaski was as significant a technological turning point in warfare as was the first use of iron plate on the *Monitor* and *Virginia*. In the angle of the southeast wall of the fort the outline of repaired breach remains. In the adjacent wall are the craters of the impact of stray shells and the ends of a few unexploded shells, rusting in the brick.

U.S.A.M.H.I.

Fort Pulaski (1900) viewed from the southeast, showing the
repaired breach in the southeastern *pan coupé*.

U.S.A.M.H.I.

The entrance of Fort Pulaski viewed from the demilune (1900).

F.P.N.M.

Aerial view of Fort Pulaski today from the southeast, showing the site of the repaired breach at the southeast angle, the damaged southeastern wall, and the position of the magazine in the northeastern corner.

The repaired *pan coupé* and southern wall of Fort Pulaski. Part of the repaired breach is visible on the right.

Southeastern face of Fort Pulaski with the repaired breach to the left. Unexploded shells are present at the base of some craters.

Site of the breach, repaired in May, 1862, in the southern *pan coupé* of Fort Pulaski. Damage to the adjacent walls is clearly visible.

F.P.N.M.

Aerial view of Fort Pulaski today from the west; the structures in the demilune were built decades after the Civil War. Arrow indicates the southeastern *pan coupé*, site of the breach.

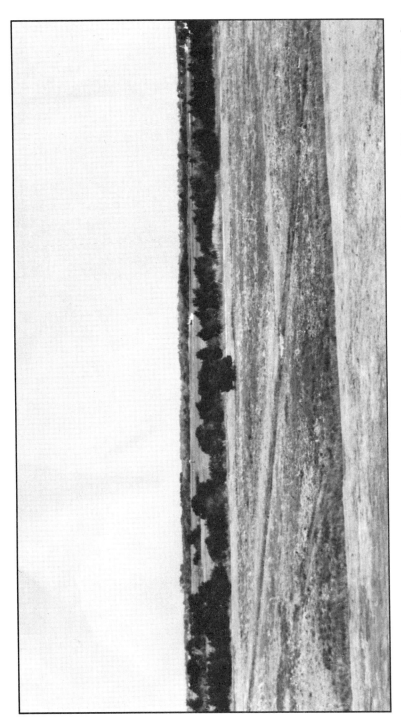

View from Fort Pulaski, at the site of the breach, looking across the southern channel of the Savannah River at Tybee Island, site of the Federal batteries (tree line on the horizon).

Parade of Fort Pulaski, viewed from the site of the breach. The northwestern magazine is in the corner where the northern and western walls join (arrow).

View of the parade and the southeastern corner (site of the breach) of Fort Pulaski today. Note the reconstructed wooden blindage to the left, protecting the door of the casemate.

$\mathcal{A}$ppendix

$\mathcal{D}$evelopment of $\mathcal{R}$ifled $\mathcal{A}$rtillery

Introduced into Europe by the Arabs in the twelfth century, cannons evolved until three centuries later heavy siege guns were in general use. Metal casting techniques improved in Europe over the next century and more light-weight, mobile pieces were developed. Cast metal shot replaced stone projectiles. Gustavus Adolphus of Sweden led the development of the light field gun and tactics in the early 1600's. The major western European countries soon founded schools of artillery and continued to improve the guns.[1]

Until shortly before the Civil War, all guns fired spherical solid shot, and gun caliber was expressed in terms of the shot's weight. However, hollow, explosive-filled shells weighed less than solid shot of the same diameter and therefore the caliber of the guns was expressed directly in inches. The invention of rifled guns and elongated projectiles made the inch system even more necessary. Forty-two, 32, 24, and 18-pounder shot was equivalent to bore diameters of 7, 6.4, 5.82, and 5.3 inches.[2]

Thus far, smoothbore artillery had to be loaded from the front, muzzle loaded, and the projectile had to freely exit the tube. Generally, a 1/10 inch difference existed between the diameter of the tube and the diameter of the ball. The difference between the interior bore of a gun tube and maximum diameter of a solid ball, "windage," affected the efficiency and accuracy of round shot. This space allowed for the escape of some of the energy of the exploding charge. In addition, the ball would bounce against the side of the tube on its way out, "balloting," which caused inaccuracy that increased with lengthening range.[3]

Material from which guns were cast also changed during the nineteenth century. Before, most guns were made of bronze. The deficiencies of bronze ordnance had become apparent during the sieges of the Peninsular Campaign of the Napoleonic

Wars. Bronze softened under rapid fire and the muzzle would begin to droop, limiting these guns to 120 rounds each 24 hours. When iron was introduced, guns could fire triple the number of shot in the same period.[4]

Small caliber smoothbore guns, the mainstay in American fortifications during the first half of the nineteenth century, were obsolete by 1860 and were being replaced by either larger caliber smoothbores or by the newly developed rifled guns.[5] Two other types of large siege and defensive guns were also in use. One of those was the howitzer, which was introduced earlier in the century. This was a smoothbore gun designed to throw large shells with a lighter charge than used by regular guns. It weighed less than guns of similar caliber and had a higher trajectory and, therefore, could reach objects with better defilade than guns.[6] The other was the mortar, a short cannon designed to throw large shells to high elevations, e.g., over walls, with a small powder charge.[7]

The "columbiad," with newly developed carriages, combined features of the gun, howitzer, and mortar. It was developed in 1811 by a young American engineer, George Bomford. The army had adopted his large caliber 8- and 10-inch columbiads by the mid-1840's. Those long, large caliber pieces could fire shot or shell with heavy charges at angles of elevation up to 40 degrees; older guns were designed for only 5- to 10- degree elevations. The increase in elevation tripled the range of shore guns. The 10-inch columbiad had a range of over three miles while the older 42-pounder gun reached about a mile. The columbiad's large caliber, long range, and high elevation made it ideal for defending narrow channels and distant roadsteads. It had become the mainstay of American coastal defense by 1860.[8]

The American Civil War fell at the beginning of a new technological era in artillery, the advent of rifled guns. Experiments proved the advantages of rifling; they awaited confirmation under wartime conditions. Rifling had been attempted since the mid-sixteenth century and had been used in small arms even earlier. The Kentucky long rifle was acclaimed for its accuracy at long range. Successful artillery rifling experiments were conducted in the 1840's and by the mid-1850's several "systems" (special spiral grooving and projectiles designed to fit) had been developed in Europe. The United States began experiments with rifled cannon in the late 1850's, but production of such guns did not begin until the outbreak of war in 1861. A few American large caliber smoothbore guns were rifled before the Civil War; however, many of these could not long withstand increased exploding pressures, and rifling smoothbores proved to be a stopgap measure until replacements could be cast.[9]

In a barrel rifled with lands and grooves, the effect of the discharge explosion is to drive the soft material at the posterior of the projectile against the lands and into the grooves, thus forcing it to "take" the rifling and impart the spin necessary to keep the projectile oriented properly during its flight. The velocity of rotation overcame the pressure of the air that tended to turn the shot over or render it unsteady during flight.[10]

The problem with muzzle loading rifled artillery is that the projectile must insert easily down the tube, even when partially fouled with powder residue, yet take the rifling when the charge ignites and the projectile is discharged. Several ingenious designs overcame this problem, among the earliest of which was the James system and Parrott piece which Gillmore used. All of the powder explosion force went into moving the projectile forward and into "taking" the rifling; energy was not lost through "windage," as with smoothbore guns firing round shot. Rifled ordnance firing a projectile of the same weight as that of a smoothbore used less than a quarter of the charge of the smoothbore because no gas escaped around the projectile; the entire charge changed into propellant gas when the soft metal, paper mache, or gutta percha section of the projectile was compressed into the grooves of the rifling.[11] Elongated projectiles had to be seated on the powder charge; if space existed between the powder and the projectile the blast would not cause the soft part of the projectile to engage the grooves. The projectile would tumble after leaving the gun and fall inaccurately short. Because artillerymen had to push their guns forward before firing, care was taken so that the projectile, round or elongated, did not slide forward after loading, leaving a space between it and the powder charge.[12]

The penetration of a masonry wall by an elongated projectile was greater than that of a ball of equal weight because the elongated projectile presented less area for wind resistance and had greater final velocity. Generally, elongated projectiles were fired at a lower initial velocity from a rifled gun than a ball of equal weight from a smoothbored gun; at short range the ball produced more penetration than the elongated projectile. As range increases, however, the penetrating power of the elongated projectile would be greater because it maintained a higher velocity. Beyond ranges of 500 to 600 yards the accuracy of the smoothbore gun was unreliable.[13]

The total effect produced by many balls upon a masonry wall was inconsiderable when compared with the effect of a rifled gun firing an equal number of elongated projectiles. British artillery expert Charles H. Owen concluded, "with the rifled gun the blows of its elongated projectiles can be repeated on the same part of the object at much longer ranges, and a wall . . . could therefore be battered with effect at ranges where balls would be practically useless." Experiments against solid oak showed that a tripling of range resulted in only a slight decrease in penetration of elongated 12-pound projectiles fired from rifled guns, e.g., 12 percent less than at 1,200 yards, while 12-pound balls with the same charge of powder lost two-thirds of their penetrating power at a similar range.[14]

Before the invention of the rifled cannon, standard military doctrine was that:

> An exposed wall may be breached with certainty at distances of 500 to 700 yards, even when elevated 100 feet above the breaching battery; and it is believed that in case of extreme necessity it would be justifiable to attempt to batter down an exposed wall from any distance not exceeding 1,000 yards; but then the quantity of artillery must be considerable, and it will require from four to seven days' firing, according to the number of guns in battery and the period of daylight, to render a breach practicable.[15]

British experiments further showed that the increased penetration of rifled projectiles was greater than theorized, and the rotation along their long axes translated into increased energy. Owen reported that a 6-inch projectile rotated 63 turns per second, and that this rate would be little reduced over three or four seconds, the time it would take a projectile to pass 1,000 yards, and would thus materially aid penetration.[16]

In series of lectures Owens further observed:

> in a smooth-bored gun several different charges may be used without effecting the accuracy of fire up to the respective ranges required; but this is not the case in a rifled gun, for if its charge be altered the velocity of rotation is changed, and with reduction of the charge for which the gun is constructed, there will usually be a loss of accuracy owing to the velocity of rotation of the shot not being high enough to preserve stability of axis during flight.[17]

Owen also noted that when a projectile strikes it penetrates until its *"accumulated or stored-up work* is destroyed." The projectile's *work* would be consumed in penetrating, fracturing, or producing vibration in the object. The penetration of a spherical projectile was proportional to its diameter, density, and to the square of its velocity on impact. The larger the ball's diameter, and the greater its density, the deeper it will penetrate for a given final velocity.[18]

The British had experimented with rifled ordnance since the beginning of the seventeenth century. Initial efforts had been unsuccessful because machinery did not exist for accurate gun tube boring and rifling. The first rifled British guns used in the Crimean War at Sevastopol were reworked 68-pounders and 8-inch cast iron guns. Projectiles frequently jammed in the bore and ruptured the unreinforced forward part of the barrel (the *chase*).[19]

Englishman William G. Armstrong developed a breech-loading rifled gun in the mid-1850's. His projectiles had metal studs, or ribs, which fit matching grooves. Between 1854 and 1857, Joseph Whitworth manufactured a breech-loading rifled gun using a peculiar hexagonal bore with similarly shaped projectiles. By 1860, both of these breech-loading English guns had been perfected. A third system for muzzle loading rifled guns used many different projectiles with a soft metal envelope or coating which expanded by the gas released at the time of detonation.[20]

With many muzzle loading "systems" the grooves could be cleaned with a moist sponge and sometimes lubricated with a greased second sponge. With the James system of projectiles the soft lead and greased canvas covering the posterior half of the projectile quickly fouled the grooves and special scrapers had to be used after a few firings.[21]

In the 1850's, the United States Army began using its limited financial and personnel resources to develop its own muzzle loading rifled artillery. Loaded from the front, the projectile was to take the rifling with minimal escape of gas. The usual system for this was a sabot ("shoe") of soft metal at the butt of the iron projectile. When the charge ignited, the sabot was jammed forward into the soft metal, squeezing it forward and laterally into the rifling grooves. The projectile was propelled forward, spinning with the pitch of the grooves and not bouncing against the interior sides of the barrel.

In 1857, Whitworth had theorized that:

> When projectiles of extraordinary weight are required, they are attainable by simply increasing the length of the projectile without increasing the diameter of the bore or rendering the piece as heavy and difficult of transport as the guns used for firing great spherical shot. In fact, guns of extraordinary diameters . . . are rendered unnecessary. I calculate that by rifling a 10-inch gun, I could fire from it a shell 5 calibers long, weighing 590 lbs. containing 48 lbs. of powder; and if the shell were made 10 calibers in length, which my experiments with the Howitzer showed to be practicable for short ranges, the shell would weigh 1,200 lbs., and contain 100 lbs. of powder.[22]

* * * * * * *

While reviewing American coastal fortifications in 1850, before experiments with rifled artillery, General Totten noted that the only "recent improvements in artillery and other military inventions and discoveries" which effected masonry forts were the use of shells in 8- and 10-inch guns. In the past, high angle mortars fired such shells. Columbiads now fired them at low angles, nearly horizontally, in the manner used for solid shot. Totten reported experiments using such shells against granite, brick, and freestone walls, finding that 32-pounder shot penetrated deeper than 8-inch shell. When the propelling charge was increased to allow the 8-inch shell to penetrate, "in every instance" the hollow iron projectile shattered against the wall. Totten concluded that only shells from 13-inch sea-coast mortars, aimed at high elevations, could be effective against masonry fortifications by penetrating deeply and producing "material ravage by their explosion."[23]

Indeed, in 1850, Totten concluded in his review of the status of American coastal fortifications that:

> The only practicable way yet discovered of demolishing a fortification, being by attaching a mine to the foot of the wall; or by dint of solid shot and heavy charges fired unremittingly, during a long succession of hours, upon the same part of the wall, in order not only to break through it, but to break through in such a manner that the weight and pressure of the incumbent mass may throw large portion of the wall prostrate. This, the shortest and best way of breaching a wall, requires, in the first place, perfect accuracy or direction; because the same number of shots that, being distributed over the expanse of a wall, would merely peel off the face, would, if concentrated in a single deep cut, cause the wall to fall; and it requires, moreover, great power of penetration in the missile—the charge of the breaching gun being for that reason, one-third greater than the common service charge. Now the requisite precision of firing for this effect is

wholly unattainable in vessels, whether shot be solid or hollow; and if it were attainable, hollow shot would be entirely useless for the purpose, because *every one of them would break to pieces against the wall,* even when fired with a charge much less than the common service charge. . . . Every hollow shot thrown against the wall of a fort or battery, if fired with a velocity affording any penetration, will unquestionably be broken into fragments by the shock.[24]

* * * * * * *

At the time of the siege of Fort Pulaski, engineer officer Quincy A. Gillmore was familiar with the reports of two recent experiments using rifled artillery against masonry walls. The British had conducted the first in August, 1860, using Armstrong's rifled guns against a Martello tower[25] in Eastbourne, England. The tower was 31 1/2 feet tall with an exterior base diameter of 46 feet and a top diameter of 40 feet. The wall of the tower varied from 7 1/2 feet thick at the base to 5 3/4 feet thick from the midsection to the top. The three rifled guns tested were a 40-pounder with 4 3/4 inch shells, an 82-pounder with 6-inch shells, and a 7-inch howitzer with 100-pound shells. At a distance of 1,032 yards the guns together fired 50 shot and plugged shells, and 108 shells, an expenditure of 10,850 pounds of metal. The three guns caused a 24-foot wide breach that included most of the interior chamber. In a similar experiment using smoothbore 68-pounders and 32-pounders, at 1,030 yards distance, the results were completely unsatisfactory. On the other hand, at a distance of 500 to 700 yards, rifled guns and smoothbore guns performed equally well.[26]

The Eastbourne experiment showed that a 40-pounder elongated rifled shot penetrated from 4 to 5 1/2 feet. In a different experiment, 68-pounder round shots fired at a Martello tower at Bexhill penetrated only from 1 to 2 feet.[27]

The Prussian Army had also conducted experiments in September, 1860, with rifled breech-loading guns, although it did not compare the effects of smoothbore guns. At a distance of 640 yards, 126 rounds of a 27-pound elongated shot caused a 32-foot breach in a three-foot thick brick wall. The projectiles penetrated the brick an average of 15 inches.[28]

Based on these experiments, Gillmore believed that rifled artillery might be successful in breaching masonry fortifications at distances too great for smoothbore artillery to be effective. Other engineer officers did not agree. Totten said of Fort Pulaski that "the work could not be reduced in a month's firing with any number of guns of manageable calibers." Brigadier General Horatio G. Wright, another West Point graduate, engineer officer, and brigade commander under General Thomas W. Sherman and the coming campaign, said that Fort Pulaski "might be buried in iron but could not be reduced if properly defended."[29] The successful reduction of Fort Pulaski would prove Gillmore right.

Abbreviations

A.C.W.	*America's Civil War*
B&G	*Blue & Gray*
B&L	*Battles and Leaders of the Civil War,* 4 vols. ed. Robert Underwood Johnson and Clarence Clough Buel. New York: The Century Co., 1888.
C.H.S.	Connecticut Historical Society
C.S.L.	Connecticut State Library
C.W.T.I.	*Civil War Times Illustrated*
D.U.	Duke University Library
F.P.N.M.	Fort Pulaski National Monument
f, ff	frame, frames (microfilm)
G.H.Q.	*Georgia Historical Quarterly*
G.H.S.	Georgia Historical Society
H.L.	Huntington Library
L.C.	Library of Congress, Manuscript Division
N.Y.H.S.	New York Historical Society

N.Y.S.L.   New York State Library

O.R.A.   *Atlas to Accompany the Official Records of the*
              Union and Confederate Armies. Washington, D.C.:
              Government Printing Office, 1891-1895.

O.R.   *War of the Rebellion: A Compilation of the Official*
              Records of the Union and Confederate Armies.
              Series 1. Washington, D.C.: Government Printing
              Office, 1880-1901.

O.R.N.   *Official Records of the Union and Confederate*
              Navies in the War of the Rebellion. Series 1.
              Washington, D.C.: Government Printing Office,
              1894-1922.

R.C.S.   *The Reports of Committees of the Senate of the*
              United States, for the Third Session of the
              Thirty-Seventh Congress. Washington, Government
              Printing Office, 1863.

R.G. 94   Record Group 94. Records of the Adjutant
              General's Office in the National Archives and
              Records Service. Register of Letters Received by
              the Office of the Adjutant General (Main Series),
              1861-1870.

S.H.C.   Southern Historical Collection, University of
              North Carolina

S.O.R.   *Supplement to the Official Records of the Union*
              and Confederate Armies. Part I. Wilmington:
              Broadfoot Publishing Company, 1994

Y.U.L.   Yale University Library

$\mathcal{E}$ndnotes

$\mathcal{C}$hapter 1

1. Samuel Jones, "The Occupation of the South Atlantic Coast by Union Troops and Bombardment and Reduction of Fort Pulaski," pp. 218-228, L.C.; Charles C. Jones, "Military Lessons Inculcated on the Coast of Georgia during the Confederate War" (Augusta: Chronicle Printing Establishment, 1883), p. 71; Milton M. Woodford, Letter, April 23, 1862, C.H.S.

2. Gilbert Sumter Guinn, "Coastal Defense of the Confederate Atlantic Seaboard States, 1861-1862: A Study in Political and Military Mobilization" (Ph.D. dissertation, University of South Carolina, 1973), pp. 67-68.

3. Emanuel R. Lewis, *Seacoast Fortifications of the United States* (Washington, D.C.: Smithsonian Institution Press, 1970), pp. 4, 7-8; J. G. Totten, *Report of General J. G. Totten, Chief Engineer, on the Subject of National Defense* (Washington: A. Boyd Hamilton, 1851), pp. 5-6, 27.

4. Totten, *Report*, p. 5.

5. Peggy Robbins, "Storm Over Fort Pulaski," *America's Civil War*, 3 (Sept., 1990):30; Roger S. Durham, "Savannah[:] Mr. Lincoln's Christmas Present" *B&G*, 8 (Feb., 1991) 12.

6. Ralston B. Lattimore, *Fort Pulaski*, (Washington, D.C.: National Park Service Historical Handbook Series No. 18, 1954), pp. 1-6.

7. Lattimore, *Ft. Pulaski*, pp. 5-6; Rogers W. Young, "The Construction of Fort Pulaski," *Georgia Historical Quarterly*, 20 (1936):41; Ian Hogg, *The History of Fortification*, (New York: St. Martin's Press Inc., 1981) p. 173.

8. Lewis, *Fortifications*, pp. 38, 52-53.

9. Totten, *Report*, pp. 70, 94.

10. Lattimore, *Ft. Pulaski*, p. 6; Young, *G.H.Q.*, 20:41.

11. Lattimore, *Ft. Pulaski*, pp. 6-7; Douglas S. Freeman, *R. E. Lee*, 4 vols., (New York, Charles Scribner's Sons, 1934) 1:94-101.

12. Lattimore, *Ft. Pulaski*, pp. 7-10; Totten, *Report*, pp. 70, 96-97; Young, *G.H.Q.*, 20:42-49.

13. Quincy A. Gillmore, *Official Report to the United States Engineer Department of the Siege and Reduction of Fort Pulaski, Georgia, February, March, and April, 1862* (New York: D. Van Nostrand, 1862), p. 9; *The War of the Rebellion: A Compilation of the Official Records of the Union and*

Confederate Armies, Series 1, 108 volumes (Washington, D.C.: Government Printing Office, 1880-1901), 6:149; Jones, L.C., pp. 230-231.

14. J. Thomas Sharf, *History of the Confederate States Navy* (New York: Rogers & Sherwood, 1887), p. 627; Charles H. Olmstead, "Fort Pulaski," *G.H.Q.* , 1 (1917):100.

15. The original company was designated "A." After it was sent to Virginia, a second company, "B," was recruited for the regiment.

16. Lieutenant Colonel William G. Rockwell, Memo, April 13, 1861, in Charles H. Olmstead Papers, S.H.C.
    The First Volunteer Regiment of Georgia should not be confused with the 1st Georgia Regulars Infantry or the 1st Georgia Independent Battalion.

17. Charles H. Olmstead, *The Memoirs of Charles H. Olmstead* (Savannah: Georgia Historical Society, 1964), p. 79; Charles H. Olmstead, "Fort Pulaski," *G.H.Q.* , 1 (1917):98-99; Julian, *C.W.T.I.*, 9:10.

18. Olmstead, *G.H.Q.*, 1:99; Olmstead, *Memoirs*, pp. 80, 99; Julian, *C.W.T.I.*, 9:10; Derry, *Georgia*, p. 15; Robbins, *A.C.W.*, 3:28.

19. Derry, *Georgia*, pp. 6, 8; Olmstead, *G.H.Q.*, 1:98-99.

20. Olmstead, *Memoirs*, p. 81; Julian, *C.W.T.I.*, 9:9-11; Robbins, *A.C.W.*, 3:28.

21. Charles H. Olmstead, Letter, January 16, 1862, S.H.C.; Olmstead, *Memoirs*, p. 81.

22. *O.R.*, 6:297; Charles H. Olmstead, Papers, April 13, 1861, S.H.C.; Guinn, "Coastal Defence," p. 124.
    Secretary of War Judah P. Benjamin would extend Lawton's command to include the entire state of Georgia, designated as the Department of Georgia, on October 21, 1861. (Guinn, "Coastal Defence," p. 219.)

23. Olmstead, *Memoirs*, p. 83.

24. *Harper's Weekly*, June 1, 1861; Theodorick W. Montfort, "Rebel Lawyer: The Letters of Theodorick W. Montfort, 1861-1865." *G.H.Q.*, 49:201; William H. Russell, *My Diary North and South* (New York: Harper and Brothers Publishers, 1863), p. 63.

25. Julian, *C.W.T.I.*, 9:12; Guinn, "Coastal Defense," p. 214.

26. Charles H. Olmstead, "The Memoirs of Charles H. Olmstead," *G.H.Q.*, 42 (1958):390; 43 (1959):183-184, 379, 382, 386.

27. Olmstead, *Memoirs*, pp. 86-87; Olmstead, *G.H.Q.*, 1:100.

28. Olmstead, *Memoirs*, p. 84; Julian, *C.W.T.I.*, 9:12-13; Charles H. Olmstead, Letter, July 22, 1861, S.H.C.; Charles J. Copp, Letter, August 21, 1861, in Aaron Wilbur Papers, S.H.C.; Cornelius M. Schoonmaker, Papers, p. 35, L.C.

29. Charles H. Olmstead Papers, Letter, June 3, 1861, S.H.C.; William D. Harden, Letter, August 8, 1861, in Charles H. Olmstead Papers, S.H.C.; *O.R.*, 6:277-288.

30. John H. Weaton, Letter, October 3, 1861, in Charles H. Olmstead Papers, S.H.C.; Charles H. Olmstead, Letter, October 31, 1861, S.H.C.

31. Williams, *Investment*, pp. 9-10, Young, *G.H.Q.*, 23:254, 256, 260; Mercer, Diary, March 2, 1862, S.H.C.; Derry, *Georgia*, pp. 59-60; Savannah, *Republican*, January 28, 1862.

32. *O.R.*, 6:304-305; Cornelius R. Hanleiter, Diary, February 1, 1862, D.U.

33. Alexander R. Lawton, Letter, November, 1861, in Charles H. Olmstead Papers, S.H.C.; Olmstead, *G.H.Q.*, 1:100; Olmstead, *Memoirs*, p. 87.
    More detailed discussion of the development of Georgia's defenses may be found in Guinn, "Coastal Defenses," pp. 115-128, 213-222, 293-310.

Chapter 2

1. *O.R.*, 6:309, 314; Freeman, *Lee*, 1:607.

2. Freeman, *Lee*, 1:608; *O.R.* 6:312-313.

3. Freeman, *Lee*, 1:609; *O.R.*, 6:311,312; Olmstead, *G.H.Q.*, 1:100; Olmstead, *Memoirs*, p. 87.
   Lee's staff consisted of Captain Thornton A. Washington, adjutant general; Captain Walter H. Taylor, assistant adjutant general; Captain Joseph C. Ives, chief engineer; Lieutenant Colonel William G. Gill, ordnance officer; and Mr. Joseph Manigault, volunteer aide-de-camp. (*O.R.*, 6:312.)

4. *O.R.*, 6:313-314; Charles C. Jones, "Military Lessons Inculcated on the Coast During the Confederate War," An Address Delivered Before the Confederate Survivors' Association in Augusta, Georgia, at its Fifth Annual Meeting, on Memorial Day, April 26, 1883 (Augusta: Chronicle Printing Establishment, 1883), p. 4; Charles H. Olmstead, Letter, November 21, 1861, S.H.C.; *O.R.*, 6:313.

5. S. F. DuPont, J. G. Bernard, A. D. Bache, and Charles Pliny Davis, *The Reports of the Committees of the Senate of the United States, for the Third Session of the Thirty-Seventh Congress* (Washington: Government Printing Office, 1863), pp. 292-294, 313-315.
   In the absence of a report by Sherman in the *O.R.*, his testimony offers his complete account of the first months of the campaign.

6. Samuel Francis DuPont, *A Selection from His Civil War Letters*, 3 vols. ed. John D. Hayes (Ithica: Cornell University Press, 1969), 1:113, 145, 181, 201.

7. Sherman, *R.C.S.*, p. 294.

8. *O.R.*, 6:185, Julian, *C.W.T.I.*, 9 (May, 1970):13; Sherman, *R.C.S.*, p. 307; DuPont, *Letters*, 1:181.

9. James H. Wilson, *Under the Old Flag*, 2 vols. (New York: D. Appleton & Company, 1912, 1:70; *O.R.*, 6:170, 175-176, 177, 178.

10. *O.R.*, 6:188; Sherman, *R.C.S.*, p. 295.

11. *O.R.*, 6:189.
    At this time Sherman had on hand nine 8-inch columbiads, six 42-pounder guns, eleven 32-pounder guns, six 24-pounder guns, four 18-pounder guns, four 12-pounder siege guns, seven 30-pounder Parrotts, two 8-inch siege howitzers, ten 24-pounder field howitzers, three 20-pounder Parrotts, one 10-inch siege mortar, ten 6-pounder field guns, two 12-pounder field howitzers, four coehorn mortars, and twenty 24-pounder casemate howitzers. All guns were mounted and had sufficient ammunition to withstand a siege. This was the armament which had been sent with his first, larger division. The armament which was to accompany his second, smaller division had not yet landed. The above mentioned artillery, along with captured Confederate ordnance, Sherman felt would all be necessary to fortify and defend his Hilton Head position. (T. W. Sherman to L. Thomas, November 30, 1861, R.G. 94, 1459-S-1861, N.A.)

12. Dupont, *Letters*, 1:257; George L. Andrew, Papers, typescript, p. 42, H.L.; John Marchand, *Charleston Blockade: The Journals of John B. Marchand, U.S. Navy, 1861-1862*, ed. C. L. Symonds (Newport: Naval War College Press, 1976), p. 98.

13. Olmstead, *Memoirs*, p. 88; Alfred H. Terry, Letter, February 2, 1862, Y.U.L.

14. Sharf, *History*, pp. 629-630; *Official Records of the Union and Confederate Navies in the War of the Rebellion*, Series 1, 27 volumes (Washington, D.C.: Government Printing Office, 1894-1922) 12:359-360, 364; *O.R.*, 6:32, 192-193; Charles H. Olmstead, Letter, November 25, 1861, S.H.C.

15. DuPont, *Letters*, 1:258; *O.R.N.*, 12:365.

16. Olmstead, *Memoirs*, p. 88; Sharf, *History*, p. 630; Charles H. Olmstead, Letter, November 11, 1862, S.H.C.; L. W. Landershine, Diary, typescript p. 2, Fort Pulaski Papers Microfilm, S.H.C.; Marchand, *Charleston Blockade*, p. 100.

17. *O.R.N.*, 12:362-365; Sharf, *History*, pp. 628-630; Charles C. Jones, *The Life and Services of Commodore Josiah Tattnall* (Savannah: Morning News Steam Printing House, 1878), pp. 130, 135; Julian, *C.W.T.I.*, 9:12; Freeman, *Lee*, 1:609.

   On February 28, 1861, Governor Brown accepted Commodore Josiah Tattnall's offer of service to his native state by appointing him senior flag-officer of the Navy of Georgia. The following month Tattnall was named commander in the Provisional Navy of the Confederate States and placed in charge of whatever navy did or might exist in the South Carolina and Georgia waters. Tattnall's task was "akin to making bricks without straw."

   He eventually formed a "mosquito fleet" by arming river steamers and few small tugs which were found along Savannah's wharves. The sidewheel steamer *Savannah*, armed with a single 32-pounder, was Tattnall's flagship. The sidewheel steamer *Huntress*, iron screw tug *Lady Davis*, sidewheel steamers *Resolute* and *Sampson*, each armed with one or two 32-pounder smooth bores or rifled guns made up the remainder of the fleet.

   With these vessels he met and quickly retired from DuPont's force which took Port Royal Sound on November 7, 1861. Tattnall was then ordered to distribute his boats among sounds near the mouth of the Savannah River to assist blockade runners expected from Great Britain, but the number of inlets vastly exceeded the number of vessels and he apparently made no such disposition.

   Second Lieutenant John N. Maffit commanded the *Savannah*, Tattnall's flag ship. Second Lieutenant J. Pembroke Jones commanded the *Resolute*; Lieutenant J. Kennard, the *Sampson*; Second Lieutenant J. Rutledge, the *Lady Davis*. Other vessels in the fleet were the *Ida* and the *Bartow*. (Jones, *Tattnall*, p. 135.)

18. Gillmore, *Siege*, p. 57; *O.R.*, 6:149, 150; 193-195; Herbert E. Barber and Allen R. Gann, *History of the Savannah District U.S. Army Corps of Engineers 1829-1989* (Savannah: United States Army Corps of Engineers, 1989), p. 219.

19. For a discussion of the development of rifled artillery see the Appendix.

20. Ripley, *Artillery*, pp. 109-110, 114, 291; Gillmore, *Siege*, p. 80.

21. Ripley, *Artillery*, pp. 17-19.

22. Ripley, *Artillery*, pp. 300-301; Gillmore, *Siege*, p. 96.
   Note that in the text Gillmore incorrectly refers to a figure "E" when explaining the shell; the correct diagram is labeled "D."

23. Gillmore, *Siege*, pp. 79-80; Ripley, *Artillery*, p. 300.

24. *O.R.*, 6:195-196; Sherman, *R.C.S.*, p. 297.

25. *O.R.*, 6:150, 193.

26. *O.R.*, 6:192-193.
   As early as October, 1861, during the preparations for the Port Royal expedition, Sherman had complained to DuPont that he had "whole regiments who do not know how to shoulder a musket, let alone firing one." (DuPont, *Letters*, 1:181.)

27. Sherman, *R.C.S.*, p. 297; *O.R.*, 6:193.

28. DuPont, *Letters*, 1:282.

29. DuPont, *Letters*, 1:264.

30. *O.R.N.*, 12:382-386.

31. *O.R.N.*, 12:382, 384-386.

32. DuPont, *Letters*, 1:271.

33. *O.R.N.*, 12:395-397.
   The fort on Green Island contained one 10-inch rifled gun, one 10-inch columbiad, two 8-inch columbiads, two 42-pounder guns and four 32-pounder guns. (*O.R.*, 6:333.)

34. Edwin W. Keen, Letter, December 20, 1861, U.S.A.M.H.I.

35. These batteries were armed with seven 32-pounders, one 42-pounder, and one 8-inch rifled gun. (Mercer, Diary, p. 4, S.H.C.)

36. This fort was armed with one 8-inch columbiad and three 18-pounder guns. (*O.R.*, 6:333.)

37. Fort Jackson was armed with one 32-pounder rifled naval gun, five 32-pounder navy guns, and three 19-pounder guns. (*O.R.*, 6:333.)

38. *O.R.*, 6:196-199, 203; *O.R.A.* (Washington, D.C.: Government Printing Office, 1891-1895), plate LXX; T. W. Sherman to L. Thomas, February 8, 1862, R.G. 94 185-S-1862, N.A.

39. *O.R.*, 6:204; *O.R.A.*, plate LXX.

40. Frederick H. Dyer, *A Compendium of the War of the Rebellion*. 2 vols. (Dayton: Morningside Bookshop, 1978), 2:1009; Stephen Walkley, *History of the Seventh Connecticut Volunteer Infantry* (Southington: n.p., 1896), pp. 38, 41; Sherman, *R.C.S.*, pp. 294-295; *O.R.*, 6:1, 207-208; *O.R.N.*, 12:415-416; DuPont, *Letters*, 1:272.

41. T. W. Sherman to L. Thomas, December 20, 1861, R.G. 94 1557-S-1861, N.A.
   This document is a detailed list of all tools, equipment, forges, extra carriages, horses, fuses, shells, shot, powder, water buckets, lanyards, etc., necessary for a land siege.

42. *O.R.N.*, 12:415-416.
   The steel-clad *Fingal* had been built in Great Britain and purchased by the Confederate government. She slipped through DuPont's blockade vessels and arrived in Savannah on November 13, 1861. She brought to Savannah 14,000 Enfield rifles, 1,000,000 ball cartridges, 2,000,000 percussion caps, 3,000 cavalry sabers, clothing, medical supplies, 1,000 short rifles with cutlass bayonets for the navy, 500 navy revolvers, 1,000,000 rounds of ammunition for the navy guns, 400 barrels of cannon powder, and four pieces of artillery. She was then loaded with cotton and ready to depart on December 20. Unable to leave, she was converted into the ironclad *Atlanta* by mid-1862, too late to effect operations against Fort Pulaski. (*O.R.*, 6:318; James D. Bullock, *The Secret Service of the Confederate States in Europe*, 2 vols. [New York: Thomas Yoseloff, 1959], 1:112, 127; William N. Still, *Iron Afloat*, [Nashville: Vanderbilt University Press, 1971], pp. 128-129.)

43. Freeman, *Lee*, 1:611; Charles H. Olmstead, Letter, November 21, 1861, S.H.C.; Olmstead, *G.H.Q.*, 1:102; Olmstead, *Memoirs*, pp. 90-91.
   On February 19, a 120-foot length of raft drifted down the Savannah River. Made of timbers fourteen inches square and forty feet long, each section was 25 timbers wide. Federal engineers on Tybee salvaged it for future gun platforms. (*O.R.N.*, 12:500.)

44. *O.R.*, 6:319, 320, 321, 327.
   Wright held a seat in the Confederate Congress and would be absent in early February; he resigned his commission on February 14, 1862. Lieutenant Colonel Lewis J. Parr took command of the regiment. [Robert K. Krick, *Lee's Colonels*, 2nd ed., (Dayton: Press of Morningside Bookshop, 1984), pp. 256, 353.]

45. Robert E. Lee, *Recollections and Letters of General Robert E. Lee* (New York: Doubleday, Page & Company, 1904), pp. 54-55; Freeman, *Lee*, 1:609-610, 614; DuPont, *Letters*, 1:lxxiii; Clifford Dowdey and Louis H. Manarin, ed. *The Wartime Papers of R. E. Lee* (Boston: Little, Brown and Company, 1961), p. 82.

46. *O.R.*, 6:327; Lee, *Recollections*, p. 54; Dowdy and Manarin, *Papers*, p. 89; Freeman, *Lee*, 1:615.

47. *O.R.*, 6:327.

48. Freeman, *Lee*, 1:615; Charles H. Olmstead, Letter, November 25, 1861, S.H.C.; *O.R.*, 6:33.

49. *O.R.*, 6:332-333.

50. Charles H. Olmstead, Letter, November 20, 1861, S.H.C.; Olmstead, *Memoirs*, p. 91; John C. Pemberton, *Pemberton Defender of Vicksburg* (Chapel Hill: The University of North Carolina Press, 1942), p. 27.

51. L. W. Landershine, Diary, typescript, pp. 1-2, Fort Pulaski Papers Microfilm, S.H.C.; Schoonmaker, Papers, pp. 39-40, L.C.

52. *O.R.*, 6:345, 347-348; A. L. Long, "Seacoast Defenses of South Carolina and Georgia," *Southern Historical Society Papers*, 1 (January-June, 1876):106.

53. *O.R.*, 6:351.

54. Sharf, *History*, pp. 630-631; Jones, *Tattnall*, p. 143.

55. *O.R.*, 6:265, 362.

56. Sharf, *History*, p. 632.

57. Savannah *Daily Morning News*, January 1 and 13, 1862; Derry, *Georgia*, pp. 21-23; Olmstead, *Memoirs*, pp. 82, 89.

58. Olmstead, *Memoirs*, p. 96.

59. Horace Porter, Letter, January 16, 1862, L.C.; Marchand, *Confederate Blockade*, p. 107; Woodford, Letter, January 26, 1862, C.H.S.; Schoonmaker, Papers, pp. 31-32, L.C.
    By the time General Benham had arrived in the department, the story had developed that the gun had been a Blakely. (Henry W. Benham, "U.S.Army Generals' Reports of Civil War Service, 1864-1887," 10:f. 503, N.A.)

60. L. W. Landershine, Diary, January 7, 1862, Fort Pulaski Collection Microfilm, S.H.C.

61. Gustavus V. Fox, *Confidential Correspondence of Gustavus Vasa Fox*, ed. Robert M. Thompson and Richard Wainwright, 2 vols. (New York: Naval History Society, 1918), 1:90-93.

62. *O.R.N.*, 12:443; Cornelius M. Schoonmaker, Papers, p. 26, L.C.
    Percival Drayton was the brother of Confederate Brigadier General Thomas Drayton, commander of the southern-most military district in South Carolina.

63. T. W. Sherman to L. Thomas, December 30, 1861, R.G. 94 1623-S-1861, N.A.; Sherman, *R.C.S.*, pp. 295-296.

64. Rowena Reed, *Combined Operations in the Civil War* (Annapolis: Naval Institute Press, 1978), pp. 9-10, 44; *O.R.*, 6:209.
    On December 28, DuPont wrote a friend, William Whetten, that criticism of Sherman was unjustified. Although Savannah might have been taken immediately after Port Royal fell, it could not have been held. DuPont felt that Sherman had insufficient men to have accomplished more than he had, especially considering the sorry state of most of his volunteer troops. (DuPont, *Letters*, 1:291-294.)

65. *O.R.*, 6:211.

66. *O.R.*, 6:214; R.G. 94 1623-S-1861 T. W. Sherman to L. Thomas, December 30, 1861, N.A.

_C_hapter 3

1. *O.R.N.*, 12:460-461.

2. Fox, *Correspondence*, 1:94-96.

3. Alonzo Williams, *The Investment of Fort Pulaski* (Providence: Personal Narratives Rhode Island Soldiers and Sailors Historical Society, 1889), p. 12-14.

4. Williams, *Investment*, pp. 15-17, Wilson, *Old Flag*, 1:79-80; Sherman, *R.C.S.*, p. 299.

5. *O.R.*, 6:85, 141, 215-216; Wilson, *Old Flag*, 1:80.

6. Williams, *Investment*, pp. 18-20; *O.R.*, 6:141, 147, 216; *O.R.*, 14:320; *O.R.N.*, 12:478; Gillmore, *Siege*, pp. 11-12; Wilson, *Old Flag*, 1:80-81; Sherman, *R.C.S.*, p. 299.

7. *O.R.N.*, 12:468.
   Isaac Tattnall, not to be confused with the commodore, had an excellent knowledge of the Georgia coastal waterways and he served DuPont usefully in the South Atlantic Blockading Squadron. (DuPont, *Letters*, 1:306, fn. 21.)

8. *O.R.*, 14:324-325; *O.R.N.*, 12:469-470.

9. *O.R.N.*, 12:491-492; Thomas W. Sherman, "U.S. Army General's Report of Civil War Service, 1864-1887," 4:ff. 49-51, N.A.; Sherman, *R.C.S.*, pp.. 299-300.

10. *O.R.N.*, 12:485.
    In an interview with Surgeon George Andrew, Sherman indicated "he had been ready on the 16th of January for a movement on Savannah which could hardly have failed of satisfactory results, but the Navy Department was not prepared with the necessary transportation." (George C. Andrew, Papers, Typescript p. 37, H.L.)

11. *O.R.*, 6:219; *O.R.N.*, 12:491-493; Wilson, *Old Flag*, 1:83-84; Samuel Wolcott, Letter, January 12, 1862, in William Prince Collection, U.S.A.M.H.I.
    The New York *Evening Post* of January 24, 1862, headed a story "Savannah in Danger: Opening of a New Water Approach to the City" and revealed the discovery of a "new water course" by means of which "Savannah can be reached without passing Ft. Pulaski." The *Evening Post*, showing exemplary discretion, did not name the channel "for obvious reasons." DuPont requested a general order from the Navy Department to deal with the publication of such stories. DuPont later learned that a naval officer had sent a similar story, together with maps, to the Philadelphia *Daily Evening Bulletin*; DuPont ordered the officer home. (DuPont, *Letters*, 1:322, fn. 11; 322-323.)
    Sherman ordered the holding of all mail for two weeks to prevent plans for the ascent up the Savannah River from leaking out. (Adrian Terry, Letter, February 1, 1862, Y.U.L.)

12. *O.R.*, 6:151; *O.R.*, 14:320-321; Williams, *Investment*, pp. 22-23; Adrian Terry, Letter, January 3, 1862, Y.U.L.

13. Horace Porter, Letter, January 19, 1862, L.C.

14. Thomas W. Sherman, "U.S. Army General's Report of Civil War Service, 1864-1887," 4:ff. 49-51, N.A.; Sherman, *R.C.S.*, p. 299; *O.R.*, 6:219-220.

15. *O.R.N.*, 12:493-494; Savannah *Republican*, January 31, 1862.

16. Gillmore, *Siege*, p. 59.

17. *O.R.*, 6:367.

18. Freeman, *Lee*, 1:622; Dowdey and Manarin, *Papers*, pp. 103, 106; Lee, *Recollections*, pp. 60-61.
    His father, General Henry Lee, had been returning from the West Indies where he had gone for health reasons. He had landed at Cumberland Island and died a few days later. (Lee, *Recollections*, p. 60.)

19. Savannah *Republican*, January 10, 1862.

20. "George" to "My Dear Sister," Letter, January 12, 1862, Confederate Miscellany I, Emory University Library; L. W. Landershine, Diary, January 12, 1862, Fort Pulaski Papers Microfilm, S.H.C.

21. L. W. Landershine, Diary, January 13, 1862, Fort Pulaski Papers Microfilm, S.H.C.

22. L. W. Landershine, Diary, January 25, 1862, Fort Pulaski Papers Microfilm, S.H.C.; James M. Green, Letter, February 22, 1862, in Robert C. Ogden Papers, L.C.

23. Savannah, *Republican*, January 30, 1862; Hanleiter, Diary, January 19 and 21, 1862, D.U.

24. *O.R.N.*, 12:512; Dowdey and Manarin, *Papers*, p. 107; Freeman, *Lee*, 1:623-624; also see *O.R.*, 6:376, 379.

25. Savannah *Republican*, January 27, 1862.

26. *O.R.*, 6:83.
    Pending the finalization of plans about Savannah and Fort Pulaski, General Sherman had ordered that *"no mail whatever"* should leave for the North. By February 4 there were 31,000 pieces of mail piled there waiting to go. (Joseph R. Hawley, Letter, February 6, 1862, L.C.)

27. *O.R.*, 6:83; *O.R.N.*, 12:493-494, 524, 527; George C. Swathel, Diary, January 27 and 28, 1862, C.S.L.; L. W. Landershine, Diary, January 27, 1862, Fort Pulaski Papers Microfilm, S.H.C.; Montfort, *G.H.Q.*, 49:205; Savannah, *Republican*, January 28, 1862.
    Eventually, one mile of land and "submarine" telegraph wire would be removed. (*O.R.*, 6:141.)

28. *O.R.N.*, 12:494; *O.R.*, 14:321; L. W. Landershine, Diary, January 21 and 28, 1862, Fort Pulaski Papers Microfilm, S.H.C.

29. *O.R.N.*, 12:494.

30. *O.R.N.*, 12:494-495.

31. *O.R.*, 14:327-328; Sherman *R.C.S.*, p. 300.

32. Hanleiter, Diary, January 29, 1862, D.U; *O.R.N.*, 12:494; 523-525, 526-528; *O.R.*, 6:84; *O.R.*, 14:321; Savannah *Republican*, January 28 and 31, 1862; Jones, "Lessons," p. 4; Savannah *Daily Morning News*, January 29, 1862; Olmstead, *Memoirs*, p. 94; L. W. Landershine, Diary, January 28, 1862, Fort Pulaski Papers Microfilm, S.H.C.; Swathel, Diary, January 28, 1862, C.S.L.; Adrian H. Terry, Letter, February 2, 1862, Y.U.L.; Jones, *Tattnall*, p. 144.
    General Wright viewed the firing of Tattnall's fleet and concluded that batteries located where the gunboats were would cause danger, but not serious risk, to Confederate vessels supplying the fort. Wright felt that "the position from which to cut off communication between the fort and Savannah by way of the river must therefore be sought higher up." (*O.R.N.*, 12:523-525, 526-528; *O.R.*, 6:83-84.)

33. Thomas W. Sherman, "U.S. Army Generals' Reports of Civil War Service, 1864-1887," 4:f. 52, N.A.

34. Horace Porter, Letters, February 3 and 16, 1862, L.C.; Adrian Terry, Letter, January 25, 1862, Y.U.L.

35. T. W. Sherman to L. Thomas, February 8, 1862, R.G. 94 185-S-1862, N.A.

36. *O.R.*, 6:221.
    Sherman recognized the need to link the islands of his command and on January 8 requested that Cyrus W. Field be sent to join Tybee, Port Royal, St. Helena, and Otter Island by "electric cable." (T. W. Sherman to L. Thomas, January 8, 1862, R.G. 94 41-S-1862, N.A.)

37. *O.R.*, 6:2.

38. Sherman was coming under criticism in the newspapers for inaction. He and DuPont were purported to have frequent disagreements; such was alleged in the Philadelphia *Intelligencer*, to which Sherman responded in late January "the most friendly and cordial feelings and entire harmony of action" existed between the two men. DuPont, in a January 9 letter to a friend stated that "our relations, both official and personal, have never been other than most cordial." (DuPont, *Letters*, 1:313.)

39. *O.R.*, 6:224.

40. *O.R.*, 6:225.
    McClellan regarded the capture of Fort Pulaski and the closing of the Savannah River and its port city as extremely important. He regarded the occupation of Fernandina as desirable. He even felt that occupying St. Augustine "by way of an interlude" might be worthwhile. Sherman's emphasis, McClellan felt, should be in the direction of Charleston and he urged Sherman to concentrate his energies and enlarging forces in that direction. "To gain Fort Sumter and hold Charleston is a task well worthy of our greatest efforts and considerable sacrifice. That is the problem I would be glad to have you study. Some time must elapse before we can be in all respects ready to accomplish that purpose." (*O.R.*, 6:224.)

41. *O.R.*, 6:226.
    Sherman's request for 10,000 additional men was denied by McClellan. Again, McClellan recommended that Sherman reduce Fort Pulaski in preference to attempting to take Savannah.

42. Theodorick W. Montfort, "Rebel Lawyer: The Letters of Lt. Theodorick W. Montfort, 1861-1862," *G.H.Q.* 49 (1965):84; Savannah *Republican*, January 28, 1862; Jones *Tattnall*, p. 144.

43. Hanleiter, Diary, February 2, 1862, D.U.

44. Joseph R. Hawley, Letters, March 15 and 21, 1862, L.C.

45. George G. Lyons, Letter, February 23, 1862, N.Y.H.S.; Tredwell W. Remson, Letter, February 23, 1862, L.C.; Aaron H. Ingraham, Letter, March 14, 1862, N.Y.S.L.

46. James H. Wilson, Letter, February 20, 1862, in the James B. McPherson Papers, L.C.

47. *O.R.*, 6:85; *O.R.*, 14:328; *O.R.N.*, 12:505; Savannah *Republican*, January 31, 1862.

48. *O.R.N.*, 12:523.

49. *O.R.*, 14:321, 328-329; *O.R.*, 6:86, 151; Gillmore, *Siege*, p. 15.
    For Beard's maps, see *O.R.A.*, CXXXV-B, 5 & 6.

50. Horace Porter, Letter, February 3, 1862, L.C.

51. *O.R.*, 6:86.

52. *O.R.*, 6:374; *O.R.N.*, 12:505-506.

53. *O.R.*, 6:373, 374; *O.R.N.*, 12:495, 496-497.

54. Gillmore, *Siege*, p. 16; Montfort, *G.H.Q.*, 49:87.

55. Walkey, *7th Conn.*, p. 41; Henry C. Glines, Diary, February 1, 1862, Y.U.L.; Samuel Wolcott, Letter, February 15, 1862, William Prince Collection, U.S.A.M.H.I.

56. Alfred H. Terry, Letter, January 18, 1862, Y.U.L.
    Colonel Serrell, 1st New York Engineers, brought word from Washington, D.C. of Terry's nomination when he returned to Tybee, about April 1. (Adrian Terry, Letter, April 1, 1862, Y.U.L.)

57. Horace Porter, Letter, January 16, 1862, L.C.

58. Milton M. Woodford, Letter, January 26, 1862, C.H.S.

59. Adrian Terry, Letter, January 3, 1862 (added to on January 13, 1862), Y.U.L.; Horace Porter, Letter, January 16, 1862, L.C.

60. Horace Porter, Letter, January 16, 1862, L.C.

61. Alfred H. Terry, Letter, February 22, 1862, Y.U.L.
    Colonel Terry's brother Adrian also wrote home that "the banks of a creek about two miles from camp give us any number of oysters, which with rice, hominy and various preparations of flour called slap-jacks and soft-tommy & c. constitute the bulk of our provisions." (Adrian Terry, Letter, January 15, 1862, Y.U.L.

Surgeon George L. Andrew, with United States Sanitary Commission, recalled the acres of oyster banks. "A soldier waded out and fished up a chunk of oysters large as half a bushel measure and laid it on the coals. As soon as the hissing of escaping steam indicated that the oyster was in the right condition, the mass was turned over and most delicious of my experience in oyster eating was the result. By the time these had been disposed of, the mass was ready to be turned over again and soon nothing was visible by a heap of shells. (George L. Andrew, Papers, Typescript p. 30, H.L.)

62. Marchand, *Charleston Blockade*, pp. 98-100, 103-104.

63. Adrian Terry, Letter, January 15, 1862, Y.U.L.
    A map is included in the letter.

64. Joseph R. Hawley, Letters, February 15 and March 3, 1862; George L. Andrew, Papers, typescript p. 41, H.L.

65. Landershine, Diary, January 30, 31, February 1, 3, 1862, Fort Pulaski Papers Microfilm, S.H.C.; *O.R.*, 6:85; Savannah *Republican*, January 1, 1862.

66. Savannah *Daily Morning News*, February 8, 1862; Landershine, Diary, February 7 and 10, 1862, Fort Pulaski Papers Microfilm, S.H.C.; Marchand, *Charleston Blockade*, pp. 100, 101.

67. *O.R.*, 6:376.

68. *O.R.*, 6: 379-380, 390; Derry, *Georgia*, p. 84.

69. Hanleiter, Diary, February 10 and 22, 1862, D.U.

70. Landershine, Diary, February 11, 1862, Fort Pulaski Papers Microfilm, S.H.C.; Montfort, *G.H.Q.*, 49:88, 89, 93.

71. *O.R.*, 6:381-382, 384-385, 396-398.

72. *O.R.*, 6:386-387, 391, 396; Mercer, Diary, March 3, 1862, S.H.C.

73. Freeman, *Lee*, 1:625-626; see *O.R.*, 6:390, 393-394, 398, 400, 402-404, 406; Dowdey and Manarin, *Papers*, pp. 120-121.

74. *O.R.N.*, 12:498; Sherman, *R.C.S.*, p. 301.

75. *O.R.N.*, 12:498.

76. Charles K. Cadwell, *The Old Sixth Regiment, Its War Record, 1861-1865* (New Haven: Tuttle, Morehouse & Taylor, 1875), pp. 30-33; Martin Emmons, Letter, March 3, 1862, D.U.; George C. Swathel, Diary, C.S.L.; *Supplement to the Official Records of the Union and Confederate Armies*, Part I, vol. 1, p. 434.

77. T. W. Sherman to L. Thomas, December 15, 1861, R.G. 94 275-S-1862, N.A.

78. E. W. Serrell to A. Lincoln, April 13, 1861, with attached undated newspaper clipping, R.G. 94 1767-S-1861, N.A.

79. T. W. Sherman to L. Thomas, January 22, 1862, R.G. 94 182-S-1862, N.A.; Quincy A. Gillmore, "U.S. Army Generals' Reports of Civil War Service, 1864-1887," 9:f. 548, N.A.
    Gillmore would be confirmed as "Brigadier General of Volunteers" on April 28, 1862.

80. T. W. Sherman to G. B. McClellan, February 26, 1862, R.G. 94 275-S-1862, N.A.
    Gillmore was appointed on January 27, 1862. (*O.R.*, 14:324.)

81. Q. A. Gillmore to J. G. Totten, February 7, 1862, R.G. 94 275-S-1862 N.A.
    Commodore DuPont wrote a glowing recommendation to Senator John Sherman on May 2, 1862, urging the confirmation of Gillmore. "The public service will be benefited and a deserving and skillful officer rewarded by its confirmation [by the United States Senate]. (DuPont, *Letters*, 2:30.)

82. G. A. Gillmore to J. G. Totten, February 7, 1862, filed with 1491-S-1861, R.G. 94, 63-G-1862, N.A.

83. James H. Wilson, Letter, February 20, 1862, in James B. McPherson Papers, L.C.

84. New York Citizen, August 17, 1867.

85. New York *Citizen*, August 17, 1867; Wilson, *Old Flag*, 1:87.

Chapter 4

1. Quincy A. Gillmore, "U.S. Army Generals' Reports of Civil War Services, 1864-1887," 9:f. 548, N.A.; *O.R.*, 14:321-325; Gillmore, *Siege*, p. 13; Williams, *Investment*, p. 24; Quincy A. Gillmore, "Siege and Reduction of Fort Pulaski," *Battles and Leaders of the Civil War*, 4 vols. ed.Robert Underwood Johnson and Clarence Clough Buel (New York: The Century Co., 1888), 2:5; *O.R.* 6:141-143.

    Sherman later testified, "I become so tired of the delay that I gave General Viele orders to go into the river, and land, and erect the battery, whether the navy would assist him or not. (Sherman, *R.C.S.*, p. 301.)

2. Abraham J. Palmer, *The History of the Forty-eighth Regiment New York State volunteeers in the War for the Union. 1861-1865* (Brooklyn: Published by the Veteran Association of the Regiment, 1885), p. 28; James M. Nichols, *Perry's Saints or the Fighting Parson's Regiment in the War of the Rebellion* (Boston: D. Lothrop and Company, 1886), pp.77-78; Tredwell W. Remson, Letter, February 23, 1862, L.C.; Miscellaneous Civil War Papers #150, p. 5, S.H.C.; *O.R.*, 14:321.

3. Gillmore, *Siege*, pp. 15-16, Plate 1; Nichols, *Perry's Saints*, pp. 81-82; Palmer, *48th N.Y.*, p. 31; James M. Green, Letter, February 22, 1862, in Robert C. Ogden Papers, L.C.; Aaron H. Ingraham, Letter, February 2, 1862, N.Y.S.L.; Miscellaneous Civil War Papers #150, p. 8, S.H.C.; *O.R.*, 14:322, 329-331.

    Regimental historian Palmer, writing almost a quarter of a century later, remembered "Who that recalls that lugging of logs will not feel his shoulders ache to this very day?" (Palmer, *48th N.Y.*, p. 31.) Another member of the 48th New York recalled:

> Many of the boys here received injuries they will never recover [from]. Imagine a heavy pitch pine log about a foot in diameter and thirty feet long. Now there is standing along the opposite sides of it two lines of boys in blue. They stoop down and with the words ["]altogether *now*["] they rise with the log clasped in their arms and place it on their shoulders. With faces red from the lifting they march forward keeping step as best they can until some one suddenly steps in a depression in the ground and suddenly a weight which he cannot bear comes upon a comrade. The log rolls and tumbles to the ground: a squad of soldiers with torn blouses and scratched and bleeding hands and arms, with battered knees and wounded feet and toes is scattered around cursing crying and laughing. But after a few minutes rest the heavy burden is again lifted to the lame and aching shoulders and the tiresome march resumed until the log is thrown upon the pile at the landing. The shoulders ache now to think of this labor we endured day after day. (Miscellaneous Civil War Papers #150, p. 9, S.H.C.)

4. *O.R.*, 14:321.

5. Palmer, *48th N.Y.*, p. 32; Nichols, *Perry's Saints*, p. 82; *O.R.*, 6:141.

6. Williams, *Investment*, p. 33.

7. Miscellaneous Civil War Papers #150, p. 9, S.H.C.; Gillmore, *Siege*, pp. 16-17; Gillmore, *B&L*, 2:5.; *O.R.*, 14:325, 326-327, 330, 331.

8. Gillmore, *Siege*, p. 17; Gillmore, *B&L*, 2:5; *O.R.*, 6:143.

9. Williams, *Investment*, pp. 31-33; *O.R.*, 6:152; *O.R.*, 14:322, 331-333.

10. Marchand, *Charleston Blockade*, p. 102; Nichols, *Perry's Saints*, pp. 83-84; Palmer, *48th N.Y.*, p. 32; Miscellaneous Civil War Papers #150, p. 11, note, S.H.C.

11. Gillmore, *Siege*, p. 18; Miscellaneous Civil War Papers #150, pp. 10-11, S.H.C.; Williams, *Investment*, p. 34; *O.R.*, 6:143; *O.R.*, 14:326.

12. Gillmore, *Siege*, pp. 59-60; *O.R.*, 14:322; Horace Porter, Letter, February 16, 1862, L.C.

13. *O.R.*, 14:142, 326; Nichols, *Perry's Saints*, p. 85; James M. Green, Letter, February 22, 1862, in Robert C. Ogden Papers, L.C., *O.R.S.*, 1:435.

14. Gillmore, *Siege*, pp. 19-20, 60-61; Jones, pp. 221-222, L.C.; Williams, *Investment*, p. 35; Wilson, *Old Flag*, 1:84-85.

15. Williams, *Investment*, pp. 35, 37; *O.R.*, 14, 323; Gillmore, *Siege*, pp. 19-20, 60-61; Jones, pp. 221-222, L. C. Wilson, *Old Flag*, 1:84-85; Miscellaneous Civil War Papers #150, p. 11, S.H.C.; *O.R.*, 6:142.

16. *O.R.*, 14:326, 333; Palmer, *48th N.Y.*, p. 33.

17. Williams, *Investment*, p. 39; Gillmore, *Siege*, pp. 60-61; *O.R.N.*, 12:501.

18. Marchand, *Charleston Blockade*, p. 101.

19. *O.R.N.*, 12:501, 504, 654; Gillmore, *Siege*, p. 17; Joseph R. Hawley, Letter, March 3, 1862, L.C. Hawley's letter to his wife includes a diagrammatic map showing the site of the hulk.

20. Gillmore, *B&L*, 2:6; Landershine, Diary, February 14, 1862, Fort Pulaski Papers Microfilm, S.H.C.; Olmstead, *Memoirs*, p. 92; Gillmore, *Siege*, p. 20; *O.R.*, 6:144; *O.R.*, 14:323.
    Marchand, on Tybee Island, observed the "small steamer hugging the southern shore." The battery on Jones Island fired six shots, "but she escaped and anchored under the protection of Fort Pulaski." (Marchand, *Charleston Blockade*, pp. 105-106.)

21. *O.R.N.*, 12:500, 555, 556; *O.R.*, 6:90-91; DuPont, *Letters*, 1:330; Gillmore, *Siege*, pp. 20-21; Miscellaneous Civil War Papers #150, p. 12, S.H.C.; James H. Wilson, Letter, February 20, 1862, in James B. McPherson Papers, L.C.; Horace Porter, Letter, February 16, 1862, L.C.; Marchand, *Charleston Blockade*, p. 107; *O.R.*, 14:323; Olmstead, *G.H.Q.*, 1:101; Olmstead, *Memoirs*, p. 93; Landershine, Diary, February 14, 1862, Fort Pulaski Papers Microfilm, S.H.C.; DuPont, *Letters*, 1:308.

22. Marchand, *Charleston Blockade*, p. 103.

23. *O.R.*, 6:389.

24. Gillmore, *Siege*, pp. 21, 61-62; Jones, p. 222, L.C.; *O.R.*, 6:142, 143, 153, 389; *O.R.*, 14:323, 327; Nichols, *Perry's Saints*, pp. 86-87; Williams, *Investment*, pp. 41, 42.

25. Williams, *Investment*, pp. 45-47, 49.

26. Martin Emmons, Letter, April 16, 1862, D.U.

27. Jones, pp. 222-224, L.C.; Gillmore, *Siege*, pp. 21, 62; Gillmore, "U.S. Army Generals' Reports of Civil War Service," vol. 11:f. 550, N.A.; *O.R.*, 6:143, 146; *O.R.*, 14:323; Nichols, *Perry's Saints*, pp. 86-87; Williams, *Investment*, p. 42; Montfort, *G.H.Q.*, 49:93, 94, 95, 200, 202, 324, 325, 327.

28. Mercer, Diary, March 4, 1862, S.H.C.; Nichols, *Perry's Saints*, pp. 88-92, James M. Green, Letter, February 22, 1862, in Robert C. Ogden Papers, L.C.

29. T. W. Sherman to G. B. McClellan, February 23, 1862, Houghton Library, Harvard University; *O.R.*, 6:235.
    On February 16, DuPont had described for Sherman the force he would be using to take Fernandina; Sherman was "astonished at the number." (DuPont, *Letters*, 1:324.)

30. *O.R.*, 6:223-224; *O.R.N.*, 12:502-503, 504; DuPont, *Letters*, 1:328 fn. 17, p. 430; Milton F. Perry, *Infernal Machines* (Baton Rouge: Louisiana State University Press, 1965), p. 30.

31. T. W. Sherman to L. Thomas, February 15, 1862, R.G. 94 221-S-1862, N.A.

32. *O.R.N.*, 12:552-554.

33. Tredwell W. Remson, Letter, February 23, 1862, L.C.; Laurin B. Drake, Letter, February 23, 1862, in David Howell Collection, U.S.A.M.H.I.; Landershine, Diary, February 22, 1862, Fort Pulaski Papers Microfilm, S.H.C.; Montfort, *G.H.Q.*, 49:200; Hanleiter, Diary, February 22, 1862, D.U; Marchand, *Charleston Blockade*, p. 109.

34. Jones, "Lessons," pp. 5-6.

35. Jones, "Lessons," p. 6; Jones, L.C., pp. 230-232; Gillmore, *Siege*, p. 67; *O.R.*, 6:149; Williams, *Investment*, pp. 10-11; Deary, *Georgia*, p. 88.

36. *O.R.*, 6:394.

37. *O.R.*, 6:393-394.

38. Lee, *Recollections*, pp. 64-65.

39. Sharf, *History*, pp. 636-637, *O.R.N.*, 12:842; Jones, *Tattnall*, pp. 145-147.

40. Olmstead, *Memoirs*, p. 94.

41. *O.R.*, 6:2; DuPont *Letters*, 1:344.
    On March 1, Amelia and Cumberland Islands were abandoned; Captain James S. Blalin's Company A, 26th Georgia, was moved to Savannah. (Derry, *Georgia*, p. 86.)

42. *O.R.*, 6:235-236; DuPont, *Letters*, 1:344 fn. 3; Fox, *Correspondence*, 1:108-109.

43. Fox, *Correspondence*, 1:110.

44. Ibid.

45. T. W. Sherman to L. Thomas, December 23, 1861, R.G. 94 1545-S-1861, N.A.; *O.R.*, 6:237.
    Sherman had requested on January 9, 1862, that two additional companies of the 3rd Rhode Island Volunteers, being recruited as heavy artillery, be sent to him as field (light) artillery batteries, each equipped with six guns. The regimental commander concurred. (T. W. Sherman to L. Thomas, January 9, 1862, R.G. 94 58-S-1862, N.A.)
    Sherman was outraged that the five light draught steamers he had been asking for since November 15, 1861, had not arrived, although he knew that they had left New York long ago. Further, he had not received a single boat or wagon. Until these arrived, he added it would be "impracticable to move away from the island coast any large force." (T. W. Sherman to L. Thomas, February 5, 1862, R.G. 94 189-S-1862, N.A.)

46. *O.R.*, 6:237; General Order No. 5, John E. Bryant Papers, D.U.; John E. Bryant, Letter, March 14, 1862, D.U.

47. *O.R.*, 6:97-100.

48. E. L. Viele to Hiram Birney, Letter, March 12, 1862, Hiram Birney Papers, H. L.
    Viele was unsuccessful and his wife joined him on Daufuskie shortly thereafter.

49. *O.R.N.*, 12:641, 654; Levi Pinner, Letter, March 22, 1862, The South Caroliniana Library; Charles P. Lord, Letter, March 25, 1862, Duke University Library; Landershine, Diary, March 19, 1862, Fort Pulaski Papers Microfilm, S.H.C.; Montfort, *G.H.Q.*, 49:210.

50. George C. Swathel, Diary, C.S.L.

51. Martin Emmons, Letter, March 3, 1862, Duke University Library.

52. Cadwell, *Sixth Regiment*, pp. 34-35; *O.R.*, 6:144.

53. *O.R.*, 6:144.

54. Mercer, Diary, March 3, 1862, S.H.C.

55. Lee, *Recollections*, p. 66.

56. *O.R.*, 6:400-402; Freeman, *Lee*, 1:628.

57. Mercer, Diary, March 3, 10, 14, 1863, S.H.C.; Hanleiter, Diary, March 10, 1862, D.U.

58. Jones, *Tattnall*, p. 148.

59. Mercer, Diary, March 23 and 27, 1863, S.H.C.; Hanleiter, Diary, March 24, 1862, D.U.; *O.R.N.*, 12:663, 664; DuPont, *Letters*, 1:391.

60. *O.R.*, 6:407, 414; Guinn "Coastal Defense," p. 351.
    On March 19, 1862, Trapier was relieved of command and sent to Decatur, Alabama, to report to General Albert S. Johnston. Colonel William S. Dilworth was assigned temporary command of the Department of Middle and Eastern Florida. (*O.R.*, 6:413.)

61. Landershine, Diary, March 15, 1862, Fort Pulaski Papers Microfilm, S.H.C.

62. Mercer, Diary, March 19 and 20, 1862, S.H.C.; Jones, *Tattnall*, pp. 150-151.

63. *O.R.N.*, 12:641-642, 652.

64. *O.R.N.*, 12:654, 662-663, 669-670, including a sketch of the ironclad, 674; Cadwell, *Sixth Regiment*, p. 34; Dupont, *Letters*, 1:314, 394, 396; *O.R.*, 6:112-113; Charles G. Halpine, Letter, April 6, 1862, H.L.; *O.R.*, 6:112.
    On March 15, General Mercer had authorized Captain Pritchard to go into Savannah and "offer to construct a floating [ironclad] battery." (Mercer, Diary, March 15, 1862, S.H.C.)
    The ironclad was built on the hull of the *Fingal*.

65. *O.R.N.*, 12:687-688; DuPont, *Letters*, 1:394.

66. *O.R.*, 6:245.

67. *O.R.*, 6:245-247.
    Between January 31 and February 10, twelve 13-inch siege mortars and beds were shipped from the New York Arsenal. (J. W. Ripley to L. Thomas, February 20, 1862, R.G. 94 202-S-1862, N.A.)

68. *O.R.*, 6:247.

69. *O.R.*, 6:248.
    When DuPont learned of Hunter's appointment, he wrote his wife (March 23): "I shall regret Sherman; his peculiarities I am now accustomed to—his integrity, officer-like qualities, and manly firmness, on the whole, are not to be questioned." (DuPont, *Letters*, 1:385.)

70. *O.R.*, 6:253-254.

71. *O.R.*, 6:254.

72. *O.R.*, 6:255.

Chapter 5

1. Quincy A. Gillmore, "U.S. Army Generals' Reports of Civil War Service, 1864-1887," 11:f. 549, N.A.; *O.R.*, 6:146, 152; *O.R.*, 14:323; Jones, pp. 224-225, L.C.; Gillmore, *B&L*, 2:2; Charles P. Lord, Letter, April 13, 1862, D.U.; Alfred H. Terry, Letter, February 22, 1862, Y.U.L.

2. Gillmore, *Siege*, p. 23; Walkey, *7th Conn.*, p. 41.

3. Gillmore, *Siege*, pp. 25-26; Thomas B. Brooks, Letter, February 28, 1862, Fort Pulaski Papers Microfilm, S.H.C.; *O.R.*, 14, 324.

4. Gillmore, *Siege*, pp. 62-63; Joseph R. Hawley, Letter, March 3, 1862, L.C.

5. Gillmore, *Siege*, p. 64.

6. Henry C. Glines, Diary, February 21, 22 and 25, 1862, Y.U.L.

7. Gillmore, *Siege*, pp. 25, 63; Joseph R. Hawley, Letter, March 3, 1862, L.C.

8. Gillmore, *Siege*, pp. 63-64.

9. Olmstead, *Memoirs*, p. 95.

10. Horace Porter, Letter, March 2, 1862, L.C.

11. Henry W. Benham, "U.S. Army Generals' Reports of Civil War Service, 1864-1887," 10:ff. 495-498, N.A.

   Benham would persist in referring to Gillmore's rank as "captain" throughout all of his writings about this period of time.

   In the letters which survive, Terry makes no mention of Porter's conversation with Gillmore.

12. New York *Citizen*, August 17, 1867.

   When Gillmore saw the newspaper article, he wrote Lieutenant Thomas B. Brooks, of Company A, 1st New York Volunteer Engineers, who had served Gillmore as his sole assistant engineer on Tybee Island and later as major and aide de camp on Gillmore's staff in South Carolina, to prove "that you were with me when I selected the positions for all the batteries on Goats Point; that my object and aim was to get these batteries and all others as near Ft. Pulaski as possible, and in order to get nearer to the Fort than Tybee to be examined." Gillmore had written Porter for a disclaimer; he dismissed Wilson's and O'Rorke's comments since these two men were not under Gillmore's command until after the battery sites had been selected. (Quincy A. Gillmore, Letter August 23, 1867, in Thomas R. Brooks Papers in Fort Pulaski Microfilm Collection, S.H.C.)

13. A. B. Ely, "Letter to Editors of Boston *Daily Advertiser*," in Henry W. Benham, "U.S. Army Generals' Reports of Civil War Service, 1864-1887," 10:ff. 658-659, N.A.

14. Joseph R. Hawley, Letter, March 5, 1862, L.C.

   Lieutenant Thomas B. Brooks, of the 1st New York Volunteer Engineers provides details of the construction of the platforms, rivetting, embrasures, magazines, and splinter proofs in Gillmore, *Siege*, pp. 81-95 and plate 4.

15. Joseph R. Hawley, Letter, March 3, 1862, L.C.; Samuel Wolcott, Letter, March 3, 1862, William Prince Collection, U.S.A.M.H.I.

16. Henry C. Glines, Diary, March 7, 10, 11, 12 and 13, 1862, Y.U.L.

17. Milton M. Woodford, Letter, March 9, 1862, C.H.S.

18. Milton M. Woodford, Letter, March 10, 1862, C.H.S.

19. Henry C. Glines, Letter, March 10, 1862, Y.U.L.

20. Joseph R. Hawley, Letter, March 10, 1862, L.C.; Henry C. Glines, Diary, March 15, 18 and 19, 1862, Y.U.L.

21. Captain Charles E. Palmer wrote a friend: "I am again with the regiment, which happy reunion took place nearly a month ago, though it seems scarcely a week. We hold up our hands in silent praise. The mental suffering endured under the rule of King Major Gardiner for the four months we were under his supervision is impossible to express on paper. I will say he is a jackanapes, & if I ever get home I will amuse you of an evening by telling some of his freaks." (Charles E. Palmer, Letter, April 5, 1862, Paper, G.H.S.)

22. Adrian Terry, Letter, March 19, 1862, Y.U.L.

23. Horace Porter, Letter, March 20, 1862, L.C.

24. Horace Porter had commented on Shunk's problems as early as January 16, 1862. (Horace Porter, Letter, January 16, 1862, Y.U.L.)

25. Joseph R. Hawley, Letter, March 20, 1862, L.C.

26. Henry C. Glines, Diary, March 21 and 22, 1862, Y.U.L.; Joseph R. Hawley, Letter, March 21, 1862, L.C.

27. Joseph R. Hawley, Letter, March 21, 1862, L.C.; Henry C. Glines, Diary, March 22, 1862, Y.U.L.

28. Olmstead, *G.H.Q.*, 1:102.

29. Savannah *Republican*, March 19, 1862.

30. Landershine, Diary, March 22, 1862, Fort Pulaski Papers Microfilm, S.H.C.

31. Henry C. Glines, Diary, March 24 and 28, 1862, Y.U.L.

32. Adrian Terry, Letter, March 24, 1862, Y.U.L.; *O.R.N.*, 12:704; DuPont, *Letters*, 1:400.

33. *O.R.*, 6:122-123; George A. Mercer, Diary, April 6, 1862, S.H.C.; Savannah *Republican*, April 1 and 2, 1862; Horace Porter, Letter, April 2, 1862.

34. *O.R.*, 6:121-122, *O.R.N.*, 12:700.

35. Savannah *Republican*, April 1, 1862; Savannah *Daily Morning News*, April 1, 1862; M. J. Solomon, Scrapbook, D.U., p. 163; George A. Mercer, Diary, April 6, S.H.C.
    On April 2, Federals landed on Skidaway Island. Men of the Georgia Hussars (Captain W. H. Wiltberger, Company D, 2nd Battalion Georgia Cavalry) went forward to ascertain the state of affairs and found the island had been left abandoned. (Hanleiter, Diary, April 2, 1862, D.U.)

36. *O.R.*, 6:120-121.

37. Samuel Wolcott, Letter, March 30, 1862, William Prince Collection, U.S.A.M.H.I.

38. Samuel Wolcott, Letter, March 30, 1862, William Prince Collection, U.S.A.M.H.I.

39. Montfort, *G.H.Q.*, 49:214.

40. Landershine, Diary, April 2, 1862, S.H.C.

Chapter 6

1. Joseph R. Hawley, Letter, March 21, 1862, L.C.

2. Charles E. Palmer, Letter, April 5, 1862, G.H.S.

3. Adrian Terry, Letter, April 1, 1862, Y.U.L.

4. Henry W. Benham, "U.S. Army Generals' Reports of Civil War Service, 1864-1887," 10: f. 495 and Appendix A, f. 634, N.A.; Charles G. Halpine, Letter, March 29, 1862, H.L.
   Halpine found himself "squire of dames" to Mrs. General Viele and Mrs. Col. Serrell as well as to "a very pretty little innocent young thing—Miss Hinks" who was Mrs. Serrell's guest. (Charles G. Halpine, Letter, March 29, 1862, H.L.)

5. *O.R.*, 6:254, 257; Charles G. Halpine, Letter, March 31, 1862, H.L.

6. *O.R.*, 6:258; Charles G. Halpine, Letter, March 31, 1862, H.L.

7. DuPont, *Letters*, 1:400.

8. Fox, *Correspondence*, 1:117; DuPont, *Letters*, 1:396.

9. DuPont, *Letters*, 1:396, 397.

   On April 3, Sherman wrote DuPont: "I am highly gratified with your good will and kind feelings and shall ever remember them, but you must indeed excuse [me] from any demonstration whatever, whether dinner or anything else. I really am not in that happy state of mind to satisfy what is due to your kind and generous thoughts and feelings.

   "You know that I told you last winter that I did not know what they meant if it was not to ruin me. They are determined to do it, I should suppose." (DuPont, *Letters*, 1:398.)

10. Horace Porter, Letter, April 2, 1862, L.C.

11. DuPont, *Letters*, 1:399-400; New York *Times*, April 14, 1862.

12. *O.R.*, 6:259; Henry W. Benham, "U.S. Army Generals' Reports of Civil War Service, 1864-1887," 10:f. 495, N.A.; Quincy A. Gillmore, "U.S. Army Generals' Reports of Civil War Service, 1864-1887," vol. 11:f. 551, N.A.

13. *O.R.*, 6:259-260; Henry W. Benham, "U.S. Army Generals' Reports of Civil War Service, 1864-1887," 10:f. 495, N.A.

14. *O.R.*, 6:259-260.

15. *O.R.*, 6:146; Henry C. Glines, Diary, April 1, 1862, Y.U.L.

16. Henry C. Glines, Diary, April 2 and 3, 1862, Y.U.L.; Horace Porter, Letter, April 2, 1862, L.C.

17. Landershine, Diary, April 4, 1862, Fort Pulaski Papers Microfilm, S.H.C.

   Gillmore later reported that after the fort surrendered, the Confederates told him that they knew the specific site of two batteries—Sherman and Burnside. (*O.R.*, 6:158.)

18. Montfort, *G.H.Q.*, 49:324-325.

19. Landershine, Diary, April 6, 1862, Fort Pulaski Papers Microfilm, S.H.C.; Montfort, *G.H.Q.*, 49:328.

20. DuPont, *Letters*, 1:400; Landershine, Diary, April 5, 1862, Fort Pulaski Papers Microfilm, S.H.C.; *O.R.*, 6:120-121, 154, 262; *O.R.N.*, 12:700.

21. *O.R.*, 6:260, 262, 265.

22. *O.R.N.*, 12:704.

23. Fox, *Correspondence*, 1:116-117; New York *Times*, April 14, 1862.

24. *O.R.N.*, 12:713, 718.

25. Charles P. Lord, Letters, April 8 and 13, 1862, D.U.; Henry C. Glines, Diary, April 4 and 5, 1862, Y.U.L.; New York *Times*, April 14, 1862.

26. George L. Andrew, Papers, Typescript p. 52, H.L.

27. *O.R.*, 6:263; D. Hunter to L. Thomas, April 6, 1862, R.G. 94 475-S-1862, N.A.

28. *O.R.*, 6:260, 261.

29. *O.R.*, 6:136, 142, 159, 261.

   Major Oliver T. Beard, in command of Battery Hamilton on Bird Island, had made a reconnaissance of Long Island. He located a site suitable for a land battery about one and one-half miles from Fort Pulaski. The site, protected from observation from the fort by large clump of tall cane, consisted of a strip thirty yards wide. (*O.R.*, 6:261.)

First Lieutenant James H. Wilson visited Turtle Island and had located a battery site 2 1/8 miles from the fort. The distance from a suitable landing place on the Wright River, across the marsh, would be five hundred yards. The labor would be "exceedingly heavy" and the difficulties would exceed anything experienced thus far on Tybee Island. (*O.R.*, 6:262.)

Maps were included with both reports, were not published with the reports, and are not included in the microfilm edition of the *Letters Received by the Office of the Adjutant General (Main Series) 1861-1870.*

On April 4, Benham directed Viele to begin preparations to construct a four gun battery on Long Island. He wanted the battery completed in less than eight days. Viele immediately agreed and planned to use a 10-inch and an 8-inch mortar which he had available; Benham had offered four columbiads, two each of similar bore. (*O.R.*, 6:264-265.)

30. New York *Times*, April 14 and 20, 1862; *O.R.*, 6:135-137.

31. Landershine, Diary, April 9, 1862, Fort Pulaski Papers Microfilm, S.H.C.

32. *O.R.N.*, 12:717, 718; Charles G. Halpine, Letter, April 6, 1862, H.L.; New York *Times*, April 14, 1862; DuPont, *Letters*, 1:405.

DuPont had a few light moments during these last few days of the siege. On April 6, he wrote his wife, "fortunately now and then something ludicrous occurs which keeps us up by a hearty laugh. The last was the arrival of Mrs. General Viele—a *fast* New York woman and a habitué of Newport, etc.—who suddenly appears here in the *Atlantic* and rushes over to Daufuskie with high notions of a general's "headquarters," no doubt expecting chasseurs "a la porte" and so on; finds herself on a mud bank, with a trunk as large as a small cottage, two children, and a French maid; looks around for a flashy staff of officers and discovers a few forlorn individuals quite out at the elbows, whose principal costume consists of fishermen's boots, up over the knees and covered with awful-looking blue greasy mud. The only thing showing life and animation being the sand flies, at this season the avant-garde of the mosquitoes." (DuPont, *Letters*, 1:405.)

33. *O.R.N.*, 12:721.

34. Henry C. Glines, Diary, April 7 & 8, 1862, Y.U.L.

35. Henry C. Glines, Diary, April 7 and 8, 1862, Y.U.L.; Charles G. Halpine, Letter, April 8, 1862, H.L.

36. New York *Times*, April 19, 1862; *O.R.*, 6:266; R.G. 94 475-S-1862 D. Hunter to L. Thomas, April 6, 1862, N.A.; Charles G. Halpine, Letter, April 6, 1862, H.L.

37. D. Hunter to J. W. Ripley, April 7, 1862, R.G. 94 493-S-1862, N.A.; Horace Porter, Letter, April 2, 1862, L.C.

38. Gillmore, *B&L*, 2:7; Gillmore, *Siege*, p. 64; Walkey, *7th Conn.*, pp. 43-44.

39. Milton M. Woodford, Letter, April 17, 1862, C.H.S.

40. George L. Andrew, Papers, Typescript p. 53, H.L.

41. Henry W. Benham, "U.S. Army Generals' Reports of Civil War Service, 1864-1887," vol. 10:ff. 497-498, N.A.; Gillmore, *Siege*, pp. 57-58; New York *Times*, April 19, 1862; Joseph R. Hawley, Letter, March 21, 1862, L.C.

The officers staffing each battery are listed in the Gillmore's *Siege and Reduction of Fort Pulaski.*

42. Gillmore, *Siege*, pp. 23-24.

43. Gillmore, *Siege*, pp. 23-24, 27; New York *Times*, April 19, 1862.

44. Gillmore, *Siege*, p. 26.

45. *O.R.*, 6:156-157; New York *Times*, April 20, 1862; Gillmore, *B&L*, 2:7.

46. DuPont, *Letters*, 1:409; Henry W. Benham, "U.S. Army Generals' Reports of Civil War Service, 1864-1887," vol. 10:ff. 498-499, N.A.; Horace Porter, Letter, April 17, 1862, L.C.

Chapter 7

1. Landershine, Diary, April 10, 1862, Fort Pulaski Papers Microfilm, S.H.C.; Olmstead *G.H.Q.*, 1:102-103.

2. Landershine, Diary, April 10, 1862, Fort Pulaski Papers Microfilm, S.H.C.

3. Wilson, *Old Flag*, 1:88.

4. *O.R.*, 6:134-135.

5. *O.R.*, 6:134-135; Wilson, *Old Flag*, 1:88-89; Olmstead, *G.H.Q.*, 1:103; Charles H. Olmstead, Report, April 12, 1862, Fort Pulaski National Monument; Landershine, Diary, April 10, 1862, Fort Pulaski Papers Microfilm, S.H.C.
   Landershine says Wilson was met by Lieutenant Rowland and Sergeant Boyd. (Landershine, Diary, April 10, 1862, Fort Pulaski Papers Microfilm, S.H.C.)

6. Olmstead, *Memoirs*, p. 96; Landershine, Diary, April 10, 1862, Fort Pulaski Papers Microfilm, S.H.C.

7. New York *Times*, April 19, 1862.

8. Wilson, *Old Flag*, 1:87-88; *O.R.*, 6:145, 146; Walkey, *7th Conn.*, p. 44; Horace Porter, Letter, April 11 and 17, 1862, L.C.; Olmstead, *Memoirs*, p. 96; DuPont, *Letters*, 1:415; New York *Times*, April 19, 1862; Charles H. Olmstead, Letter, April 11, 1862, Fort Pulaski National Monument.

9. Horace Porter, Letter, April 17, 1862, L.C.

10. Horace Porter, Letter, April 17, 1862, L.C.; *O.R.*, 6:145; Gillmore, *Siege*, pp. 64, 76-77.

11. Henry W. Benham, "U.S. Army Generals' Reports of Civil War Service, 1864-1887," 10:f. 500, N.A.

12. Henry W. Benham, "U.S. Army Generals' Reports of Civil War Service, 1864-1887," 10:f. 500, N.A.; Henry C. Glines, Diary, April 10, 1862, Y.U.L.; Milton M. Woodford, Letter, April 14, 1862, C.H.S.; Horace Porter, Letter, April 11, 1862, L.C.; New York *Times*, April 19, 1862.

13. Henry W. Benham, "U.S. Army General's Reports of Civil War Service, 1864-1887," 10:ff. 501-502, N.A.

14. Gillmore, *B&L*, 2:7, 9; DuPont, *Letters*, 1:409, 421; Henry W. Benham, "U.S. Army Generals' Reports of Civil War Service, 1864-1887," 10:ff. 499, 501-502, N.A.; *O.R.*, 6:134, 136, 146, 160; New York *Times*, April 19, 1862.
   Turner was Assistant Commissary of Subsistence to Hunter and a trained artillerist from the 1st Artillery, U.S. Army (New York *Times*, April 19, 1862).
   The sailors had been sent ashore to be available on April 10 but had not been used. They camped on the beach beyond range of the Confederate guns. (DuPont, *Letters*, 1:415.)

15. Henry W. Benham, "U.S. Army Generals' Reports of Civil War Service, 1864-1887," 10:f. 501, N.A.; *O.R.*, 6:136; New York *Times*, April 19, 1862.

16. Landershine, Diary, April 10, 1862, Fort Pulaski Papers Microfilm, S.H.C.; Milton M. Woodford, Letter, April 14, 1862, C.H.S.; Horace Porter, Letter, April 17, 1862, L.C.

17. Henry W. Benham, "U.S. Army Generals' Reports of Civil War Service, 1864-1887," 10:f. 502, N.A.

18. *O.R.*, 6:145, 158; Adrian Terry, Letter, April 16, 1862, Y.U.L.

19. *O.R.*, 6:142, 147.

20. Henry W. Benham, "U.S. Army Generals' Reports of Civil War Service," 10:ff. 495-496, N.A.; *O.R.*, 6:136.

21. A. B. Ely in letter to "Editors of the Boston *Daily Advertiser*, in Henry W. Benham, "U.S. Army Generals' Reports of Civil War Service, 1864-1887," 10:f. 659, N.A.; Henry W. Benham, "U.S. Army Generals' Reports of Civil War Service," 10:ff. 495-496, N.A.; *O.R.*, 6:136.

22. Olmstead, Letter, April 11, 1862, F.P.N.M.; Landershine, Diary, April 10, 1862, Fort Pulaski Papers Microfilm, S.H.C.

23. Olmstead, *G.H.Q.*, 1:103-104.

24. Olmstead, *G.H.Q.*, 1:103.

25. Savannah *Daily Morning News*, April 11, 1862.

26. Hanleiter, Diary, April 10, 1862, D.U.; Mercer, Diary, April 11, 1862, S.H.C.

27. Thomas Monaghan, "Only a Private. A Sketch of the Services of Thomas Monaghan, of the Forty-Eighth N.Y. Regiment" (Boston: Pratt Brothers, n.d.), p. 6; Aaron H. Ingraham, Letter, April 10, 1862, N.Y.S.L.

28. Henry W. Benham, "U.S. Army Generals' Reports of Civil War Service, 1864-1887," 10:ff. 504-505, N.A.; *O.R.*, 6:136, 145; New York *Times*, April 20, 1862; Walkey, *7th Conn.*, p. 45; William M. Davidson, Letter, April 15, 1862, G.H.S.; Gillmore, *Siege*, pp. 72, 74, 75, 80; Mercer, Diary, April 11, 1862, S.H.C.

29. *O.R.*, 6:145; Olmstead, *Memoirs*, p. 98.

30. Savannah *Daily Morning News*, April 12, 1862; Savannah *Republican*, April 12, 1862; William M. Davidson, Letter, April 15, 1862, G.H.S.

31. New York *Citizen*, August 17, 1867; *O.R.*, 6:137; New York *Times*, April 19, 1862 (Gillmore's April 12 report); Henry W. Benham, "U.S. Army Generals' Reports of Civil War Service, 1864-1887, 10: f. 507, N.A.

32. Henry W. Benham, "U.S. Army Generals' Reports of Civil War Service, 1864-1887," 10:f. 506, N.A.

33. *O.R.*, 6:137; Gillmore, *B&L*, 2:9; Henry W. Benham, "U.S. Army Generals' Reports of Civil War Service, 1864-1887," 10:f. 507, N.A.; New York *Citizen*, August 17, 1867; New York *Times*, April 19, 1862.

34. Gillmore, *B&L*, 2:9.

35. Undated newspaper clipping, microfilm reel 22, Joseph R. Hawley Papers, L.C.; Adrian Terry, Letter, April 16, 1862, Y.U.L.

36. Adrian Terry, Letter, April 16, 1863, Y.U.L.

37. George L. Andrew, Papers, Typescript, pp. 54-55, H.L.

38. Horace Porter, Letter, April 17, 1862, L.C.; Adrian Terry, Letter, April 16, 1862, Y.U.L.; New York *Times*, April 19, 1862, *O.R.*, 6:166.

39. Thomas Monaghan, "Only a Private," p. 6; Nichols, *Perry's Saints*, pp. 95-96; Cadwell, *Sixth Regiment*, p. 37; also see *O.R.*, 6:137.

40. Olmstead, Letter, April 11, 1862, F.P.N.M.

41. Olmstead, *G.H.Q.*, 1:104; Olmstead, *Memoirs*, p. 98.

42. *O.R.*, 6:167; Savannah *Republican*, April 23, 1862; Mercer, Diary, April 14, 1862, S.H.C.

43. Jones, "Lessons," p. 9.

44. Olmstead, Report, April 12 and 16, 1862, F.P.N.M.
    Although Gillmore gave Olmstead a map to enclose with his report to Lawton, it was removed by military censors before the colonel's report was forwarded on April 16.

Colonel Olmstead prepared a second report of the bombardment and capture of Fort Pulaski, clearly written after his exchange, which was published in the Augusta *Daily Constitutionalist* of November 23, 1862. (*O.R.S.*, 1:439-443.)

45. Mercer, Diary, April 14, 1862, S.H.C.

46. Undated newspaper clipping, microfilm reel 22, Joseph R. Hawley Papers, L.C.

47. Henry W. Benham, "U.S. Army Generals' Reports of Civil War Service, 1864-1887," 10: ff. 507-508, N.A.; Horace Porter, Letter, April 11, 1862, L.C.; Adrian Terry, Letter, April 16, 1862.
    Statistical data for each battery, the number of projectiles fired, problems, etc. can be found in Gillmore, *Siege*, pp. 70-80.

48. Henry W. Benham, "U.S. Army Generals' reports of Civil War Service, 1864-1887," 10:f. 509, N.A.; *O.R.*, 6:137.
    The party consisted of Major Halpine; Captain Ely and Captain Hawes, Adjutants and Aides to Benham; Lieutenant Irwin of the Navy; Lieutenant Colonel James F. Hall, New York Volunteer Engineers; and Captain Louis H. Pelouse, Inspector General of the Department. (New York *Times*, April 19, 1862.)

49. George L. Andrew, Papers, Typescript, p. 56, H.L.

50. New York *Times*, April 19, 1862; Landershine, Diary, April 11, 1862, Fort Pulaski Papers Microfilm, S.H.C.; Henry W. Benham, "U.S. Army Generals' Reports of Civil War Service, 1864-1887," 10:ff. 508-510, N.A.
    Gillmore was accompanied in the boat by his aide, Captain Badeau.

51. *O.R.*, 6:139-140.

52. Henry W. Benham, "U.S. Army Generals' Reports of Civil War Service, 1864-1867," 10:f. 510, N.A.; DuPont, *Letters*, 1:421; New York *Times*, April 19, 1862.

53. Robbins, *A.C.W.*, 3 (Sept., 1990):31; Olmstead, *Memoirs*, p. 100; Landershine, Diary, April 10-11, 1862, Fort Pulaski Papers Microfilm, S.H.C.; Gillmore, *B&L*, 2:9-10.
    "As the officers, some 20 or more had in succession handed in their side arms, one, among the last, came up saying, 'I have no sword, here is my sash, you can have that,'—throwing it upon the pile of swords. This however was returned to him, by Ely, with a statement that his sash was not required, if he had no sword. The next day, however, the sword, without doubt belonging to this officer, was found *concealed* in the Fort, and was handed to Capt. Ely, and proved to have been one of rebel manufacture at their arsenal at Macon, G.—a tolerable imitation of our own uniform sword, ornaments on the blade, and inscribed, as made by one 'Freeman,' and 'present to his brother, Lt. Freeman, of the Oglethorpe Lt Infantry,' the regiment that garrisoned the Fort." (Henry W. Benham, "U.S. Army Generals's Reports of Civil War Service, 1864-1887," 10:f. 512, N.A.)

54. *O.R.*, 6:135.
    The most complete roster of Confederate officers and men surrendered in Fort Pulaski may be found in the Hughes-Folsom papers in the G.H.S. Additional names and information can be found in the *Savannah Republican*, April 15, 1862; Savannah *Daily Morning News*, April 29, 1862; Solomon, *Scrapbook*, pp. 185-186, D.U.; New York *Times*, April 23, 1862; Olmstead, *G.H.Q.*, 1:101; Olmstead, Letter, April 11, 1862, F.P.N.M.; Olmstead, Report, April 12, 1862, G.H.S.; Olmstead, *Memoirs*, pp. 90, 96; George Bell, *G.H.Q.*, 22:170-171.

55. New York *Times*, April 19, 1862.

56. Olmstead, Letter, April 11, 1862, F.P.N.M.

57. DuPont, *Letters*, 1:422; Adrian Terry, Letter, April 16, 1862, Y.U.L.

58. Henry W. Benham, "U.S. Army Generals' Reports of Civil War Service, 1864-1887," 10:ff. 510-511, N.A.; New York *Times*, April 19, 1862; *O.R.*, 6:137.
    In his August 11, 1867, letter published in the New York *Citizen*, Benham stated:

I authorized him [Gillmore] to go over to the fort also, where he, in connection with yourself [Halpine] and Captain Ely, the Adjutant Generals of his superior officers, arranged, as I understood it, the terms of surrender, as had been directed.

Alfred B. Ely, Benham's assistant adjutant general, recalled that after Benham had told Gillmore to go with Halpine and him to receive Pulaski's surrender, Gillmore took a separate boat, "arrived first at the fort, and negotiated the terms according to his directions [from Benham] and left." (Alfred B.Ely, "Letter to the Editors of the Boston *Daily Advertiser*," in Henry W. Benham, "U.S. Army Generals' Reports of Civil War Service, 1864-1887," 10:ff. 661-662, N.A.

Halpine made no mention of surrender proceedings in his letters to his wife. (Charles G. Halpine, Papers, H.L.)

59. *O.R.*, 6:134, 137.

60. Seth Reynolds, Letter, April 15, 1862, Y.U.L.

61. Walkey, *7th Conn.*, p. 46; Henry W. Benham, "U.S. Army Generals' Reports of Civil War Service, 1864-1887," 10:f. 511, N.A.

62. Carroll E. Kingsley, Letter, April 30, 1862, Civil War Miscellaneous Collection, U.S.A.M.H.I.

63. William H. Harrison, Letter, May 1, 1862, Lewis Leigh Collection, U.S.A.M.H.I.; Olmstead, Letter, April 11, 1862, Fort Pulaski National Monument.

64. Milton M. Woodford, Letter, April 23, 1862, C.H.S.

65. Horace Porter, Letter, April 17, 1862, L.C.
Details of the captured ordnance and ordnance stores may be found in Gillmore, *Siege*, pp. 67-69.
A few days later Porter sent his sister a piece of the flag staff and a three by three inch piece of red bunting from the "detestable flag that so long waved over the work." Both items are attached to the letter. (Horace Porter, Letter, April 17, 1862, L.C.)

66. DuPont, *Letters*, 1:418.

67. DuPont, *Letters*, 1:418.

68. DuPont, *Letters*, 1:422-423.
For participation of the naval forces, see *O.R.N.*, 12:730-732.

69. Thomas W. Sherman, "U.S. Army Generals' Report of Civil War Service, 1864-1867," 4:f. 53, N.A.

70. Mercer, Diary, April 14, 1862, S.H.C.

71. Sharf, *History*, p. 637; New York *Times*, April 20, 1862.

72. *O.R.*, 6:145, 166.

Chapter 8

1. *O.R.*, 6:161; Gillmore, *B&L*, 2:10; Gillmore, *Siege*, pp. 70-80, plate II.

2. *O.R.*, 6:162, 164.

3. Gillmore, *Siege*, pp. 46, 64-65.

4. *O.R.*, 6:164.

5. Gillmore, *Siege*, p. 65; *O.R.*, 6:164.

6. Thomas W. Sherman, "U.S. Army Generals' Report of Civil War Service, 1864-1887," 4:ff. 54-55, N.A.

7. Ripley, *Artillery*, p. 291; Gillmore, *Siege*, p. 65.

8. *O.R.*, 6:123; Jones, pp. 238-239, L.C.

9. Gillmore, *Siege*, p. 52; *O.R.*, 6:161, 163.

10. *O.R.*, 6:163-164.

11. *O.R.*, 6:164.

12. *O.R.*, 6:146-147.

13. *O.R.*, 6:147-148; Gillmore, *Siege*, pp. 48, 50, 51.

14. Gillmore, *Siege*, p. 68.

15. *O.R.*, 6:165; Gillmore, *Siege*, p. 52.

16. George L. Andrew, Papers, Typescript, p. 54, H.L.; Gillmore, *B&L*, 2:8-9; Landershine, Diary, April 10, 1862, Fort Pulaski Papers Microfilm, S.H.C.; Gillmore, *Siege*, p. 52.

17. *O.R.*, 6:148.
   Written October 20, 1865.

18. James H. Wilson, Letter, April 30, 1862, in James B. McPherson Papers, L.C.

19. Jones, "Lessons," pp. 7, 9-10.

20. Thomas W. Sherman, "U.S. Army Generals' Report of Civil War Service, 1864-1887,", 4:ff. 53-56, N.A.

21. *O.R.*, 6:134.

22. Henry W. Benham, "U.S. Army Generals' Reports of Civil War Service, 1864-1887," 10:f. 513, N.A.
   On April 14, General Benham sent a friend in Boston a "portion of the rebel flag of Fort Pulaski captured by a part of the troops of my division on Friday last. The 11th is the *anniversary* of the fire upon Fort Sumter by the rebels." The recipient, Mrs. Harrison Gray Otis of Boston, already had a fragment of the flag hauled down by surrendering Federal forces a year before. Benham concluded that "I trust to make a trio for you in due time from Sumter." (Henry W. Benham, Letter, April 14, 1862, First Corps of Cadets Collection, Boston University Library.)

23. Henry W. Benham, "U.S. Army Generals' Reports of Civil War Service, 1864-1887," 10:f. 513, N.A.; Edwin C. Merriam, Letter, April 14, 1862, C.S.L.; Schoonmaker, Papers, pp. 39-41, L.C.
   Schoonmaker included a sketch of the blindage construction. Like so many others, he sent his father "bunting taken from a rebel flag found in Pulaski after its surrender."

*C*hapter 9

1. Landershine, Diary, April 12, 1862, Fort Pulaski Papers Microfilm, S.H.C.

2. Edwin J. Merriam, Letter, April 14, 1864, C.S.L.; "Muster Role of Captain M. J. McMullan's Company of the Wise Guards from the 31st Day of August to the 31st of October, 1862, Stationed at Camp Jasper, Near Savannah, *G.H.Q.*, 1:106-107; Savannah, *Republican*, April 12 & 14, 1862; Gillmore, *B&L*, 2:10.

3. Olmstead, Letter, April 17, 1862, Georgia Historical Society; George Bell, "Diary of George Bell, A Record of Captivity in a Federal Military Prison, 1862," *G.H.Q.*, 22 (1938):170-171.

4. George L. Andrew, Papers, typescript, p. 56, H.L.; New York _Times_, April 23, 1862; Landershine, Diary, April 13, 1862, Fort Pulaski Papers Microfilm, S.H.C.; Edwin C. Merriam, Letter, April 14, 1862, C.S.L.; Olmstead, _G.H.Q._, 1:105; "Muster Role," _G.H.Q._, 1:106-107.

    The Pulaski enlisted men were transferred to Fort Delaware on July 10 and sent for exchange to Aiken's Landing on August 1, 1862. They were exchanged on April 5. ("Muster Role," _G.H.Q._, 1:106-107.)

5. R.G. 94 475-S-1862 D. Hunter to E. M. Stanton, April 14, 1862, N.A.; _O.R._, 6:134, 333; New York _Times_, April 20, 1862.

6. Henry C. Glines, Diary, April 14, 1862; Joseph R. Hawley, Letters, April 28 and May 8, 1862, L.C.

7. Walkey, _7th Conn._, p. 46; Milton M. Woodford, Letter, April 14, 1862, C.H.S.; Henry W. Benham, "U.S. Army Generals' Reports of Civil War Service, 1864-1887," 10:f. 514, N.A.; Henry C. Glines, Diary, April 14, 1862, Y.U.L.; New York _Times_, April 23, 1862 (with names).

8. Edwin J. Merriam, Letter, April 14, 1862 (continued on April 15), C.S.L.

    Sergeant Merriam enclosed a piece of the Confederate flag in his letter to his wife; the six by two and one-half inch fragment is with his papers in the Connecticut State Library.

9. _O.R._, 6:133, 135; Henry W. Benham, "U.S. Army Generals' Reports of Civil War Service, 1864-1887," 10:ff. 148-149, 517-519, N.A.; Walkey, _7th Conn._, p. 47; William H. Harrison, Letter, May 1, 1862, Lewis Leigh Collection, U.S.A.M.H.I.

10. DuPont, _Letters_, 1:424.

11. _O.R._, 6:133, 135; Henry W. Benham, "U.S. Army Generals' Reports of Civil War Service, 1864-1887," 10:ff. 148-149, N.A.

12. Henry W. Benham, "U.S. Army Generals' Reports of Civil War Service, 1864-1887," 10:ff. 516-517, N.A.

13. New York _Citizen_, August 17, 1867.

    For Gillmore's report, see _O.R._, 6:144-146; for Benham's and Hunter's reports, see _O.R._, 6:133-139.

14. Adrian Terry, Letter, April 16, 1862, Y.U.L.; Horace Porter, Letter, April 17, 1862, L.C.

15. Wilson, _Old Flag_, 1:91; James H. Wilson, Letter, April 30, 1862, in James B. McPherson Papers, L.C.

16. James H. Wilson, Letter, April 30, 1862, in James B. McPherson Papers, L.C.

17. A. B. Ely to C. Sumner, April 17, 1862, R.G. 94 78-E-1862, N.A.

18. Henry W. Benham, "U.S. Army Generals' Reports of Civil War Service, 1864-1887," 10:f. 518, N.A.; _O.R._, 14:5.

    The 8th Michigan had arrived on Tybee Island on April 8. (New York _Times_, April 19, 1862.)

19. _O.R._, 14:6, 8.

20. _O.R._, 14:6, 8; New York _Times_, April 23, 1862.

21. _O.R._, 14:8.

22. _O.R._, 14:9-11; Savannah _Republican_, April 18 and 19, 1862; Savannah _Daily Morning News_, April 18, 1862.

23. _O.R._, 14:6, 9; Dyer, _Compendium_, 2:1285.

24. _O.R._, 14:6, 9, 11; New York _Times_, April 23, 1862.

25. _O.R._, 14:11.

26. _O.R._, 14:11-12, 14; Savannah _Republican_, April 18, 1862; George A Mercer, Diary, April 23, 1862, S.H.C.

27. W. D. Smith to F. W. Capers, Letter, April 16, 1862, Confederate Miscellany Collection, April, 1862, University of Georgia.

28. Carroll E. Kingsley, Letter, April 30, 1862, Civil War Miscellaneous Collection, U.S.A.M.H.I.; Charles P. Lord, Letter, April 17, 1862, D.U.; Schoonmaker, Papers, p. 38, L.C.

29. *O.R.*, 14:4, 5, 7-9; Wilson, *Old Flag*, 1:85-86; James H. Wilson, Letter, April 30, 1862, in James B. McPherson Papers, L.C.
    The Federal dead were buried on April 17 in Beaufort. (Joseph R. Hawley, Letter, April 21, 1862, L.C.); New York *Times*, April 23, 1862 (with names of dead).

30. Henry W. Benham, "U.S. Army Generals' Reports of Civil War Service, 1864-1887," 10:f. 519, N.A.; *O.R.*, 14:5, 334-335.

31. *O.R.*, 14:335.

32. Henry W. Benham, "U.S. Army Generals' Reports of Civil War Service, 1864-1887," 10:ff. 519-520, N.A.; Robbins, *A.C.W.*, 3 (Sept., 1990):31.

33. Q. A. Gillmore to C. G. Halpine, Letter, June 27, 1862, Charles G. Halpine, Papers, H.L.; Quincy A. Gillmore, "U.S. Army Generals' Reports of Civil War Service, 1864-1887," 11:f. 560, N.A.
    On June 10, 1862, Olmstead wrote Stanton that he had just learned from the New York newspapers that a boat had been sent to Pulaski, not to transport the Confederate wounded to Savannah but to be there to exchange them for Federal prisoners held by the Confederates. This violated the terms of surrender. Olmstead learned in the same paper that Gillmore was home on furlough and the Colonel wrote him, too. Gillmore, then at West Point, New York, telegraphed back that the sick had been sent to Savannah as agreed. Olmstead was relieved until he received a letter from one of the sick prisoners dated June 1 from Hilton Head, where they had been taken some time before and where two had died. Olmstead appealed to Stanton to see that right was done to "these unfortunate men." (Olmstead, *G.H.Q.*, 1:105; Olmstead, Letter [copy], June 10, 1862, S.H.C.) Gillmore learned the details of what had happened later and notified Olmstead, then in prison in Sandusky, that he would try to rectify the matter. (Q. A. Gillmore to W. Hoffman, Letter, August 11, 1862, in Olmstead Papers, S.H.C.; Olmstead, *G.H.Q.*, 1:105.) Nothing further occurred and the wounded who survived were exchanged with the rest in the late summer of 1862. Many years later someone tried to arrange a meeting between Gillmore and Olmstead, but the latter declined. (Olmstead, *Memoirs*, p. 99; "Muster Role, *G.H.Q.*, 1:106-107.) Gillmore served as military commander of the Department of South Carolina from late June until November, 1865, and the opportunity for the meeting may have occurred then.

34. Joseph R. Hawley, Letter, April 21, 1862, L.C.
    Terry was confirmed by the Senate on April 26, 1862. (Dwight Loomis to Joseph R. Hawley, April 26, 1862, in Joseph R. Hawley Papers, L.C.)

35. Adrian Terry, Letter, April 29, 1862, Y.U.L.

36. William H. Harrison, Letter, May 1, 1862, Lewis Leigh Collection, U.S.A.M.H.I.; Henry C. Glines, Diary, April 30-May 2, 1862, Y.U.L.; Horace Porter, Letter, May 21, 1862, L.C.

37. *O.R.*, 14:338.

38. Horace Porter, Letters, May 11 and 21, 1862, L.C.; Charles G. Halpine, Letter, April 14, 1862, H.L.

39. Palmer, *48th N.Y.*, p. 40; Dyer, *Compendium*, 2:1422; *O.R.*, 14:347.

40. *O.R.*, 6:140; Cadwell, *Sixth Regiment*, p. 38; *O.R.*, 14:343; Savannah *Republican*, April 14, 1862.

41. Mercer, Diary, April 23, 1862, S.H.C.

42. Olmstead, *G.H.Q.*, 42 (1958):389; 44 (1960):198-201, 306-314, 319, 419-434; 45 (1961):46-53, 139-155.

43. A. H. Terry to C. G. Halpine, Letter, June 3, 1863, Charles G. Halpine Papers, H.L.

44. Lewis, *Fortifications*, pp. 66-67.

45. Lewis, *Fortifications*, pp. 50, 67-68.

*A*ppendix

1. Albert Manucy, *Artillery Through the Ages* (Washington: United States Government Printing Office, 1949), pp. 5-12.

2. Lewis, *Fortifications*, p. 17, fn. 15.

3. David McConnell, *British Smooth-Bore Artillery: A Technological Study* (Ottawa: Canadian Government Publishing Center, 1988), pp. 287-290; *The Ordnance Manual for the Use of the Officers of the Confederate States Army* (Dayton: Morningside Bookshop, 1976), pp. 13-18, 378.

4. H. C. B. Rogers, *A History of Artillery* (Secaucus: The Citadel Press, 1975), p. 81.

5. Ripley, *Artillery*, p. 17; James C. Hazlett, Edwin Olmstead, and M. Hume Parks, *Field Artillery Weapons of the Civil War* (Newark: University of Delaware Press, 1983), pp. 148-150.

6. Ripley, *Artillery*, p. 45.

7. Ripley, *Artillery*, p. 57.

8. Ripley, *Artillery*, p. 71; Lewis, *Fortifications*, pp. 58-59.

9. William B. Edwards, *Civil War Guns* (Harrisburg: The Stackpole Company, 1962), p. 15; Manucy, *Artillery*, pp. 14-17; Larry J. Daniel and Riley W. Gunter, *Confederate Cannon Foundries* (Union City: Pioneer Press, 1977), p. x.

10. Joseph Whitworth, *Papers on Mechanical Subjects* (London: E. & F. Spon, n.d.), pp. 38-40; Charles H. Owen, *Elementary Lectures on Artillery, Prepared for the Use of the Gentlemen Cadets of the Royal Military Academy* (Woolrich: Royal Artillery Institution, 1865), p. 35.

11. Owen, *Lectures*, pp. 109-110.

12. Manucy, *Artillery*, p. 17.

13. Owen, *Lectures*, p. 145.

14. Owen, *Lectures*, p. 145.

15. *O.R.*, 6:161.

16. Owen, *Lectures*, p. 146.

17. Owen, *Lectures*, p. 35, f.n. 1.

18. Owen, *Lectures*, pp. 142-143.

19. Rogers, *Artillery*, p. 93.

20. Rogers, *Artillery*, pp. 93-96; Owen, *Lectures*, p. 36.

21. Manucy, *Artillery*, p. 17.

22. Whitworth, *Papers*, p. 40.

23. Totten, *Report*, pp. 29-31.

24. Totten, *Report*, p. 30.

25. The name "Martello tower" refers to a small round tower in the Corsican Bay of Martello which contained one heavy gun. In 1794, it successfully beat off two heavily armed British warships without sustaining any material injury from their fire. As a result, it was subsequently felt that well-mounted shore guns were superior to a larger number of ship-borne pieces. (Totten, *Report*, pp. 33-34; Lewis, *Fortifications*, p. 42 and f.n. 45.)

26. *O.R.*, 6:161.

27. Owen, *Lectures*, p. 145.

28. *O.R.*, 6:162.

29. Joseph T. Derry, *Georgia* in *Confederate Military History Extended Edition*, ed. Clement A. Evans. (Wilmington: Broadfoot Publishing Company, 1987), p. 6; Gillmore, *B&L*, 2:1; James H. Wilson, Letter, April 30, 1862, James B. McPherson Papers, L.C.

$\mathcal{B}$ibliography

$\mathcal{M}$anuscripts*

BOSTON UNIVERSITY LIBRARY

Henry W. Benham. Letter. First Corps of Cadets Collection.

CONNECTICUT HISTORICAL SOCIETY

Milton M. Woodford. Letters, in the Churchill-Woodford Family Papers. [7th Connecticut]

CONNECTICUT STATE LIBRARY

Edwin J. Marriam. Papers. [7th Connecticut]

George C. Swathel. Diary. [6th Connecticut]

DUKE UNIVERSITY LIBRARY

John E. Bryant. Papers. [8th Maine]

Martin Emmons. Letters. [6th Connecticut]

Cornelius R. Hanleiter. Diaries 1861-1863. [Joe Thompson Artillery, Wright's Legion (38th Georgia)]

---

*Whenever a manuscript collection is not listed by the individual named, the collection is also cited.

Charles P. Lord. Papers. [8th Maine]

M. J. Solomon. Scrapbook, 1861-1863.

FORT PULASKI NATIONAL MONUMENT

Charles H. Olmstead. Letter, April 11, 1862.

Charles H. Olmstead. Report, April 12 and 16, 1862.

EMORY UNIVERSITY LIBRARY

Confederate Miscellany I. Letter, "George" to "My Dear Sister," January 12, 1861 [1862].

GEORGIA HISTORICAL SOCIETY

William Murray Davidson. Papers. [Chatham Artillery]

Charles H. Olmstead. "Fort Pulaski."

Charles H. Olmstead. Letter, April 17, 1862.

Theodorick Winfield Montfort. Papers. [Wise Guards, 1st Georgia Volunteer Regiment]

Charles E. Palmer. Papers. [7th Connecticut]

HUNTINGTON LIBRARY

George L. Andrew. Papers.

Hiram Barney. Papers.

Charles G. Halpine. Papers.

HOUGHTON LIBRARY, HARVARD UNIVERSITY

Thomas W. Sherman. Letter, February 23, 1862.

LIBRARY OF CONGRESS, MANUSCRIPT DIVISION

James M. Green. Letter, February 22, 1862, in Robert C. Ogden Papers. [48th New York]

Joseph R. Hawley. Papers.

Samuel Jones. "The Occupation of the South Atlantic Coast by Union Troops and Bombardment and Reduction of Fort Pulaski."

Horace Porter. Papers.

Tredwell W. Remson. Letter, February 23, 1862. [48th New York]

Cornellius M. Schoonmaker. Papers.

James H. Wilson. Letters, James B. McPherson. Papers.

NATIONAL ARCHIVES

Record Group 94, Records of the Adjutant General's Office, Letters Received by the Office of the Adjutant General (Main Series), 1861-1870.

Henry W. Benham. U.S. Army Generals' Reports of Civil War Service, 1864-1887, vol. 10. (microfilm)

Quincy A. Gillmore. U.S. Army Generals' Reports of Civil War Service, 1864-1887, vol. 11. (microfilm)

Thomas W. Sherman. U.S. Army Generals Reports of Civil War Service, 1864-1887, vol. 4. (microfilm)

NEW YORK HISTORICAL SOCIETY

George Greenville Lyons, Letter, February 23, 1862. [48th New York]

NEW YORK STATE LIBRARY

Aaron H. Ingraham. Papers. [48th New York]

THE SOUTH CAROLINIANA LIBRARY

Levi Pinner. Letter, March 22, 1862. [3rd Rhode Island Artillery]

SOUTHERN HISTORICAL COLLECTION, UNIVERSITY OF NORTH CAROLINA

George Bell. Diary. Fort Pulaski Papers Microfilm. [Montgomery Guards, 1st Regiment Georgia Volunteers]

Thomas B. Brooks. Letters. Fort Pulaski Papers Microfilm. [1st New York Volunteer Engineers]

Charles Lafferty. Letters. Fort Pulaski Papers Microfilm. [48th New York]

L. W. Landershine. Diary, [typescript]. Fort Pulaski Papers Microfilm. [Oglethorpe Light Infantry, Co. B, 1st Regiment Georgia Volunteers]

George A. Mercer. Diary.

Charles H. Olmstead. Papers.

Aaron Wilbur. Papers. Letters of Charles J. Copp.

UNITED STATES ARMY MILITARY HISTORY INSTITUTE

Laurin B. Drake. Letters in David Howell Collection. [1st New York Volunteer
    Engineers]

Edwin W. Keen. Letter, December 20, 1861. Civil War Miscellaneous Collection.
    [3rd Rhode Island Artillery]

Carroll E. Kingsley. Letters. Civil War Miscellaneous Collection. [7th Connecticut]

William H. Harrison. Letter, May 1, 1862. Lewis Leigh Collection. [7th Connecticut]

Samuel Wolcott. Letters. William Prince Collection. [7th Connecticut]

UNIVERSITY OF GEORGIA LIBRARY

Georgia Confederate Miscellaneous Collection, April, 1862.

YALE UNIVERSITY LIBRARY

Seth Reynolds. Letters. [7th Connecticut]

Henry C. Glines. Letters and Diary. [7th Connecticut]

Adrian Terry. Letters. Terry Family Papers.

Alfred H. Terry. Letters. Terry Family Papers.

Books and Articles

Atlas to Accompany the Official Records of the Union and Confederate Armies.
    Washington, D.C.: Government Printing Office, 1891-1895.

Barber, Henry E. and Allen R. Gann. *History of the Savannah District U.S. Army Corps
    of Engineers 1829-1989.* Savannah: United States Army Corps of Engineers, 1989.

Bell, George. "Diary of George Bell, A Record of Captivity in a Federal Military
    Prison, 1862." *Georgia Historical Quarterly,* 22 (1938):169-184. [Montgomery
    Guards, 1st Georgia Volunteer Regiment]

Bright, Samuel R. "Confederate Coast Defense." Ph.D. dissertation, Duke University, 1961.

Bulloch, James D. *The Secret Service of the Confederate States in Europe.* 2 vols. New York: Thomas Yoseloff, 1959.

Cadwell, Charles K. *The Old Sixth Regiment, Its War Record, 1861-1865.* New Haven: Tuttle, Morehouse & Taylor, 1875.[6th Connecticut]

Daniel, Larry J. and Riley W. Gunter. *Confederate Cannon Foundries.* Union City: Pioneer Press, 1977.

Derry, Joseph T. *Georgia* in *Confederate Military History Extended Edition.* ed. Clement A. Evans. Wilmington: Broadfoot Publishing Company, 1987.

Dictionary of American Biography, "Quincy Adams Gillmore," New York: Charles Scribner's Sons, 1931, vii:295-297.

Dowdey, Clifford and Louis H. Manarin, ed. *The Wartime Papers of R. E. Lee.* Boston: Little, Brown and Company, 1961.

DuPont, Samuel Francis. *A Selection from His Civil War Letters.* 3 vols. ed. John D. Hayes. Ithaca: Cornell University Press, 1969.

Durham, Roger S. "Savannah[:] Mr. Lincoln's Christmas Present." *Blue and Gray*, 8 (Feb., 1991), 8-53.

Dyer, Frederick H. *A Compendium of the War of the Rebellion.* 2 vols. Dayton: Morningside Bookshop, 1978.

Edwards, William B. *Civil War Guns.* Harrisburg: The Stackpole Company, 1962.

Freeman, Douglas Southall. *R. E. Lee.* 4 vols. New York: Charles Scribner's Sons, 1934.

Fox, Gustavus V. *Confidential Correspondence of Gustavus Vasa Fox.* 2 vols. ed. Robert M. Thompson and Richard Wainwright. New York: The Naval History Society, 1918.

Gillmore, Quincy A. *Engineer and Artillery Operations against the Defences of Charleston Harbor in 1862.* New York: D. Van Nostrand, 1865.

Gillmore, Quincy A. "Siege and Capture of Fort Pulaski." *Battles and Leaders of the Civil War.* 4 vols. ed. Robert Underwood Johnson and Clarence Clough Buel. New York: The Century Co., 1888. 2:1-12.

Gillmore, Quincy A. *Official Report to the United States Engineer Department of the Siege and Reduction of Fort Pulaski, Georgia, February, March, and April, 1862.* New York: D. Van Nostrand, 1862.

Guinn, Gilbert Sumpter. "Coastal Defense of the Confederate Atlantic States, 1861-1862: A Study in Political and Military Mobilization," Ph.D dissertation, University of South Carolina, 1973.

Hazlett, James C., Edwin Olmstead, and M. Hume Parks. *Field Artillery of the Civil War.* Newark: University of Delaware Press, 1983.

Hogg, Ian. *The History of Fortifications*. New York: St. Martin's Press, Inc., 1981.

Krick, Robert K. *Lee's Colonels*. Dayton: Press of Morningside Bookshop, 1984.

Jones, Charles C. *The Life and Services of Commodore Josiah Tattnall*. Savannah: Morning News Steam Printing House, 1878.

Jones, Charles C. "Military Lessons Inculcated on the Coast of Georgia during the Confederate War." An Address Delivered Before the Confederate Survivors' Association, in Augusta, Georgia, at its Fifth Annual Meeting, Memorial Day, April 26, 1883. Augusta: Chronicle Printing Establishment, 1883.

Julian, Allen Phelps. "Fort Pulaski." *Civil War Times Illustrated*, 9 (May, 1970):8-21.

Lattimore, Raltson B. *Fort Pulaski*. Washington, D.C.: National Park Service Historical Handbook Series No. 18, 1954.

Lee, Robert E. *Recollections and Letters of General Robert E. Lee*. New York: Doubleday, Page & Company, 1904.

Lewis, Emanuel R. *Seacoast Fortifications of the United States*. Washington, D.C.: Smithsonian Institution Press, 1970.

Long, A. L. "Seacoast Defenses of South Carolina and Georgia," *Southern Historical Society Papers* 1 (January-June, 1876):103-107.

Manchard, John B. *Charleston Blockade, The Journals of John B. Manchard, U.S. Navy, 1861-1862*. ed. Craig L. Symonds. Newport: Naval War College Press, 1976.

McConnell, David. *British Smooth-Bore Artillery: A Technological Study*. Ottawa: Canadian Government Publishing Centre, 1988.

Manucy, Albert. *Artillery Through the Ages*. Washington: United States Government Printing Office, 1949.

Monaghan, Thomas. "Only a Private: A Sketch of the Services of Thomas Monaghan of the Forty-Eighth N.Y. Regiment." Boston, Pratt Brothers, n.d. [48th New York]

Montfort, Theodorick W. "Rebel Lawyer: The Letters of Theodorick W. Montfort, 1861-1862." *Georgia Historical Quarterly*, 49 (1965): 82-97, 200-216, 324-334. [Wise Guards, 25th Georgia]

"Muster Roll of Captain M. J. McMullan's Company of the Wise Guards from the 31st Day of August to the 31st of October, 1862, Stationed at Camp Jasper, Near Savannah." *Georgia Historical Quarterly*, 1 (1907):106-107.

Nichols, James M. *Perry's Saints or the Fighting Parson's Regiment in the War of the Rebellion*. Boston: D. Lothrop and Company, 1886. [48th New York]

Official Records of the Union and Confederate Navies in the War of the Rebellion. Series 1. Washington, D.C.: Government Printing Office, 1894-1922.

Olmstead, Charles H. "Fort Pulaski." *Georgia Historical Quarterly*, 1 (1917):98-105.

Olmstead, Charles H. *The Memoirs of Charles H. Olmstead.* Savannah: Georgia Historical Society, 1964. [Serialized in *Georgia Historical Quarterly* 42 (1958) through 45 (1961)]

The Ordnance Manual for the Use of Officers of the Confederate States Army, Dayton: Morningside Bookshop, 1976.

Owen, Charles H. *Elementary Lectures on Artillery Prepared for the Use of the Gentlemen Cadets of the Royal Military Academy,* 4th ed. Woolwich: Royal Artillery Institution, 1865.

Palmer, Abraham J. *The History of the Forty-eighth Regiment New York State Volunteers in the War for the Union. 1861-1865.* Brooklyn: Published by the Veteran Association of the Regiment, 1885.

Pemberton, John C. *Pemberton: Defender of Vicksburg.* Chapel Hill: The University of North Carolina Press, 1942.

Perry, Milton F. *Infernal Machines.* Baton Rouge: Louisiana State University Press, 1965.

Reed, Rowena. *Combined Operations in the Civil War.* Annapolis: Naval Institute Press, 1978.

The Report of Committees of the Senate of the United States, for the Third Session of the Thirty-Seventh Congress. Washington: Government Printing Office, 1863.

Ripley, Warren. *Artillery and Ammunition of the Civil War.* New York: Van Nostrand Reinhold Company, 1970.

Robbins, Peggy. "Storm Over Fort Pulaski." *America's Civil War,* 3 (Sept., 1990):26-31.

Rogers, H. C. B. *A History of Artillery.* Secaucus: The Citadel Press, 1975.

Russell, William H. *My Diary North and South.* New York: Harper & Brothers, Publishers, 1863.

Sharf, J. Thomas. *History of the Confederate States Navy.* New York: Rogers & Sherwood, 1887.

Still, William N. *Iron Afloat.* Nashville, Vanderbilt University Press, 1971.

Supplement to the Official Records of the Union and Confederate Armies. Part I. Wilmington: Broadfoot Publishing Company, 1994.

Totten, J. G. *Report of General J. G. Totten, Chief Engineer, on the Subject of National Defences.* Washington: A. Boyd Hamilton, 1851.

Walkley, Stephen. *History of the Seventh Connecticut Volunteer Infantry.* Southington, n.p., 1896.

The War of the Rebellion: A Compilation of the Official Records of the Union and Confederate Armies. Series 1. Washington, D.C.: Government Printing Office, 1880-1901.

Whitworth, Joseph. *Papers on Mechanical Subjects*. London: E. & F. Spon, n.d.

Williams, Alonzo. *The Investment of Fort Pulaski*. Providence: Personal Narratives Rhode Island Soldiers and Sailors Historical Society, 1887. [3rd Rhode Island Artillery]

Wilson, James H. *Under the Old Flag*. New York: D. Appleton & Company, 1912.

Young, Rogers W. "The Construction of Fort Pulaski." *Georgia Historical Quarterly* 20 (1936):41-51.

Young, Rogers W. "Two Years at Fort Bartow, 1862-1864." *Georgia Historical Quarterly*, 23 (1939):253-264.

Newspapers

Harper's Weekly

New York *Citizen*

New York *Times*

Savannah *Republican*

Savannah *Daily Morning News*

Maps

General Highway Map: Beaufort County, South Carolina. South Carolina Department of Highways and Public Transportation, 1978.

General Highway Map: Chatham County, Georgia. Department of Transportation, Division of Planning and Programming, 1986.

General Highway Map: Jasper County, South Carolina. South Carolina Department of Highways and Public Transportation, 1969.

Gillmore, Quincy A. "Map showing the Position of the Batteries used by the U.S. Forces in the Reduction of Fort Pulaski." Plate V-3. *Atlas to Accompany the Official Records of the Union and Confederate Armies*. Washington, D.C.: Government Printing Office, 1891-1895.

Gillmore, Quincy A. "Siege of Fort Pulaski. Map of the Mouth of Savannah River and Adjacent Islands." Plate V-4. *Atlas to Accompany the Official Records of the Union and Confederate Armies*. Washington, D.C.: Government Printing Office, 1891-1895.

D'Oyley, Christopher. "Plan of Fort Pulaski, Cockspur Id, Ga, May 3, 1862." Connecticut State Library.

Poe, Orlando M. "Map of Savannah, Ga. and Vicinity. Illustrating the Operations of the Army under command of Maj. Gen. W. T. Sherman resulting in the Fall of that City December 21, 1864." Plate LXX-2. *Atlas to Accompany the Official Records of the Union and Confederate Armies.* Washington, D.C.: Government Printing Office, 1891-1895.

*J*ndex

A

Adelaide, 90
Altamaha River, Georgia, 11
Ames, Isaac, 112
Ammen, Daniel, 37
Anderson, John W., 4
Andrew, George L., 95, 97, 110, 113, 132
Armstrong, William G., 154
Atlantic, 91, 92
Augusta, 15
Augusta, Georgia, 51

B

Babcock, Samuel, 3
Bacon, Theodore, 110
Badeau, Adam, 95, 113
Badger, Frederick M., 140
Bailey, David J., 67
Bailey, James E., 31
Bailey, William G., 35, 61
Bankhead, John P., 40
Barnes, John S., 34
Bartow, 26, 40
Bartow, Francis S., 4, 5
Bartow Artillery, 37
Battery Burnside, Tybee Island, 97, 98, 105, 108
Battery Cheves, 27
Battery Daniels, 21
Battery E, 3d U.S. Artillery, 13, 66
Battery Grant, Tybee Island, 97, 98
Battery Halleck, Tybee Island, 98, 103, 108
Battery Hamilton, Bird Island, 63, 66, 67, 70, 94, 95, 142; erection, 61–62

Battery Lincoln, Tybee Island, 97, 98, 105
Battery Lyon, Tybee Island, 97, 98, 104, 109
Battery McClellan, Tybee Island, 98, 110
Battery Scott, Tybee Island, 93, 98, 103, 104, 131
Battery Sherman, Tybee Island, 98
Battery Sigel, Tybee Island, 98, 105, 108, 131
Battery Stanton, Tybee Island, 97, 98
Battery Totten, Tybee Island, 98, 108
Battery Vulcan, Jones Island, Erection, 56–61, 63, 66, 67, 70, 94, 95, 96, 142
Beard, Oliver T., 31; reconnaissance of Long and Elba Islands, 44; reconnaissance on Wrights River, 45, 58, 61, 62, 69
Beaufort, South Carolina, 13
Beaulieu, Georgia, 22, 69
Bedal, John, 66
Ben DeFord, 16, 28, 135
Benham, Henry W., 80, 90–91, 93, 94, 96, 99, 100, 104, 106, 107, 108, 112, 113, 114, 115, 137, 138, 141; visits Tybee Island, 92; plan to assault Fort Pulaski through breached wall, 109
Benjamin, Judah P., 10, 24, 26, 50
Bernard, Simon, 2, 3
Bird Island, Georgia, 95; erection of Battery Hamilton, 61–62
Birney, Hiram, 66
Black, Lieutenant ——, 36
Bluffton, South Carolina, 8, 22
Bomford, George, 152
Bonaventure Battery, 22
Brooks, Thomas B., 77, (Chapter 5, note 12)
Brown, Charlie, 66
Brown, Joseph E., 4, 10, 23, 50
Brunswick, Georgia, 11, 25, 50, 65
Brutus, 27

195